George Devey
Architect, 1820-1886

George Devey

George Devey
Architect, 1820-1886

Jill Allibone

The Lutterworth Press
Cambridge

The Lutterworth Press
P.O. Box 60
Cambridge
CB1 2NT
England

British Library Cataloguing in Publication Data

Allibone, Jill
   George Devey, architect 1820-1886.
   1. England. Architectural design. Devey, George
   I. Title
   720.92

   ISBN 0-7188-2785-6

Copyright © Jill Allibone, 1991

All rights reserved. No part of this publication may be reproduced, stored in a retrieval system, or transmitted in any form or by any means, electronic, mechanical, photocopying, recording or otherwise, without the prior permission in writing of the Publisher.

Printed by
St Edmundsbury Press

This book is dedicated to the memory of
Jill Franklin
dear friend and fellow historian of the country house
who died on 23 March
and is also for
Alexandra Emma Rhiannon
who was born on 5 April
1988

Contents

Preface	7
List of Illustrations	10
1 'George has made up his mind as to his Line of Life.'	13
2 Cottage Building	23
3 Making a Slow Start	37
4 Working for the Whigs	53
5 The Use of Photography	79
6 The Flourishing Practice	91
7 Struck Down in his Prime	119
8 'An able and accomplished architect, and a chivalrous, high-minded gentleman.'	135
Notes on Sources	142
Notes to Chapters 1-8	144
Catalogue Raisonné	150
Abbreviations	150
Catalogue	151
Index	181

Preface

George Devey made a crucial contribution to the development of English domestic architecture. Beginning as a skilled watercolourist, the business of earning a living directed him into the profession of architecture which he learnt with one of those industrious and competent practitioners who were designing and building churches and houses in the first half of the nineteenth century. He remained in this somewhat prosaic pupilage for a period of nine years before leaving for the customary continental tour, and when he returned to England and set up on his own, commissions were for some reason very slow in coming in. He was nearly thirty before he began his study of the buildings of the Weald, where the abundant trees which were the remains of the ancient forest of Anderida had led to the development of a manner of building timber-framed houses which Devey adopted and made his own. The eye of a painter made him receptive to local building methods and materials, and his designs proved most attractive to his first clients, who were nearly all landowners on a large scale. Having spent the first fifteen years of his practice designing small buildings, by the 1870s Devey's practice had expanded enormously, and at the time of his death both he and his office were busy with houses of every size, in almost every part of the country. Although his clients came of a class which abhored publicity, and thus his works were not generally known, they were known to and admired by his fellow architects; his use of the vernacular was adopted by the next generation and became the basis for the design of the traditional country house, so his influence may be said to continue even today.

Many people have helped me with my research and the writing of this book. I must mention first Jill Franklin, to whom it is dedicated, with whom I had many happy arguments, and thank my family for taking the news that I was to write about yet another Victorian architect with resignation. They have also contributed by reading the text and making suggestions. Millicent Godfrey has allowed me to use both the drawings and photographs in the Devey Collection as illustrations, and to consult both Devey's own records and the material put together by Walter Godfrey when he wrote his prize-winning essay, and I am most grateful to her for her kindness over a long period. The Devey Collection had been deposited on loan with the Drawings Collection of the British Architectural Library, RIBA, but has recently been purchased by the Institute so that the most important Devey archive will remain intact and available for reference. I must thank Ian Mackenzie-Kerr who allowed me to study his collection of early sketches by Devey, which he has now given to the Drawings Collection, Margaret Richardson, who went through my final draft and made helpful suggestions and Lord De L'Isle and Dudley who gave me much information about Devey's early work at Penshurst. My thanks go also to all those who live in Devey's houses and who have allowed me to invade their privacy, and the many librarians and archivists who have searched out papers for me and answered my questions about both the buildings and Devey's clients. Although I regret the fact that the catalogue reveals much that cannot yet be identified, the situation would have been infinitely worse without their help. I conclude by asking readers to inform me if they notice something which has been left out or indeed, anything which is wrong.

Jill Allibone

Hemsted Toll, Benenden
June 1989

Illustrations

All illustrations are from the Devey Collection unless otherwise indicated and are reproduced by the kind permission of Mrs Emil Godfrey.

Frontispiece   George Devey   (British Architectural Library)

Fig.1	John Sell Cotman *Glastonbury* 2842 Norfolk Museums Service (Norwich Castle Museum)	16
Fig.2	South Benfleet Vicarage. (Author)	20
Fig.3	Elevation of cottages signed by Thomas Barber	21
Fig.4	Design for Leicester Square, Penshurst	28
Fig.5	Cottage on the east side of Leicester Square. (Author)	29
Fig.6	Leicester Square. (Author)	30
Fig.7	Home Farm, South Park. (Author)	31
Fig.8	Barn at Home Farm. (Author)	31
Fig.9	Gateway Lodge, Penshurst. (Author)	32
Fig.10	Ashour Lodge, Penshurst. (Author)	33
Fig.11	Cottages on Rogues Hill, Penshurst. (Author)	34
Fig.12	Design for window of butcher's shop, Penshurst	34
Fig.13	Elevation of the garden front, Hammerfield, Penshurst	35
Fig.14	Sketch for Culver Hill, Penshurst	35
Fig.15	Elevation, Culver Hill, Penshurst	36
Fig.16	Elevation of south front, Penshurst Place	39
Fig.17	Game larder, Penshurst Place. (Author)	39
Fig.18	The Buckingham Building under reconstruction. (Lord De L'Isle and Dudley)	40
Fig.19	Entrance front, Betteshanger	41
Fig.20	Elevation of the garden front, Betteshanger	42
Fig.21	Garden front, Betteshanger	43
Fig.22	Design for terrace and parterre, Betteshanger	45
Fig.23	Elevation, The Cloisters, Betteshanger	46
Fig.24	Gravel Pit Lodge, Trentham. Sketch by Walter Godfrey	47
Fig.25	Sketch for Tower Lodge, Golspie. (Ian MacKenzie-Kerr)	48
Fig.26	Elevations of Tower Lodge	49
Fig.27	Buckland School	52
Fig.28	South Lodge, Mentmore. (Author)	52
Fig.29	Design for a farm in Silesia	56
Fig.30	Eythrope	57
Fig.31	Ascott, sketch perspective	57

Fig.32	Ascott, c.1878	58
Fig.33	Ascott, the entrance courtyard	59
Fig34	Ascott, the conservatory	59
Fig.35	Sketch elevation of Walmer Castle	60
Fig.36	Elevations of Dover Clock Tower	61
Fig.37	Elevation of Dover Baths	62
Fig.38	Elevation of cottages at Lullington	63
Fig.39	Whitchurch School	64
Fig.40	Benenden School. (Author)	65
Fig.41	Jarrow School	65
Fig.42	Akeley Wood	66
Fig.43	Brantingham Thorpe, before the alterations	66
Fig.44	Brantingham Thorpe. (Author)	67
Fig.45	Brantingham Thorpe, design for the new bays	68
Fig.46	Coombe Warren I	69
Fig.47	Coombe Warren II, the entrance courtyard	70
Fig.48	Kelsall Lodge. (Author)	71
Fig.49	Coombe Warren II, the south front	72
Fig.50	Elevation of the Bay House, Coombe Warren	73
Fig.51	The Dairy, Coombe Cottage	74
Fig.52	Coombe Cottage	75
Fig.53	Hall Place, the entrance front under construction	76
Fig.54	Hall Place stables. (RCHM England)	76
Fig.55	Hall Place boathouse. (RCHM England)	77
Fig.56	Send Holme. (Author)	78
Fig.57	Cottage at Fonthill	82
Fig.58	Retaining walls at the Fonthill Arch under construction	83
Fig.59	The Chafyn-Grove Almshouses	84
Fig.60	New entrance porch at Zeals House	85
Fig.61	Evangelical Free Chapel, Leigh	86
Fig.62	Design for an unidentified Station Hotel	87
Fig.63	Elevation of Macharioch House	88
Fig.64	New laundry, Penshurst Place	89
Fig.65	Grasshome	90
Fig.66	Almshouses, Watton-at-Stone. (Author)	92
Fig.67	Goldings, ground plan	93
Fig.68	Goldings, entrance front	94
Fig.69	Goldings, drawing room doorway	95
Fig.70	Wendover Vicarage	96
Fig.71	Denne Hill. (RCHM England)	97
Fig.72	Dutch House, Kew. (Author)	98
Fig.73	Broomford Manor, garden front. (Author)	99
Fig.74	Broomford Manor from the kitchen courtyard. (Author)	100
Fig.75	St Alban's Court, entrance courtyard. (Author)	101
Fig.76	St Alban's Court, garden front. (Author)	101
Fig.77	St Alban's Court, ground plan.	102
Fig.78	St Alban's Court, Gardener's House. (Author)	103
Fig.79	Double cottage, Nonnington. (Author)	104

Fig.80	Membland, entrance front	105
Fig.81	Membland, garden front	107
Fig.82	Adderley Hall. (RCHM England)	108
Fig.83	North Lodge, Adderley. (Author)	109
Fig.84	Killarney entrance courtyard. (The Irish Architectural Archive)	110
Fig.85	Killarney, ground plan	111
Fig.86	Killarney, garden front. (The Irish Architectural Archive)	112
Fig.87	Killarney, W.H. Lascelles & Co. Ltd. advertisement	113
Fig.88	Lodge to the Western Domain, Killarney.(Irish Architectural Archive)	114
Fig.89	Barton Manor, model of house and stable yard. (Author)	116
Fig.90	Barton Manor, model of entrance to stable. (Author)	116
Fig.91	The Ledgers, model of proposed additions. (Author)	117
Fig.92	Drawing for a model of a gatehouse, St. Alban's Court	118
Fig.93	Poster advertising the Spencer Estate	120
Fig.94	Design for semi-detached houses, Spencer Estate	121
Fig.95	Terrace houses, Spencer Estate	122
Fig.96	Artisan's terrace housing, Spencer Estate	122
Fig.97	No. 8, Lennox Gardens. (Author)	123
Fig.98	No. 8, Lennox Gardens, doorway. (Author)	124
Fig.99	Nos. 2, 4 & 6, Lennox Gardens. (Author)	124
Fig.100	Nos. 23 and 25, Lennox Gardens. (Author)	125
Fig.101	No. 43, Lennox Gardens. (Author)	126
Fig.102	No. 41, Grosvenor Square, the staircase hall (RCHM England)	127
Fig.103	No. 41, Grosvenor Square (RCHM England)	128
Fig.104	Houses in Cadogan Square. (Author)	129
Fig.105	New tower, Melbury House	131
Fig.106	Design for a dairy, Melbury House	132
Fig.107	Dunraven Castle	133
Fig.108	Cranbrook Lodge, Hemsted. (Author)	139
Fig.109	The Devey memorial, Minley. (Author)	140
Fig.110	Calverley Grange	161
Fig.111	Lynwood	165
Fig.112	Brickwall. (Author)	168

1

'George has made up his mind as to his Line of Life.'

The keeping of parish registers in England began in 1538 by order of Thomas Cromwell, Henry VIII's chief minister and Vicar-General; they were written at first on paper, and after 1597, on parchment. Early volumes have frequently perished, those in London disappearing with their churches in the Great Fire of September 1666. The name Devey seems to originate in Staffordshire, and the first notice of a Devey in London is in the register of St James', Dukes Place the year after the fire, when, on the 30th September a Thomas Devey married Mary Hills. Two other Deveys married in this church in 1686 and 1688, and from this parish the family spread out so that by the eighteenth century they are found at St Marylebone, Southwark, Bethnal Green, Whitechapel, Shoreditch, Westminster, Finsbury, Bishopsgate, Holborn and Ealing. In 1776 Roger Devey married Sarah Nicholls at St Clement Danes; their son Frederick Nicholls Devey was born on the 20th March 1786.[1]

Roger Devey was a brass founder and the proprietor of the business, probably commenced by his father, R. Devey & Sons, Founders, (manufacturers of Devey & Dale's Cylinder Ballvalve & Ball) of 8 Shoe Lane, Fleet Street. Frederick appears to have been their only child, or at least the only one to survive long enough to be christened. He advanced socially by becoming admitted to the legal profession as a solicitor in 1807, beginning his own practice in Quality Court off Chancery Lane in 1813, and moving the following year to 52 Dorset Street, Salisbury Square near Ludgate Circus. In 1838 he moved from here to 34 Ely Place, Holborn. As was the custom then, these addresses served as both office and home. He married Ann Egg on the 3rd September 1817 and their first child, Frederick William was born the following year. A second son, George, the survivor of twins, was born on the 23rd February 1820, and two daughters, Ann and Emma arrived in 1821 and 1823. Ann died in infancy. The surviving children continued to live with their parents until well into their adult life. The 1851 census shows Frederick, described as an attorney, George, an architect, and their sister Emma, aged 32, 31 and 27 respectively, all living at 34 Ely Place with Frederick Nicholls and Ann, aged 65 and 66, Lucy Hill, the cook, and Emily Andrew, the housemaid.[2]

Curiously, there is no record of Frederick William ever having been admitted as a solicitor, although he appears as his father's partner in *The Post Office Annual Directory* for 1853, and is there described as a solicitor in 1858. In 1859 they are both described as of Ely Place and Ealing Common, and these are the addresses given in the will of the elder Devey, which he made on the 12th September 1861. He died on the 20th April the following year, when the practice came to an end. His son then vanishes from both the business and Court sections of the *Directory*. He may have gone to Staffordshire, (although only briefly as he later moved to Hastings) as his father left him 'my freehold Estate at Walsall'; how his father came to have such a property so far from the centre of his activities in London is not known, but

Devey is a common name in that part of the county, so it may have been left to him by a relative, and sentiment may have made him leave it in turn to his eldest son. However he came by this property, he had at an early stage in his career taken one step to distance himself from the manufacture of ballvalves, by adopting (probably without the authority of the College of Arms) a coat of arms. This seems to have been of some antiquity, and a curious paper still in the possession of the family, explains the meaning of the engrailed chevron, the three annulets, the difference distinguishing them as the arms of a fifth son, and the cannon crest 'in a more intelligible tongue, giving authorities for my assertions, and leaving it to the superior judgment of my friends (the Deveys) to form an opinion upon the respectability of their Coat-of-Arms.' Devey senior used them when sealing his correspondence. His younger son did not.

Ann Egg was the daughter of Durs Egg, a Swiss gunmaker born in Basle in 1745 who emigrated to England and established himself in London in 1772. In 1814 he opened a shop at 132 the Strand, moving to the Colonade, Pall Mall, in 1818. In this same year a relative, Joseph Egg, gun and patent truss maker, opened at 1 Piccadilly. Durs Egg in Pall Mall, Joseph and his sons Charles and Henry in Piccadilly, all continued in business until the mid 1860s. Durs manufactured double-barrelled shot guns, duelling and pocket pistols, and was patronised by the Prince Regent who wrote to his brother Frederick in 1782: 'we are to try three rifle barrel guns ... one wh. was made by ye. best workman we have here; he is a Swiss German, & his name is Egge. This gun is made after Furgeson's rifle & one of ye. best guns ever was made.' Egg was to make Lord St Leger and the Prince 'new ones upon the same construction. Ye gunsmith himself says he could not possibly turn out of his hands a better gun than this.' The Prince's new gun with the Ferguson action and silver mounts hall marked 1782 is still in the Armoury at Windsor Castle. When a list of his debts was prepared for William Pitt in 1787 it showed that he owed Egg £548.[3] The gunmaker seems to have got on well with his royal customer; James Williams, who was to become Devey's partner and who had probably heard the story many times, wrote: 'It is said he was on somewhat familiar terms with His Majesty, and on one occasion, when invited to breakfast, refused on the plea that he preferred the bread and butter cut by his daughter Nancy (Mr. Devey's mother). He was thereupon ordered, the next time he was asked, to bring his daughter with him, but the worthy parent had doubts as to the moral atmosphere of the Court, so Nancy never went.'[4]

What is more interesting, however, is British patent 3903 granted by George III on the 24th October 1815 to Durs Egg and Jean Samuel Pauly, another Swiss who was in business as a gunmaker in Paris in 1808, and who came to England in 1814. This patent was not, as might have been anticipated for some refinement of the gunmakers' craft, but for 'Certain Aerial Conveyances, and Vessels to be steered by Philosophical or Chemical and Mechanical Means.'[5] It was the first in England for any kind of airship. What was proposed was a fish-shaped balloon on a rigid frame with a moveable tail made of whalebone and silk for steering and 'fins, feathers, fans or wings for propulsion' operated either manually or mechanically. Ascent and descent were to be controlled by a box filled with water or sand moved towards the nose or tail by ropes and pulleys; the contents acted as ballast and could be discharged. The passengers were to travel in a gondola slung below all this. Construction began in 1816 in a shed at Knightsbridge 100 feet long and with doors from top to bottom. This prototype was about 85 feet long and 32 feet high and was called the *Dolphin*. It had a wooden frame with an external envelope and an internal balloon made of varnished gold-beaters' skin in layers, obtained, it was said, from the hides of 70,000 oxen. Tickets at a guinea each were sold for a view of 'one of the ascensions' of what became popularly known as 'Egg's Folly'. It never ascended and was said to have cost him over £10,000. Pauly died before it was completed.

The manufacture of guns is a matter of blacksmithing, their enrichment is a matter of art. The process of engraving and inlaying the patterns which decorated the finer pieces required considerable skill in design, and it is therefore not surprising that Egg's son, Augustus Leopold, inherited his father's artistic gift and became a painter. He was born in 1816, studied at Sass's Academy in Charlotte Street, and later at the Royal Academy Schools. He became an Associate in 1849, and a Royal Academician in 1861, but in 1837 he joined with John Philip, Richard Dadd, W.P. Frith and others, and founded an association which they called The Clique. This group of young men were determined to reform the stuffy and self-interested traditionalism of the Academicians, who they felt were deliberately excluding them from membership, so denying them hanging space at the exhibitions and thus the commissions which they hoped would result from this publicity. Egg's subjects were at first historical genre taken from English history and literature such as his *Life and Death of Buckingham,* scenes from *Romeo and Juliet, The Winter's Tale* and *The Taming of the Shrew.* However, when the Pre-Raphaelite Brotherhood was founded in 1848 Egg befriended the members, adopted some of their techniques, and became interested in painting scenes of contemporary life such as the *Past and Present* triptych, painted in 1858, which is by way of being a commentary on the Matrimonial Causes Act passed the previous year. This had made divorce, previously only obtainable by Act of Parliament and therefore a prerogative of the wealthy, available to the middle classes.[6] Egg met Charles Dickens in 1847 and almost immediately joined in the amateur theatrical tours organised by him, in which Douglas Jerrold, George Cruikshank, John Leech, Mark Lemon and other writers and artists took part. Egg both acted and designed the costumes: 'The dresses are a perfect blaze of colour, and there is not a pocket-flap or a scrap of lace that has not been made according to Egg's drawings to a quarter of an inch.'[7] In 1853 he accompanied Dickens and Wilkie Collins, the novelist son of William Collins R.A. and brother of the Pre-Raphaelite follower Charles Allston Collins, on a tour of Italy, and was greatly regretted by them when he died ten years later.

Ann had been born in 1785, and so was considerably older than Augustus. With this family background it is most probable that she was also gifted artistically, and that it was from from his mother that George inherited his talent for, and interest in painting. Having a young uncle only four years older than himself actively involved with the politics of the art world must also have excited his interest and it seems more likely that his enthusiasm for painting was aroused by what was going on in his immediate family circle rather than his brief period as a pupil of John Sell Cotman, as has been previously suggested.[8]

The Devey boys were educated together, and were first sent to a school run by the Revd J.A. Baron at Stanmore. Both entered King's College School in the autumn term of 1832, aged respectively fourteen and twelve, and George left at the end of the spring term of 1835. As they were not nominated by a Proprietor, their father paid a one guinea entrance fee and nine guineas for a half year's tuition for each boy. King's College had been founded by Royal Charter on the 14th August 1829 and opened on the 8th October 1831 in a building designed by Robert Smirke on the east of Somerset House.[9] It was the Established Church's response to the foundation of University College, London, which had aroused concern in the Church of England by being non-sectarian. Both institutions were designed to fill the educational gap between the working-class Mechanics Institutes and the Universities of Oxford and Cambridge which were only open to the wealthy upper classes. This gap was at the time most inadequately filled by the endowed grammar schools, which were in such a state that they had to be regulated by the Grammar Schools Act of 1840, and the public schools such as Harrow and Rugby. The abuses prevalent at these boarding schools were to be countered in time by the example of Dr Arnold who had been appointed to the mastership of Rugby in 1827. King's College was divided into two sections, for older and younger boys, the junior department being at first housed in the basement. Administered by a General Court of Governors and Proprietors, it was intended that an education equivalent to that of the old grammar schools

Fig.1 Glastonbury

should be offered, to day boys only, with a curriculum which also would ground the boys in general knowledge and prepare them for the professions. It was very succesful in attracting the attention of middle-class fathers who were either professional men themselves or in business, and an idea of the sort of boy educated there is shown by the surprising number of future architects who passed through the school: E.M. Barry, William Burges, Arthur Cates, Nockalls Johnson Cottingham, J.D. Crace, Henry Crisp, F.W. Cumberland, Sir William Emerson, H.B. Garling, William Lightly, Jacob Wrey Mould, Arthur Shean Newman,

William Niven, Edmund Scott, R. Phené Spiers, Gervase Wheeler, John Whichcord junior and of course Devey. In 1840 a Department of Civil Engineering and Architecture was founded with a course on Civil Architecture which was taught at a fee of £31.10.0. per annum which would have made the College even more attractive to young men intending to be architects.[10]

There were six classes in the school, and the subjects taught were Religious Instruction, the customary Latin and Greek, French, Mathematics, History, Geography, English Language and Literature, and Elocution. Extras offered were fencing and sword exercises taught by Signor Henry Angelo (Fencing Master to H.M.'s Forces), Hebrew, German, Italian, Spanish, Natural Philosophy, the Principals and Practice of Commerce, and Drawing. John Sell Cotman was appointed Professor of Drawing in 1834. He had been recommended for the post by Sir Francis Palgrave and the architect William Wilkins, who was also a Norfolk man, and was taken on at a salary of £100 a year plus a guinea extra for every pupil enrolled after the first hundred. He had 185 students at the start, this number rising within a month to 200, all taught in classes of about 50 boys.[11] His teaching was, under these circumstances, necessarily perfunctory, as William Michael Rossetti remembered: 'Mr. Cotman's course of instruction did not extend far beyond giving us pencil-sketches, often his own, to copy...'[12] This had been his method with his private pupils and over 2,000 such drawings were in existence before he went to the College, and this number was doubled, with the help of his children, before he died in 1842. Each pupil was given a drawing with a laconic 'Copy this'. The boys pricked through the design onto paper below and used the resulting pattern as an aid to making an accurate copy; shading they had to accomplish on their own. (Fig.1) It was a soul-destroying exercise leading to boredom and mischief. The classes were too large to be manageable and attempts by Cotman and his assistant (this was his son Miles Edmund, providing unpaid help) to maintain discipline failed until his final threat: 'Gentlemen, I cannot go on thus. You must be silent or I must leave the room.' This apparently quietened things down.[13]

Devey's earliest known drawings are half a dozen sketches mounted in two bound volumes of autographs presented to the Headmaster of King's College School, the Revd J.R. Major, at Christmas 1834 and 1835. One is a view of a castle on the banks of a loch, and another a group of figures in invented historical costume; there is a lugger in a stiff breeze, a sketch of church and parsonage, and of a cottage in a wood.[14] None are particularly remarkable productions and he was only sixteenth in his class in drawing. Little more is known about his school-days; James Williams wrote: 'he used modestly to say that he was never considered to be a very capable youth ... George seldom spoke of his school days, but the impression left is that the time there must have been somewhat irksome to anyone of his temperament.' The school had the reputation of being a bit rough, but then most were at that time. Nevertheless, the *Report from the Council* already referred to gives particulars of a prize-giving held on the 29th June 1833, when the prizes were presented by the Archbishop of Canterbury, who was Visitor of the College. George was awarded fifth prize for his classwork and a prize for French. In May the following year he came top of the fifth Class and Frederick William gained the first prize for German, so they showed some ability. When they left, Frederick, as we have seen, became a lawyer. George wanted to be a painter.

Given the fact that he had been taught by Cotman for only a year and under the most trying circumstances, it is surprising that Cotman's style and his usual choice of subject matter, ancient and vernacular buildings, dominated his own to such a great extent. But this may have happened later. As mentioned above, Devey was more likely to have been impressed by his Uncle Augustus, supported by Durs Egg's considerable means (despite the failure of the *Dolphin*), an angry young painter on his way, already feeling thwarted by the establishment as represented by the Royal Academicians, and altogether an exciting person to emulate. But his father would have none of this 'for in the early part of the last century it was hardly thought of as respectable enough to be classed with the professions.'[15] The elder Devey may well have been on his dignity as a professional man, whereas Durs Egg, however successful, was in trade. Furthermore, he was probably not as wealthy as Egg and unwilling to support his son through the years during which he would be trying to create a name for himself. Clearly the young man's future was a matter of family debate from the time he left school in the spring of 1835 until the autumn of 1837. We do not know how he occupied himself during this period, but if it is true that he was taught watercolour painting by James Duffield Harding, it probably happened then.[16] Harding, though not so great a man as Cotman, was probably a better teacher, and had done much to further the teaching of art in schools and the training of art masters, and he had published books on teaching drawing by direct observation of nature rather than the mechanical copying methods of the overworked Cotman. He was greatly admired by John Ruskin, and thus probably better known to the layman than Cotman would have been.

Frederick Nicholls Devey had acted for over ten years for the Revd George Richard Boissier, curate first of Chiddingstone and then of Penshurst in Kent. On the 18th December 1832 he was appointed Boissier's receiver, and from his correspondence it appears that he managed Boissier's financial affairs, which seem to have been chaotic. Bossier was the 'gentleman, the reverse of rich, (who) had been recommended to consult Mr. Frederick Devey ... with reference to the recovery of some property, which had almost been given up as lost, partly on account of the lapse of time and the difficult tangle into which things had got, and partly because the client was poor; however, after endless investigation, and with little chance of payment, the faithful solicitor succeeded in recovering a large estate, which put the needy client into very comfortable circumstance.'[17] Boissier remained in difficulties despite this success. Indeed as late as January 1858, George Devey came to his rescue with a loan of £100 which was only repaid by Boissier's widow after his death in 1866. From time to time the solicitor received small gifts of game from his client, and on the 11th September 1837 he wrote with thanks for two brace of birds and concluded the letter: 'I know you will be glad to hear that George has made up his mind as to his Line of Life, and that last week he entered upon the probationary Interval which preceeds positive Adoption. And what do you think the line is ? But setting anyone to guess is viler than punning; so I hasten to tell you - an Architect and Surveyor.'[18]

The man to whom Devey went as pupil after this 'probationary Interval' was Thomas Little, who had a prosperous, no nonsense sort of practice which would appeal to a businessman. Little, born in 1802, was thus in his mid-thirties when Devey came to him. Coutts Stone, who became Devey's life-long friend was also a pupil at this time, and Little probably took them on as much for the help they could give him in the running of a busy practice as for the premiums their fathers undoubtedly paid. Little himself had been a pupil of Robert Abraham and begun as an architect and surveyor, but gradually restricted himself to architectural work only. He is described in his obituary as 'an excellent draughtsman, and a man of great talent and perseverance. He was much appealed to as an arbitrator, his strict honour and integrity being known.'[19] His office was at 36 Northumberland Street, New Road, off Trafalgar Square.

Devey was to remain with Little a surprisingly long time, certainly far beyond the usual period a youngster would expect to remain in pupilage, and it was not because he was a slow learner. It is probable that at the end of his formal training he passed from being a pupil to being a paid assistant, and in view of his obvious talent, a much-favoured employee. The contract drawings dated 1844 for the Nunhead Cemetery, Peckham, show how soon and how greatly he came to exceed his master in the matter of draughtsmanship. It is not possible to establish exactly what work Little had in hand during the first five years that Devey was with him, but designs hung in the Royal Academy exhibition in 1840 show that he worked at White Knights, Berkshire, for which he made a *Design for entrance to Botanic Gardens*, and built a grand house at 13 Hyde Park Gardens for T. Assheton Smith Esq. We also know of 'houses and manufactories' in Oxford Street for Messrs Gillow the upholsterers & Messrs Collins. However, this was a time when Devey himself was successful in having some paintings accepted by the Royal Academy. In 1841 he contributed: *Design; Cottage near Southampton*. The following year it was *Design; Garden entrance* and *Design; Mansion - Italian style*. In 1843 his *Design; Entrance to a Cemetery &c* was probably his own scheme for the Nunhead Cemetery Competition, which Little won.[20] The drawings for the cemetery are the first set of designs in which Devey's participation can be seen, both in acting as witness to the signing of the contract drawings, and in the drawings themselves. He does not seem to have helped with another set of designs for a road improvement scheme and the rebuilding of a shop and dwelling at No.1 Princes Street (now Wardour Street), Leicester Square prepared for a Robert Sampson in c.1840-3.[21]

The Nunhead drawings consist of the competition design, contract drawings and working drawings for two chapels. The cemetery had been laid out by the London Cemetery Company which attached its seal on appropriately black wax to the contract drawings. It had been consecrated in 1840 and laid out by the Company's architect James Bunning who also designed the gates and lodges. Little's chapels, for unconsecrated and consecrated ground, the latter octagonal, have survived, and they are his most interesting designs. At the same time he received commissions for two substantial churches, All Saints, St John's Wood and St Andrew's, Fairlight in Sussex, which was rebuilt by rich visitors to Hastings in the teeth of the objections of the local congregation who were greatly attached to 'their old church wherein the rude forefathers of the hamlet worshipped for many ages, and around which many take their eternal rest'.[22] St. Andrew's is Early English with a west tower and beacon turret. All Saints was built in 1845-6 and enlarged and generally improved in 1852-4. It is unambitious Perpendicular carried out in Kentish ragstone with Bath stone dressings, the standard materials for London churches at this time, and ones which did not wear well in the polluted atmosphere. Devey signed both the original design drawing on which the estimates were based, in March 1845, and the contract drawings on the 3rd June 1845. The only other work which we know the office was engaged with at this time was the stables for Mr Dickinson in Curzon Street, where forty horses were kept. This would have been a job after Devey's heart. Throughout his life he was devoted to horses and when he had his own, visited them daily in the stables with titbits of carrot. *The Builder* praised the ventilation of the Curzon Street stables without naming the architect which caused Little to protest to the editor: 'As professional services are too often forgotten in descriptions of new buildings, I am sure you will take an early opportunity of stating that these stables were executed from my plans and superintendance.'[23]

In 1846, Devey, who had now been in Little's office for nine years, set off on a continental tour with Coutts Stone. Quite a number of sketches and watercolours by both young men, whose work at this stage is not readily separated, have survived, and their route can be followed. They crossed from Dover to Belgium and visited Brussels, where Devey sketched a number of the lead-covered onion-shaped belfry turrets of the kind he designed later for Coombe Warren and Killarney. They then travelled up the Rhine by way of Bingen, Heidelberg and Strasbourg, on to Lago Maggiore, Bologna, Verona, Venice, Mantua, Rome and Naples. In Rome, Devey was quite overwhelmed by the Sistine Chapel. From here they went on to Greece, which is confirmed by the last of Devey's Royal Academy exhibits. In 1847 he showed *Arch of Titus, Rome &c.*, and in 1848, *On the Acropolis, Athens 1846*. James

Fig.2 South Benfleet Vicarage

Williams remembered that there were not many drawings left from this tour 'but what remain are exceptionally good, especially those made in Venice and Athens.' The address given for his previous exhibition entries had been that of his father's house, 34 Ely Place; now it was 16 Great Marlborough Street where he rented an office; he had started in practice on his own.

We know that he had difficulty in finding clients. Luckily, what was obviously a most happy relationship with Little ensured that he had something to do. He continued to work for him on a part-time basis, first on St Mary's, Church End, Willesden and then on Paddington cemetery. St Mary's church was in a ruinous state, partly through neglect and partly through parish altercations and litigation. The survey drawings were made in 1848, but the designs for the restoration, mostly by Devey, were not prepared until 1851. After the objections of the pew-holders had been met, the south aisle was rebuilt, a porch added and new windows and doorways in Bath stone inserted throughout.[24] Devey also made the designs for Paddington Cemetery at Willesden in 1854-5, with Episcopal and Dissenters' Chapels, walls, gateways and lodges for the burial board of the parish of Paddington. This is all good, standard Gothic Revival stuff, but not as exciting a design as that for Nunhead.[25]

Of Devey's own commissions during this period we know very little and only one building can now be identified. (Fig. 2) This is the vicarage at South Benfleet, Essex built for the Revd H.R. Lloyd, of whom nothing is known, in 1846. Godfrey records the fact that his perspective of a parsonage at South Benfleet was rejected by the Royal Academy.[26] This has disappeared, but three sheets of plans and a section have survived, and this building is a most useful demonstration of the way Devey set about the design of such a thing before he came to know the traditional buildings of the Weald. It is constructed of rubble stone with squared up quoins; two gables of differing size face the road, there is a round-headed central doorway and to the right of this an overscaled chimney breast cutting into the gable. The offsets of this and a large angle buttress on the left are finished with red tiles, there is a string course of red brick, and two rows of bricks are inserted under the eaves. Devey is already using the diagonally set red brick chimney stacks which were to become so characteristic of his small buildings, and these, together with the substantial and strong treatment of the details set this parsonage apart from the sort of thing which would have been produced by many other architects of this period.

Apart from this, it must be said that there are a number of early drawings for unidentified cottages and small houses, including one for a doctor rendered in both the Italian villa and Tudor styles, but these schemes are most fragmentary, and generally only a single plan or elevation remain. A contract drawing for a pair of cottages in the vernacular style, dated February 1850 and signed by the builder Thomas Barber, was clearly made after he had begun at Penshurst, and the difference between this and South Benfleet is immediately apparent. Unfortunately these cannot be identified. (Fig.3) But Devey could still relapse into his earlier style as two later sets of contract drawings show; they are dated 1856 and signed by Richard Collins who worked at Penshurst, so although also unidentified, they were

Fig.3 Elevation of cottages signed by Thomas Barber

presumably built in west Kent. They show Devey designing in a very plain manner, with perhaps a touch of Gothick, in other words in a style indistinguishable from that used by his contemporaries for cheap cottages, and again demonstrate the change which occured when he began to look at Wealden buildings and found sympathetic clients.[27] Besides these small efforts he had written a paper on the removal of domestic and factory smoke from the atmosphere, which he suggested should be done by using the sewers as flues but this slightly impractical proposal seems to have gone no further than a letter to *The Builder*.[28] All in all this was a bleak period; that he had still to work for his old employer in his mid-thirties must have been galling, but things were slowly to improve.

2

Cottage Building

At this point the Revd Mr Boissier came up trumps. Walter Godfrey's index of Devey's clients mentions his name with a note: 'Very early work, old friend and intro' G.D. to Lord De L'Isle'.[1] Godfrey later expanded this in his biographical essay describing Devey's father as: 'a man of ability and of a high minded nature, to whose persistent and successful efforts (quite disinterested) in following up and substantiating the claim of a friend to certain properties, his son is said to have owed his first introduction to distinguished patronage, benefiting by the gratitude which his father had inspired.'[2] Boissier lived at a house called Oakfield at Smart's Hill both during his curacy of Penshurst, an appointment which he gave up in June 1852, and during his retirement. He had previously been curate at Chiddingstone but did not strike the more fastidious parishioners as being quite out of the top drawer: 'In the evening we had a service & a sermon from Mr. Boissier — he is a very indifferent performer — one of the lowest *class* of Clergyman that I ever heard in the Pulpit for generally the Anglican clergy are Gentlemen.'[3]

Devey was commissioned by him to carry out some small works which cannot now be identified, due to the large additions that have been made to Oakfield over the years. Whatever they were, they were obviously satisfactory and Boissier took the trouble to present his *protegé* to the two most important landowners in the neighbourhood, Lord De L'Isle and Dudley of Penshurst Place and Lieut. General Sir Henry Hardinge, Governor General of India 1844-8, hero of the Sikh War and the owner of South Park. Both employed him, first, Lord De L'Isle, on the restoration of, and additions to a group of cottages at the entrance to Penshurst churchyard, called Leicester Square. This was so succesful that after the death of the 1st Baron in 1851, Sir Philip Sidney, the 2nd Baron, continued to employ Devey until the mid 1870s, using him for restoration work at Penshurst Place, improvements in the village, and estate cottages. Then Hardinge had him enlarge and improve the buildings at South Park Home Farm, build the Chafford Arms and a new vicarage at Fordcombe, and provide a lych gate for St Peter's. It was the work at Leicester Square and Home Farm, in which Devey first employs the style and materials which were based upon the vernacular buildings of the Weald, that enabled him to formulate a style of building which was to characterise his own work. This work was to have a demonstrable effect on the younger architects who adopted old buildings as models for domestic architecture, rejecting the borrowings from mediaeval ecclesiastical buildings, the Tudor period and the Continent, which were common practice for most architects of this time.

Two separate themes meet here, both of which were to be of great importance in Devey's early career; they are the increase of cottage building on country estates and the rise in popularity of English genre painting. We will consider the matter of cottage building first.

The life of the English agricultural labourer in the late eighteenth and early nineteenth centuries had little to do with 'Merrie England' and the idealised vision of English rural life invented by popular historians.[4] There had been a period of rapid improvement in farming methods, which in counties like Norfolk, under the instruction of Thomas Coke of Holkham, had increased its output by a hundred per cent in twenty years. There was need of such an increase for the population had doubled in the past hundred years and the wars with France and Napoleon's 'Continental System' obliged the English to feed themselves or starve. Improvements in stock rearing and rotations of crops were matched by a reorganisation of the way the land was managed. Eighteen hundred enclosure bills went through Parliament in the period 1796-1815 with the approval of all but the dispossessed. 'A great portion of unstinted common lands remain nearly as nature left them, appearing in the present state of civilisation and science as filthy blotches on the face of the country, especially when seen under threatening clouds of famine.'[5] The blotches were, in fact, partly the old open fields, and partly commons and manorial wastes. The open field system had involved the peasant in the cultivation of his own strips of land, and the common had afforded him grazing and fuel. The compensatory allotments which replaced these ancient rights required fencing and draining, processes frequently beyond the means of the poor man, who was forced to sell his field to his richer neighbours. Where he had been to a great extent self-supporting, he now relied on wages. Those who had squatted on the wastes received nothing. Once enclosed, the landowners preferred to let their property in large holdings, which was both convenient from an administrative point of view, and in accord with good farming practice. The rural poor, particularly in the south, where there were few factories to take on the unemployed, were now more than ever under the control of the farmers, and already low wages were further depressed by the Berkshire magistrates, meeting at Speenhamland in 1795, when, instead of setting a minimum wage, which they had the power to do, a subsistence rate was arrived at dependent upon the price of corn and the size of the worker's family; the difference between this and the actual wage received to be made up out of the Poor's Rate. The result of this, was that by the time of Waterloo, one-fifth of the rural population was on relief and the Poor's Rate had increased from £700,000 in 1750 to £8,000,000 in 1818. When the war ended three things had happened; the labour market was flooded with returning soldiers, the Government ceased to buy the food which had previously fed the army, and imports of European and American grain brought down farming profits until these were protected by the Corn Laws. Good harvests in England in 1813 and 1815, and in France in 1814 brought prices sharply down and farmers were unable to pay their rents and loan interest. Matters were compounded in 1816, the worst summer in memory, when unemployment led to riots and rick burning, but 1817 was a good year and things got better; this slow progress continued until the repeal of the Corn Laws in 1849 began another period of agricultural depression.

But the labourers did not benefit from this steady improvement. Speenhamland and starvation wages led to the Swing riots which began in Kent in August 1830 and lasted until the end of the year. Not only were the poor unfed, but their living conditions were dreadful, in hovels built of mud or stones and branches, roughly thatched with bracken, heather or whatever material was locally available. It is doubtful if William Cobbett much exaggerated their state: 'Look at these hovels, made of mud and straw, bits of glass, or of old cast-off windows, without frames or hinges, frequently, but merely stuck in the mud wall. Enter them, and look at the bits of chairs or stools; the wretched boards tacked together, to serve for a table; the floor of pebble, broken brick, or of bare ground'. These stood on unclaimed, unenclosed patches of land or on strips between the road verges and the field hedges and they bore little resemblance to John Ruskin's view of the ideal cottage, which was based not, as he imagined, on a peasant's home, but on a yeoman's farmhouse: ' The principal thing worthy of observation in the lowland cottage of England is its finished neatness. The thatch is firmly pegged down, and mathematically levelled at the edges; - The whitewash is stainless, and its rough surface catches a side light as brightly as a front one: the luxuriant rose is trained gracefully over the window; and the gleaming lattice, divided not into heavy squares, but into small pointed diamonds is thrown half open, - The light wooden porch breaks the flat of the cottage face by its projection; and a branch or two of wandering honeysuckle spread over the low hatch.'[6] This highly idealised view was given pictorial expression by painters like Myles Birket Foster and Helen Allingham, whose timber-framed cottages with brick noggin and substantial chimney breasts are emphatically not buildings put up by the poor, though they may have been living in them at the date when they were painted. The poor labourers' hovels have entirely disappeared.

Even the more substantial farm cottages were desperately primitive: two walls, two gables with a fireplace in each, a central door leading to two rooms, perhaps with a garret above. And the stock of these had been depleted: 'Twenty years ago, during the war, landed proprietors found it most profitable to pull down cottages and let their lands in large farms; and that they should follow the course which they found most lucrative was very natural. It is just as natural, in the present times, for them to return to the cottage system, in order to save the rent of the land being eaten up by the poor's rate.'[7] This was hardly altruistic but the situation was beginning to cause concern among the country gentry and the plight of the poor and its consequences were recorded in John Claudius Loudon's periodical, *The Gardener's Magazine*. John H. Moggeridge of Monmouthshire wrote: 'Twenty years experience as a magistrate ... have fully confirmed in my mind the suspicion I had from general observation ... that the moral and political degradation of the labouring classes in this county, generally, is more the effect of the circumstances in which they have been placed, than of any positive and unavoidable necessity; and far less the result of their own indifference or criminality, than of the imperfection and errors of that state of society of which they form an essential, but a most oppressed and unjustly treated portion.'[8] The Conductor, that is, Loudon himself, took up the theme in 1832:

> The depressed state of the agricultural population in England, the consequent pressure of poor-rates in some places, and the outrages of incendiaries in others, have forced the attention of the landed proprietors to the means of ameliorating, or at least quieting for a time, their territorial population; and, in consequence we have heard, for upwards of a year, of cottages being repaired, and land allotted to cottages at moderate rents throughout most of the English counties. Within the last six months the alarm occasioned by the cholera has caused increased attention to be given to the subject of comfortable cottages for agricultural labourers, and to that of the conditions of the poor generally; cleanliness, warmth proper ventilation, and wholesome food being found the best preventives of that disease. [9]

So bad housing had as its consequences criminal and riotous behaviour, political unrest (the French Revolution was still very much within living memory), and the harbouring of disease. Loudon informs his readers that he has a collection of nearly 200 designs for cottages which could be inspected, copies of these, and the services of 'a young architect' could be had at a moderate charge.[10] Cottage building became a preoccupation of the landed classes as a measure of self-protection and also as a means of display. A man living in a grand house did not wish to see hovels at his gate; rehousing his tenants could demonstrate his good taste, philanthropy, and also be a measure of the wealth which allowed the building work to take place. This situation led to the production of large quantities of pattern books in the first half of the nineteenth century, many written and illustrated by architects, or would be architects, of no consequence, but some by men of considerable ability.[11] By the time Devey began work in Kent a great programme of rebuilding in the village and on the estate was well and truly under way.

The parallel between the revival of interest in vernacular architecture and the beginnings of British genre painting was first made some years ago.[12] A change in the type of patron was in part responsible for this. The wars with France had put a stop to the Grand Tour for twenty years, and it was never re-established as part of the education of a gentleman. Part of the object of the Tour had been the acquisition of paintings, either new works by painters who had established themselves at Paris or Rome, or Old Masters which were actively marketed, often by these same practising painters. But now the upper classes had practically ceased collecting, and had been replaced by men with new money, but without the education to distinguish between the genuine article and the false attributions or out and out fakes which had been asiduously promoted by the less scrupulous sort of dealer. A number of these new collectors burnt their fingers badly and their plight was taken up and publicised by Samuel Carter Hall, the editor of *The Art-Journal*, and was brought more particularly to general notice by a number of court cases. The alarm these caused, and a quite natural dislike of being swindled, led to collectors in the early 1850s turning almost exclusively to new paintings by living artists. These new patrons got their money from trade. John Sheepshanks, who left his collection to the South Kensington Museum had a share in the family woollen mill in Leeds. Daniel Wade Acraman, a Bristol iron founder, built up a collection of Dutch and Flemish landscape and genre paintings, and then began to collect the work of local artists. Robert Vernon, whose paintings were given to the Nation in 1847, had made a fortune supplying horses to the British armies during the Napoleonic wars. Joseph Gillott, who surpassed them all in his collecting activities, invented and manufactured the steel pen nib (and was consequently known to his employees as 'His Nibs'), Elhanan Bicknell dealt in whale oil, Albert Grant was a Company promoter and the creator of London's Leicester Square, and William Wells was a retired 'Company's captain' in the East India Company's service. He had made two of the two year voyages to China, first as second officer of the *Lascelles* in 1792-3 and then as master of the *Albion* in 1794-95, and the considerable profits customarily made by the ship's captain on such enterprises enabled him to go into partnership with his brother as the proprietors of the Blackwall Docks. His friend, the painter Joseph Farington wrote in his diary 'Mr. Wells might have had the Husbandry of as many Indiamen as he might have chosen, and have gained two millions, but he would not avail himself of the opportunities offered to him.'[13] As it was, he had quite sufficient wealth to pursue his interests.

Wells had bought Redleaf, an estate just to the north of Penshurst Place and by 1839 had created a famous garden.[14] He also bought paintings, and his collection demonstrates the transition from the collecting of Old Masters to the collecting of the work of contemporary painters. He had magnificent examples of the former, such as Van Dyke's *Three Heads of Charles I*, which he sold to George IV in 1822, and *The Enchanted Castle* by Claude Lorrain, which he kept until his death; these are now respectively in the Royal Collection at Windsor Castle and the National Gallery. But the hall at Redleaf was hung with Landseers, and Redleaf was treated by Landseer as his second home in the 1830s, particularly when he was recovering from some sort of nervous breakdown.[15] Among these paintings were *The Stone Breaker, A Highland Interior, Ptarmigan, Low Life, High Life, The Shepherd's Grave, Falcon, Hooded Falcon, None but the Brave deserve the Fair, The Sanctuary*, bought from him by Queen Victoria as a birthday present for Prince Albert, and *The Decoyman's Dog and Duck*. The subjects of these paintings raise another point; not only did this new type of patron lack the knowledge which would have allowed them to discriminate between forgeries and genuine Old Masters, they also lacked the education which would have made history painting and mythologies, the chief subjects of High Art, attractive to them. Landscape painting was not highly regarded, as John Constable was to discover, and was thought to be mere copying. What was becoming popular was a form of sentimental rustic genre painting which owed its inspiration to the lesser seventeenth century Dutch masters, such as Teniers, Ostade and Terboch, which were collected by the Prince Regent, John Walter II, chief proprietor of *The Times*, Noel Desenfans, who was collecting on behalf of King Stanislaus of Poland, whose pictures remain together at the Dulwich Gallery, and others in the early part of the century. This type of small cabinet painting and their rural subjects were the inspiration of George Moreland, who produced idealised and picturesque scenes of country life, and David Wilkie who took a more robust and realistic view in paintings such as his *Blind Man's Bluff* of 1812. What they were producing, however, was something more acceptable to Victorian collectors and approved by Ruskin 'such work ...as these men have done, or are doing, is entirely good in its influence on the public mind: and may, in thankful exultation, be compared with the renderings of besotted, vicious, and vulgar human life perpetrated by Dutch painters, or with the deathful formalism and fallacy of what was once called 'Historical Art'.'[16] Moreland and Wilkie were followed in their choice of subject matter by a group of painters who were frequent guests at Redleaf: E.W. Cooke, Thomas Sidney Cooper, W.P. Frith, Frederick Goodall, J.C. Horsley, F.R. Lee, Patrick Nasmyth, Richard Redgrave, J.M.W. Turner and Thomas Webster. Of these, Goodall, Horsley, Lee, Nasmyth and Webster specialised in rustic genre, and Horsley and Webster, with the brothers F.D. and George Hardy, G.D. O'Neill and the mysterious A.E. Mulready who may have been an illegitimate son of William, settled for some time in Kent and formed the Cranbrook Colony, using local people as sitters, and real cottage interiors as backgrounds for paintings such as F.D. Hardy's *The Clergyman's Visit* and Webster's *Roast Pig*.[17]

William Wells died in 1847, leaving Redleaf and its contents to his nephew, another William or Billy Wells, who sold some paintings within a year or so, but kept most. Devey may quite likely have visited Boissier at Penshurst before the Redleaf *habitués* dispersed after their host's death, and in view of his known interest in paintings it is more than likely that Boissier would have introduced him to Wells and his guests. He would thus have met a group of men who not only visited and sketched at Penshurst Place, Hever Castle, Knole and Ightham Mote, all grand places which provided backgrounds for Horsley's historical paintings which he set in the sixteenth or seventeenth century, but also, the smaller houses and cottages in the neighbourhood which provided the backgrounds for their genre paintings. Their interest in this sort of building and the materials which gave them their character may well have been communicated to the young Devey.

Even if he was introduced to Wells as a possible patron, as was to be the case with Lord De L'Isle and Hardinge, Wells did not give him any work. He had chosen in the past to design any cottages he required himself, and had built two at least, which were illustrated by Loudon.[18] They are his Penshurst Lodge, which was built for the head gardener Joseph Wells (father of H.G. Wells) and what Loudon calls a Cyclopean cottage for the under gardener. The Lodge is an L shaped building built of ragstone found on the estate, with pierced and carved bargeboards and a pantile roof. The cottage is altogether more of a rum design, the ground floor is constructed of irregular sandstone blocks, a vertical manifestation of crazy paving which Wells seems to have invented, above which there is close studding with the initials WW incorporated on the southern gable.The roof here is tiled, and both small buildings had the roof slopes in two sections, running into the main gable in the lower part, and into a gablet above. These designs are a world away from those produced by Devey ten years later, and are good examples of the *cottage orné*, one of the choices then available to improving landowners, amongst designs in the Gothic in all its manifestations, the Italian villa, the Swiss chalet and so forth.[19] Yet when he first began, Devey produced designs not dissimilar from Wells' attempts. Some of the early versions of the eastern cottage on Leicester Square have all the features of the *cottage orné*. It was the development in the design of this one small building which was to take English domestic architecture forward into the vernacular revival.

Leicester Square lies between St John the Baptist, Penshurst and the road. It consisted of a pair of cottages, with a third forming a bridge between them and framing the entrance to the churchyard. That on the west is a first floor hall house, now divided in two; it is half-timbered and planked, in a manner resembling plank and muntin partitioning more usually found in interiors. The rooms in the bridge are reached by an external flight of stairs with a gable, most probably by Devey, as he uses a similar arrangement at Home Farm. Here he was required to add two more cottages to the south of the existing group, thus extending the Square towards the road, and a particularly complete set of drawings survive, which show how the design began, and was amended. The first scheme was for a substantial stone and rough-cast house of three storeys with two oriel windows overlooking the road. This, with its fretted bargeboards and moulded brick chimney stacks, is very much in the manner of the architects' pattern books already referred to. Later versions show him simplifying the design. (Fig.4) As finally built, it is clear that he has learnt lessons about scale, restricting decorative details, and the value of local building materials. (Fig.5) The principal gable facing the Square is tile hung, that part nearest the road is ragstone on the ground floor, rough-cast above with vertical

Fig.4 Design for Leicester Square, Penshurst

Fig.5 Cottage on the east side of Leicester Square

studding in the gables. Two cottages were built on the opposite, west side. That on the Square is stone with rough-cast above, the corner chamfered and the roof hipped above the corner, the first example of an arrangement which was to be typical of Devey's style. This seems to derive from a watercolour sketch of an old house at Boulogne which is reproduced in the *Royal Institute of British Architects Journal* of 7 June 1930. The cottage running west of this has a timbered first floor; in both buildings the first floor is jettied and at this stage Devey's knowledge of the vernacular was not sufficient to avoid the occasional solecism. The brackets supporting this rest upon stone corbels of a distinctly ecclesiastical profile. (Fig.6) Judging from watermarks and dates on the drawings, Devey worked on this group from 1848 to 1851, and just over ten years later, Richard Norman Shaw and William Eden Nesfield visited Penshurst, drew the hall house and took note of Devey's additions.

At South Park Home Farm the barn has the date 1850 carved on a cross beam. Here Devey added on to some existing farm buildings, placing the new barn at the end of the farmyard, and flanking this with ancillary byres, sheds and sties. He also added a chimney breast with a couple of diagonally set stacks to the farmhouse, but it is the outbuildings which are important here, and are those in which the influence of John Sell Cotman's drawings of old cottages and the sketches of the Penshurst painters can most plainly be seen. (Fig.7) The barn has the wagon entrance set off-centre to the left, with a balcony in the gable above and a couple of dormers to the right lighting the loft. This is reached by steps rising in two flights

Fig.6 Leicester Square

beneath a small tiled roof abutting the gable, similar to those already noticed at Leicester Square. This feature is borrowed from the Archbishop's stables opposite the Palace in Maidstone. (Fig.8)

There are among the drawings in the Devey Collection a number of early watercolours which show his increase in competence in his chosen style. This clearly was based upon what he could see about him in the Weald, but the present day observer is hard put to it today to find the sort of building that would have interested him. Much has been pulled down, and more restored, added to, and turned into country houses for the middle classes. It must be stressed that Devey's study of small domestic buildings as an architectural source in the late 1840s seems to be unparalleled. Many books by architects and antiquarians, from Rickman onwards, had made the study of churches and the Gothic Revival a common pursuit of both the professional man and the amateur, but interest in cottages really only developed at the turn of the century.[20] A few papers in the County archaeological societies' publications, and a book by Ralph Nevill on *Old English Cottage and Domestic Architecture in South West Surrey*, published in 1889, were the precursors of a number of publications of which *Old Cottages and Farmhouses in Kent and Sussex* by W. Galsworthy Davie and the architect E. Guy Dawber, published in 1900, is typical. There are, however, two collections of drawings which helpfully show buildings that are either no longer standing or have been much altered; they are the sketches and notebooks of William Twopenny which were deposited in the British Museum after his death in 1873. These were made from about 1820 to the 1840s. The other is the drawings in the J. Fremlyn Streatfield Collection now in the possession of the Kent Archaeological Society. This had been begun as a preparation for a third revision of Edward Hasted's *History of Kent* by Thomas Streatfield and continued by his son after his death in 1848. Comparison of the drawings in these collections with Devey's early designs show how carefully he looked about him. One typical example, the contract drawing for unidentified cottages already mentioned, dated February 1850 and signed by Thomas Barber shows the

Cottage Building 31

Fig.7 Home Farm, South Park

Fig.8 Barn at Home Farm

Fig.9 Gateway Lodge, Penhurst

attention he paid to the use of local materials, which are specified by notes: 'rough cast, weatherboarding, plastering' and so on. (Fig.3) In addition there are the bound volumes of watercolours presented to the Institute by Devey's executors, one of which consists almost entirely of sketches of chimneys, both in England and abroad. A repertoire of useful variants was being established.

Both his aristocratic patrons were pleased with his work. Hardinge went on with the buildings in Fordcombe already mentioned, and with the West Lodge, South Park, which was built in 1853-4. The 2nd Lord De L'Isle continued with works in the village and on the estate until the late 1870s, when he was obliged to stop due to yet another period of agricultural depression, brought on by appalling weather and competition from Prairie wheat, Argentinian beef and Australian lamb, the latter brought in by the new refrigerated steamships. He built the Gateway Lodge, (Fig.9) Ashour Lodge, (Fig.10) and a number of triple cottages on the estate, of which the most remarkable was one on Rogue's Hill which is designed as a 'Wealden House' with a supposed central hall recessed behind eaves braces, between gables

Fig.10 Ashour Lodge, Penshurst

which are tile hung, with some rows of shingles at the apex. (Fig.11) Other work for Lord De L'Isle in the village included the improvement of the butcher's and saddler's shops, and the rebuilding of the Medway Bridge. (Fig.12)

He acquired other clients in the neighbourhood, George Field of Ashurst Park for whom he designed two lodges in 1864, and the consecutive owners of Swaylands, Edward Cropper and George Drummond, for both of whom he made large additions to a nondescript house which had been built by William Woodgate in 1842. However the most interesting commission was from James Nasmyth. Nasmyth was trained as an engineer, invented the steam hammer, and was an excellent example of the Victorian industrialist who built up a fortune from nothing. When he retired he bought a small house just south of Redleaf, which had been built by one of William Wells' visitors, Frederick Lee R.A., and which he renamed Hammerfield. This was in 1856, and he called upon Devey to build on a large addition which was completed in 1859. Lee's house was of diapered red brick with a slate roof and a single gable on the southern front. Devey's extensions consisted of a two-storey bay on the old house,

Fig.11 Cottages on Rogues Hill, Penshurst

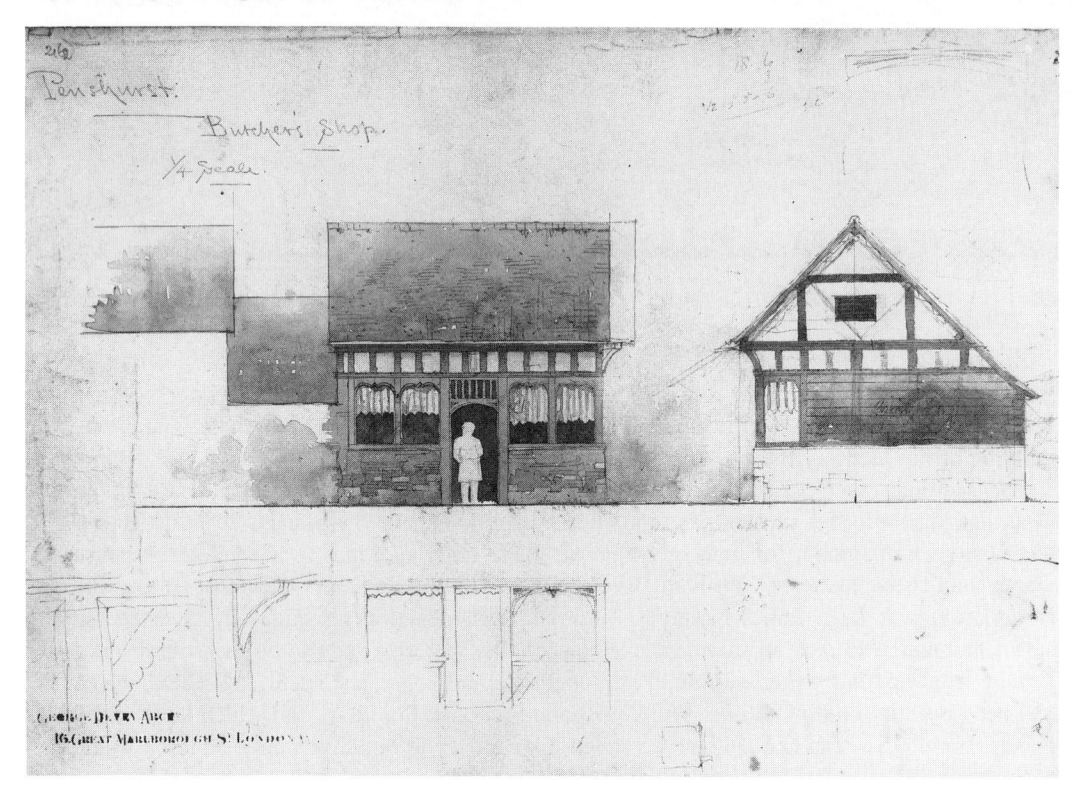

Fig.12 Design for window of butcher's shop, Penshurst

Fig.13 Elevation of the garden front, Hammerfield, Penshurst

Fig.14 Sketch for Culver Hill, Penshurst

Fig.15 Elevation,Culver Hill, Penshurst

and a westward range with a loggia and a couple of gables, half-timbered and tile hung, with a canted corner at the extremity, as at Leicester Square. (Fig.13) There is a roof walk protected by a balustrade, diamond-shaped leaded lights and shutters. The sketch for this is one of Devey's most attractive watercolours, perhaps too attractive, it is on the brink of slipping into the *cottage orné*, and the house itself has an extraordinary and unhappy decorative feature, thin barley sugar shafts with flowery capitals supporting one of the gables. These do not appear in Devey's design and must be an unwelcome intervention on the part of either the client or a local craftsman. But such prettification is not the case with the gardener's cottage he designed for Nasmyth, now called Culver Lodge, for which a charming sepia sketch survives (Fig.14), though it was finally built to a simpler design. (Fig.15) Neither was it to be the case with the two other works he had in hand at this time, the restoration of Penshurst Place and the rebuilding of Betteshanger.

3

Making a Slow Start

Devey's work on the estate and in the village of Penshurst can be easily identified, even without the P.S. date stones with which they were inevitably marked, despite the belief expressed in some quarters that they demeaned the occupants as 'those external ornaments, which, like the crested buttons on a livery suit, proclaim the dependence of the possessor.'[1] But his work on Penshurst Place itself is exceedingly reticent and not readily distinguished from the old fabric.

The condition of Penshurst Place in the early nineteenth century was distressing. There had been a failure of the male line in 1743 and the estate had passed to Mrs Elizabeth Perry, niece of the 7th and last Earl of Leicester, and then to her daughters Mary and Elizabeth Jane, when that part of the estate and house contents which belonged to Mary were sold. Mrs Perry's husband, William, made numerous alterations, replaced the old windows with sashes, even in the great hall, and put a Palladian window into the Record Tower. The younger daughter, Elizabeth Jane, married Sir Bysshe Shelley of Castle Goring, where he had built a truly remarkable house to the designs of John Biagio Rebecca, the son of the painter, in about 1795 to 1815. Combining the best of both worlds by having a Gothick entrance front of stone and flint, with battlements, machicolations, round towers and Perpendicular windows, and a Palladian garden front standing on a colonnade and decorated with Coade stone reliefs, this was their preferred residence, and when John Carter visited Penshurst in 1805 it was empty. 'When a mansion of such consequence as Penshurst becomes deserted (as is the case as this day), a melancholy gloom seems to pervade the whole pile; and it may be truly said with regard to this place, a 'rope of sand' now holds its venerable walls from being thrown to the earth: come but another breath of necessitous demand, and the whole mass is no more! The way has been shewn how to lay the first stroke at these time-revered foundations. Not long ago part of the North front was taken down, and the materials disposed of for some hundreds.'[2] This was the range to the east of the King's Tower which had been pulled down and sold to James Burton, the retired builder and father of Decimus, whose architect Joseph Parkinson used the materials in the building of Mabledon on the outskirts of Tonbridge. However, Elizabeth Jane's son John assumed the additional name of Sidney and was created a baronet of Penshurst in 1818; both events showed that he cared for the house and intended to make it his home; he set in hand a programme of repair and rebuilding.

He employed his father's architect, and Rebecca began with the restoration and redecoration of the private apartments in the north and west ranges. He created a new entrance on the north front which, with part of the west front, was refaced in a design with thin Tudor detail, all in a cleanly cut pale stone most dissimilar to that in the mediaeval building. The designs for these additions were exhibited in the Royal Academy in 1818 and 1820. Then in 1831 Sir John made over the house to his eldest son Philip Charles, who had been created Baron De L'Isle and Dudley by William IV as a consequence of his marriage to Lady Sophia FitzClarence, one of the King's and Mrs Jordan's illegitimate daughters. Philip rebuilt as stables the range east of the King's Tower, the loss of which had been so deplored by Carter, and added the entrance lodge on the Leigh road. This was put up in 1834 and is almost certainly to the designs of Rebecca. And there matters rested until 1843 when the upper part of the kitchen tower was rebuilt and made higher, apparently for purely aesthetic reasons. This minor work was probably undertaken by a local builder, perhaps Henry Constable whose family building firm worked in Penshurst throughout the nineteenth century.

Rebecca died in 1847, and the 1st Lord in 1851. Being now without an architect for the house and having observed Devey's work at Leicester Square, the 2nd Lord De L'Isle set him to work on a restoration of Penshurst Place which was to continue over a number of years. There is reason to suppose that even if Rebecca was still alive he would not have been chosen for the new campaign of works. By the mid-century the attenuated and fanciful Gothick style applied by him was falling into disrepute. During the 1830s a new generation of architects had been establishing themselves, who rejected the ecclesiastically based and essentially decorative Gothick of which the Wyatts were the best known practitioners, and Rebecca a relatively humble follower, in favour of a style which they had developed from the study of the archaeology of mediaeval buildings.[3] Less than twenty years after it was carried out, Rebecca's work would have seemed painfully inappropriate, but probably for reasons of cost, it had to remain, and still does, demonstrating most usefully the difference between attitudes to building formed in the eighteenth century, and the new care for congruity between the original building and later additions or repairs.

Financially speaking, Devey began his work at Penshurst at a very bad time, this coinciding with the agricultural depression which followed the repeal of the Corn Laws. Fortunately the estate does not seem to have been hard hit by this, and the sequence of works begun in the village by the 1st Lord was continued by his son without a break. Some financial help may have come from from his sister, the Hon. Mrs Hunloke, who was to employ Devey both at Wingerworth and for her mansion in Lennox Gardens, and who was in receipt of a considerable income from her coal mines at Clay Cross in Derbyshire. Her private fortune enabled her to help to pay for improvements to her old family home, and a steady sequence of works was maintained from the 1850s until the end of the century.[4]

Luckily many of the plans and elevations for the first programme of work undertaken by Devey have survived. (Fig.16) In the house there was a rearrangement of the offices following the demolition of a low range of buildings which ran south from the corner of the Buckingham building, and the undercroft, four (originally five) bays by two of quadripartite vaulting supported on octagonal piers, was divided into cellarage on the north and a servants' hall on the south, 'unfortunately' as J.H. Parker remarked when he conducted the Kent Archaeological Society over the building in 1863. The division, which remains to this day, destroys a fine mediaeval space. The looseboxes and stalls in the range east of the King's Tower were rearranged, and it was proposed that a new carriage house and looseboxes should to be built on either side of an archway leading from the stable yard into the laundry yard. This was not done and at a later date carriages and additional stabling were placed in a new courtyard to the south-east of the house and an octagonal game larder built at the north-east corner of this. (Fig.17) A new laundry, replacing some lean-to sheds, was built on the former site of the old kitchens at the east end of the great hall, with a large stone rainwater cistern put in above a new east door. Throughout the building Mr Perry's sash windows with small panes, were

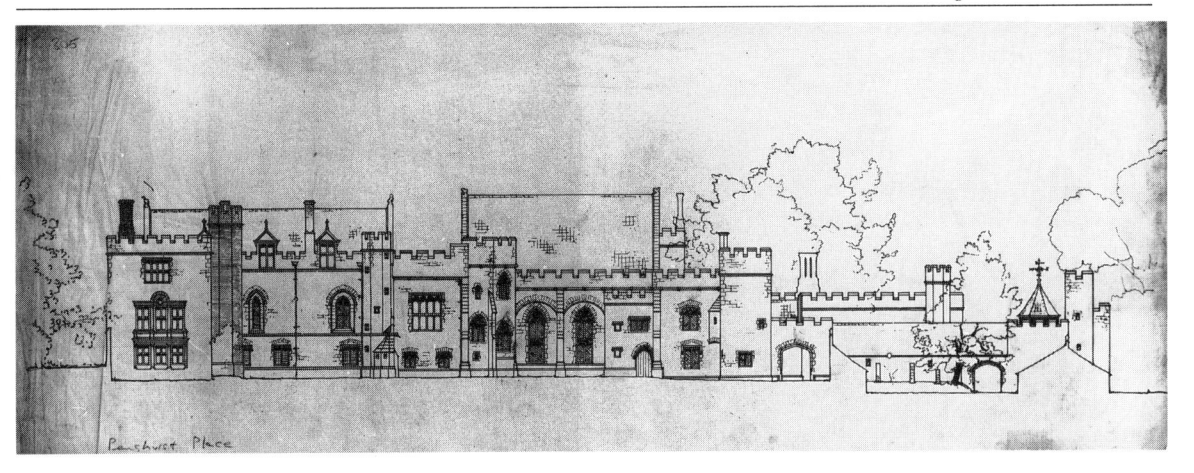

Fig.16 Elevation of south front, Penhurst Place

Fig.17 Game larder, Penshurst Place

Fig.18 The Buckingham Building under reconstruction

removed and replaced with mullions, transoms and tracery. Oddly, the Palladian window was left alone, and only removed in the inter-war period. A triple arcade and steps down to the Belvedere terrace were proposed for the Record Tower, but not executed. This was the first phase. Later, Devey was to restore the Buckingham Building which had been badly damaged by fire and rebuilt in an unsympathetic manner. 'The end wall' said Parker 'was in such a bad state that it was obliged to be taken down and rebuilt, but every stone was carefully marked, and replaced in its original situation, under the direction of Lord De L'Isle himself, and his architect Mr Devey, to whom I am indebted for much valuable assistance on the present occasion. As this wall is four feet six inches thick, the rebuilding of it with so much care was no slight operation, and due credit should be given for the pains bestowed. The word 'restoration' is odious to the ears of archaeologists, as it is so often synonymous with the entire destruction of all historical interest; but in the present instance the building has really been restored to what it was originally.'[5] A particularly good sequence of photographs of this operation has survived, one of which shows it, from the garden, in a state of some decay, with two of the original windows blocked and a sash window inserted. Another is particularly interesting as it actually shows the rebuilding mentioned by Parker in progress, the partly demolished walls surrounded by a muddle of scaffolding, and neat piles of stone and tiles are stacked within convenient reach. (Fig.18) Such a major reconstruction meant new floors, ceilings and panelling in Queen Elizabeth's and the Tapestry Rooms, and the Pages' Room was also panelled, given a wooden ceiling and fitted out with shelves for the display of china.

Fig.19 Entrance front, Betteshanger

The upper floor, known as 'the Barracks' was converted into menservants' bedrooms. At the time of the Society's visit a new floor was being put into the Sunderland Room, a guest chamber above the buttery and pantry, and Devey later designed the panelling, fireplace and overmantel of the Little Library.

He was consulted about the garden as soon as work began; a plan of the grounds and park is numbered '15' in the sequence of drawings. From this it appears that William Andrews Nesfield had been asked for advice, which is not unexpected as he had already worked on the gardens at South Park in the late 1840s, when his brother-in-law Anthony Salvin had been there seeing to the building of the trophy hall in which Hardinge's Indian souvenirs, which included two huge brass Sikh cannon and a replica of the gates of the temple at Amritsar, were displayed. Devey suggested the construction of a new drive giving a gradual rise from the Leigh Lodge to the King's Tower instead of the rise and fall in level which then existed, and the thickening of clumps of trees by the planting of 'Scotch fir or evergreen trees (not shrubs)'.[6] An unwanted hollow was to be disguised by gorse bushes and part of the lawn was to levelled for a parterre. A 'Principal Parterre' was to be centred on the drawing room window and differences in level in the lawn south of the house were to be marked by yew hedges.

If Devey could consider himself fortunate in the introductions he had obtained at this date, they were to be quite exceeded by the work which his next important client was able to put his way. Sir Walter James, Bart., later 1st Baron Northbourne was the stepson of Hardinge,

Fig.20 Elevation of the garden front, Betteshanger

and the heir to a fortune and the Langley Hall estate in Berkshire. In 1841 Sir Walter married Sarah Caroline, the youngest daughter of Cuthbert Ellison of Hebburn in Co. Durham, a neighbourhood which Ellison had left for Juniper Hill, Mickleham when the coal mines from which he had obtained a fortune had ruined the landscape about him.[7] James rented Redleaf for a year from Billy Wells, and in 1850 bought the Betteshanger estate near Deal in east Kent. Betteshanger House had been built by Robert Lugar for F.E.Morrice before 1828; it was a symmetrical two-storey villa residence and had pairs of bay windows on the south and east fronts, steep gables and scrolled bargeboards, and a low service wing to the west. James first employed Salvin on some quite considerable internal alterations, new stables, a new lodge, and his contributions to the general good of the neighbourhood, a village school at Northbourne, and the restoration of St Mary's Betteshanger, which was completed in 1853. But he was clearly unhappy about the Cockney villa look of his house and abandoned Salvin for Devey, who he had seen at work over the previous five years. That he would have preferred an old house is shown by his diary, in which he regrets the fact that Somerhill, a Jacobean mansion near Tonbridge, had come on the market the year after he was established at Betteshanger, and he set about a reconstruction which was to turn his thirty-year-old home into something which was to look as if it had stood and been subjected to additions over some hundreds of years. The rebuilding of this house took place over a period beginning in about 1856 and continuing until at least 1899, long after Devey's death. They must have got on excellently. James was a talented landscape painter and watercolourist who had exhibited at the Royal Institution and shared Devey's interest in horses; 'While at Christ Church his love of horses induced him to live principally with hunting men; but this did not in those days, and certainly not in his case, imply any neglect of his studies.'[8]

Work began on the entrance front. The front door was moved from its original, central position to one side, and now opened into an ante room which led into a grand staircase hall, which was furnished with an organ and used as a sitting room. A *porte cochère* with a gabled roof was placed to the right of a range of three Dutch gables, the central gable had an oriel window and another was placed above the entrance. A stepped gable formed the termination of the service wing. (Fig.19) At the rear this wing was lowered to emphasise the importance of the main part of the house, and the three-storey James Tower with an attached octagonal stair turret, a two-storey quadrant bay and another rectangular bay window were added. (Fig.20) Cut flint and stone were used on the quadrant and brick for the other. All windows were of plate glass with substantial mullions and a single transom. The materials used in the James Tower are calculated to impress as a Tudor building on mediaeval foundations. It is of ragstone to first-floor level with a chimney breast of stone, tumbled brickwork and brick quoins, the ragstone rises unevenly into the brick wall above, laid in English bond. Beyond this was a small building described on the plan as the 'New Washhouse' but which was in fact to be a dairy fitted with painted tiles and marble shelves on stone shafts. These were imports from the north as a commemorative plaque records: 'The fittings of the dairy were removed from Hebburn Hall Co. Durham and placed in this building erected for the purpose by Cuthbert Ellison 1855.'

The second phase was carried out in 1861 and consisted of the recasting of the main part of the house. This is another early case in which photographs of work in progress have survived; Godfrey recalled Devey's delight in the process of building and fondness for having his houses photographed when under construction and still surrounded by scaffolding.[9] (Fig.19) Unfortunately few of these have survived the eighty intervening years, but they still

Fig.21 Garden front, Betteshanger

form an intriguing corpus of material which will be discussed later. The house was rebuilt with pairs of Dutch gables on the east and south fronts, to which he added wide two-storey bays which greatly increased the size of the rooms within. (Fig.21) Such gables were characteristic of a number of small buildings in east Kent and elsewhere whose builders had borrowed from Flemish houses on the other side of the Channel. The Dutch House at Kew, Raynham Hall, Norfolk, Swakeleys near Ickenham, and Broome Park near Barham, south of Canterbury are the grandest examples, but Devey seems to have been more attracted by lesser models, such as the now demolished Fairfax House in Putney High Street, of which he kept a picture in his office, and a number of farmhouses at Sarre, Guilton and Reading Street near Broadstairs. The significance of these gables was recalled by Percy Stone after Devey died: 'In the start for a better state of things with regard to domestic style, which has been ably followed up by Mr. R. Norman Shaw, R.A., Devey may almost be called the pioneer; and it may be interesting to know that he first used the Dutch gable in the additions to Lord Northbourne's country house at Betteshanger, in 1856'.[10]

And he had not only been looking at red brick houses with shaped and Dutch gables. He has also noticed the local building materials. In this rebuilding and in the *porte cochère* which was built slightly later he uses yellow stock brick with ragstone dressings chequered in part with flint flushwork, which is used decoratively in diamond-shaped panels on the largest southern bay. This combination occurs on the Fisher gate in Sandwich and Devey was to suggest its use again when he produced his designs for Walmer Castle. Betteshanger also has the first example of another of Devey's favourite decorations, a head in a tondo, no doubt modelled by the firm of Mabey, in this case that of Queen Victoria framed by roses, a thistle and a shamrock. Whilst later examples are in red terracotta like the models from which they are copied, that is the medallions containing the heads of Roman emperors modelled by Giovanni de Maiano for Cardinal Wolsey's work at Hampton Court and those on the Holbein Gate in Whitehall, demolished in the eighteenth century but known through the engravings of George Vertue, this example is ochre in colour, to match the brick in which it is set. The *porte cochère* has a small oriel above the entrance, and a more complicated oriel rises above the garden door in two storeys with a demi cupola above. All the windows were altered, and again given robust mullions, some arched, transoms and plate glass.

Later alterations were less substantial, the two-storey semi-circular bay on the entrance front, a reduced version of those on the entrance front of Burton Agnes, of which Devey had a series of photographs, and which became a favourite feature of Devey's, recurring in mansions such as St Alban's Court, put up in the 1870s, and at the same time the decorative bargeboards and pargetting were added to the rear gable of the service range and the upper part of the *porte cochère* was rebuilt, becoming Tudor, with finials and with a more pointed gable. In 1882 the Ellison Tower at the extreme right of the entrance front was added, with a cupola above the staircase turret, as was the ventilating cupola above the kitchen. The drawing for this is dated August 1881. Work on the offices was continued after Devey's death, and is recorded by date stones of 1893 and 1899.

As at Penshurst, Devey advised upon the re-landscaping of the garden, organising a descent from a gateway in the entrance courtyard down by steps, terraces, parterres and balustrades decorated with urns, to the church of St Mary which James had had restored in the Norman style by Salvin, and which he was immensely pleased to have so close as to be in and part of his garden. (Fig.22) James was a most devout man who at this time in his life tried to attend church every day, and who tormented himself with self-recrimination, with his idleness, and lack of a sense of direction. He also worried about the houses of his employees, and about the conditions of the poor in the Eastry Union workhouse. Devey designed a number of estate cottages. Some very plain double cottages in flintwork and brick were

Fig.22 Design for terrace and parterre, Betteshanger

estimated for at £240 but the most attractive example is the large lodge now known as The Cloisters, which has a door approached through an arcaded porch, a two-storey bay window and a substantial brick chimney stack with attached bread oven on the side nearest the road. Materials used are stone, rough-cast and patterns of tile hanging in the front gable. (Fig.23) He was also the architect of the workhouse chapel, put up at the expense of a group of gentlemen headed by Sir Walter and his eldest son. This stands on a piece of land opposite the entrance to the workhouse and is a simple design in the Early English style, built of stone and with a bell-cote on the west gable.[11] James's building works did not end there. Devey was later asked to improve the parsonages at Betteshanger and Ripple, to build a cottage hospital on the outskirts of Eastry, and to work on the churches at Northbourne and Ham.

Fig.23 Elevation, The Cloisters, Betteshanger

Now, Sir Walter James was a Liberal, Member of Parliament for Hull from 1837 to 1847, and a close and devoted friend of W.E. Gladstone and his family. It was due to him that Devey was to develop a practice which was based upon the Liberal connection, through an introduction to Lord Granville who was to become Lord Warden of the Cinque Ports with his official residence at Walmer Castle. This led in turn to Devey obtaining work from many members of Gladstone's cabinets and other prominent Liberals such as the banker, B.W. Currie. This lucky chance and the work which it produced is discussed in the next chapter which deals with his rapidly expanding business in the 1860s and the 1870s. However, one greatly distinguished Liberal client began to employ him when work on Betteshanger was barely under way. This was the Duke of Sutherland, whose wife Harriet was Mistress of the Robes and confidante to Her Majesty the Queen. Devey was introduced to the Duke, who was a cousin of Lord Granville, by Lord De L'Isle.

The Duke of Sutherland had four principal country residences: Cliveden in Buckinghamshire, Trentham, Staffordshire, Dunrobin Castle in Sutherland, and Lilleshall in Shropshire. All had been rebuilt as the Sutherland fortunes, founded on coal, canals and later the railways, increased; Lilleshall by Wyatville in the 1820s, Trentham and Dunrobin by Charles Barry in 1834-40 and 1844-50, and Cliveden, again by Barry, after a fire in 1850-1.[12] Devey was employed on each estate. He began at Cliveden in 1857, by designing Woodgate Cottage for the Duchess, and the Windsor and Taplow Lodges at much the same time, then Ferry Cottage in 1861. This was followed by additions to Spring Cottage, an octagonal Gothick tea room beside the Thames, designed by Peter Nicholson for the Duchess of Orkney in 1813. Another set of designs, still kept in the estate office, are for a cow house. The house now known as Seven Gables is also by Devey, but this was built in 1879 for the Duchess's son-in-law, the 1st Duke of Westminster who bought Cliveden after her death in 1868. At Lilleshall he produced designs for a double cottage again Wealden and not in a local vernacular style. It may not have been built, and if it was, it cannot yet be identified.

At Trentham his work was again confined to small estate works, cottages, designs for recasting dull brick farmhouses, again in the Wealden style, and the new Gravel Pit Lodge. (Fig.24) It must be remarked that half-timbering and tile hanging do look exceedingly out of place in a region where the usual building material is red brick. He also built the school at Tittensor, the first of many village schools built for local landowners. The agent at Trentham was Thomas Roberts, that at Dunrobin was William Fowler, to whom Devey explained his way of supervising the works when not on site: 'The parts coloured and inked are the only parts authorised to be erected at present. Perhaps you will be so kind as to send me back these Drawings when you have made the necessary Tracings from them for carrying

Fig.24 Gravel Pit Lodge, Trentham. Sketch by Walter Godfrey

out the Works. Mr. Roberts the Surveyor on the Staffordshire Estates sends me Tracings of details made out to a large scale by himself and then I am more easily enabled to make such alterations as I think best and return them at once - '[13] Most of the designing seems to have been carried out at a distance, but Devey did go to Scotland in March 1858, to see about a shooting lodge Lord Elcho was thinking of building at Achfarry near Lairg, an estate which he rented from the Duke. George Loch, the Duke's Commissioner wrote to Fowler 'Lord Elcho had been advising with Mr. Devey (the Gentleman who made the drawings in your possession for the new house proposed for you) in respect to the new Shooting Lodge about to be erected at Altnarynie, but the latter has a difficulty in advising without having seen the site, and with much spirit he has proposed to go down immediately to Suthd. at his own expense, for that purpose. He will leave London on Monday next the 1st. March and if all goes well, will cross by the Littleferry boat on Wednesday.'[14] The designs and specification were ready and sent north in June, but the local factor reported that they would cost twice as much as anticipated, and asked Fowler to amend them to make them 'quite intelligible to the contractors of this country.' The lodge was not built.

Fig.25 Sketch for Tower Lodge, Golspie

Fig.26 Elevations of Tower Lodge

Fowler's new house was Tower Lodge, Golspie, and when Devey left for Dunrobin he took with him more drawings for the conversion of the Old Barn into cottages and for a Grieve's cottage 'both of which sketches are thought much of.' Fowler was asked to show him round Dunrobin and to accompany him to the west coast, but bad weather delayed this trip and he spent some days at the Castle working on various schemes. Tower Lodge was an attempt by Devey at the Scottish Baronial, a style which was to be rather unkindly described by one critic as 'all mustard with no beef'.[15] There is a sequence of designs for this house which combined living accommodation with an office, in all of which the most striking feature was a round tower with a conical roof. They begin with a charming watercolour sketch (Fig.25) and conclude with a design close to what was eventually built. (Fig.26) This is an obvious reference to Dunrobin Castle as remodelled by Barry. Also in Golspie is Moray House, built to Devey's designs, in stone, a restrained effort with crow-stepped gables, after the tenant's (a Mr Begg) original designs had been rejected by the estate: 'You will at once see how entirely inadmissible it is — it is the worst style of suburban villa.'[16] There were a number of other small works, including the new dairy, now converted into a house, and the venison larder in the Castle grounds. The 2nd Duke died in 1861 but work continued for the 3rd Duke which included designs for the approaches to the railway station at Dunrobin which consisted of a bridge and carriage drives sweeping round a statue of the 2nd Duke. The railway did not arrive until 1869, and when it did, a simple station was built and Devey's grand scheme was abandoned.

The beneficial effects of the chalybeate well at Strathpeffer had been promoted since early in the century by Dr Thomas Morrison, who built a Pump Room in 1819. By 1838 a 'drinking season' extending from May to October had been established, and a Poor's House capable of accommodating fifty of the less well-to-do was completed in 1839. The development of the spa proceeded independently of the landowner until 1861 when Anne, the 3rd Duchess of Sutherland, who had been created Countess of Cromartie in her own right, called upon Devey to make plans for laying out Strathpeffer with new roads, building plots for private houses and hotels, and for additions to the Pump Room, all intended to make the town a well-appointed spa in competition with such establishments in England and on the Continent. Devey prepared a town plan and drew an aerial perspective showing the hoped-for effect, which was printed and circulated as an advertisement; a copy hangs in the estate office at Castle Leod to this day.[17] It was a relaxed piece of planning, incorporating without fuss the few existing houses and disposing the substantial building plots along gently curving roads. There was no attempt to provide houses for the common people, and the size of the plots shows that it was the wealthy middle classes that the Duchess and her advisers hoped to attract. No overall rules as to the style of house to be built seem to have been imposed, but there must have been some vetting of the designs, for the estate had now made an investment both in Devey's fees and the cost of laying out the roads, which they would wish to protect. Devey's specification for additions to the Pump Room, which has been demolished, is dated April 1861. These included a new and grander entrance, a wooden veranda running round that part of the building which contained the baths, circular dormers and a louvred cupola for ventilation. Devey put in his account in 1868 so his contribution to the development must have been complete by then.

The Sutherlands were at this period Devey's most valuable clients, not only for the amount of work they gave him, but because of the benefit of having his work, particularly buildings like lodges, where they would be on view to the many guests entertained by the Duke and Duchess at their various houses. Devey's buildings were quite distinct from the usual run of estate work and would have been noticed and discussed, and his name consequently put before other landowners who were possible clients. That he valued the connection becomes clear in a letter he wrote to Fowler about some designs for rebuilding a farm which had not been carried out: 'has Langdale Farm House been built according to the plans I made, if so what did it cost and how has it turned out - What was the cost of altering Old Barn into cottages - and what did the Grieve's house at Culmaily cost - although I do not charge his Grace the usual commission on these things, still they are useful to me as a guide what to charge for them.'[18]

But this was still all very small stuff. The 1850s cannot have advanced Devey's career as much as he might have hoped, and Percy Stone had heard from his father of the disappointment and frustration which his friend felt at this time. The biggest jobs, Penshurst Place and Betteshanger, were carried out piecemeal and he was not to obtain a major commission for a country house until 1866 when Charles Pilgrim employed him on the building of Akeley Wood. He was then aged forty-six. Still he felt himself sufficiently established to join his professional association and became a Fellow of the Royal Institute of British Architects in 1856. Unfortunately, the bound volume of nomination papers for that year is missing, so we do not know who proposed him.

One other personal matter added to his unhappiness. His study of Wealden architecture took him to Chiddingstone to look at and to draw the row of old houses opposite the church called Chiddingstone Street. Boissier had been curate at Chiddingstone and no doubt introduced him to the Vicar, the Revd W.E. Hoskins to whose daughter Flora Margaret Elizabeth, Devey became engaged to be married. This did not last and in 1857 Flora married Newton William Streatfield, a member of the family that had lived at Chiddingstone Castle since the sixteenth century. Streatfield also became a clergyman, and was ordained in 1861, becoming curate of Speldhurst in 1862 and incumbent of Lamorbey near Sidcup in 1864. This was heartbreaking enough but Devey again proposed and was rejected a second time after Streatfield's death in 1866. Godfrey refers to 'certain divergences, - in their trend of opinion' which may have been due to Devey's unorthodox religious beliefs, no doubt unacceptable to the daughter of a minister of the established Church. Later in life he was to become a member of the Revd Charles Voysey's Theistic Church. Voysey had been suspended from his curacy of St. Mark's, Whitechapel after preaching a sermon 'Against Everlasting Hell' - 'this dismissal was to me and mine almost a sentence of death. I had been hunted about from one parish to another, always on the ground of heresy.' In 1869 proceedings were brought against him and he was deprived of his living in 1871. In 1882 he referred to 'my ten years work as a Theist outside the pale even of Christendom.'[19] Devey did not get over his broken engagement. When he came to make his will in 1882 he left Flora the considerable sum of £5,000, but with some apprehension that it might not be acceptable 'in case the said Flora Streatfield ... should object (on account of the engagement so cruelly broken off between us) or decline to accept' £1,000 was to go to her daughter Ethel, £2,000 to her son Arthur, and £2,000 to the Revd Charles Voysey 'for the advancement of his noble religious views'. That he could make such an arrangement a quarter of a century later, and still fear that he might be snubbed, is a measure of how badly he was hurt.

Fig.27 Buckland School

Fig.28 South Lodge, Mentmore

4

Working for the Whigs

Lord Stafford mines for coal and salt,
The Duke of Norfolk deals in malt,
Lord Douglas in red herrings;
But noble name and miles of land,
Palace, and park, and vassal band,
Are pow'rless to the notes of hand,
Of Rothschild or the Barings.[1]

The Rothschild family's connection with the Vale of Aylesbury seems to have begun very shortly after the death of Nathan Mayer, the founder of the London branch of the bank, in 1836. There is no reason to doubt the truth of the story that his widow observed that her four sons, Lionel, Anthony, Nathaniel and Mayer Amschel were becoming rather stout, and that she encouraged them to take exercise in the socially acceptable form of hunting. There were three established foxhunts in the neighbourhood at this time, the Old Berkeley, the South Oxfordshire and the Hertfordshire, all attracting visitors to a country which included Creslow Great Ground, at the time the largest unenclosed field in England. Nineteenth century literature is inclined to sneer at the newly rich who attempted to break into the ranks of society by taking up the sport, and the Rothschild's advent into the Vale probably led to Robert Smith Surtees' joke that the territory of the old 'Hit-im and Hold-im shire' was called 'Jewdea'.[2] They were, however, not to be deterred, and established their own hounds, first taking over a pack of harriers that a Mr Adamson had kennelled at Hastoe above Tring, and later establishing the Rothschild staghounds, hunting carted deer. Their acceptance in the hunting fraternity was only slightly hindered by the 2nd Duke of Buckingham who knew and detested their political views as notorious free traders and warned them off his land.

The family had acquired seven estates within eight miles of the centre of Aylesbury by the 1870s, in a carefully calculated campaign. James James of James and Horwood, solicitors of Aylesbury became lawyer, general man of business and agent for each of the Rothschilds as they moved into the neighbourhood.[3] He was first employed by Mayer Amschel who had begun by purchasing some land at Ledburn in 1844, and then took advantage of the agricultural depression which followed the repeal of the Corn Laws in 1846, which caused almost immediate financial difficulties to landowners who were frequently already over-stretched, to rapidly increase his holdings.[4] James recognised that the Rothschilds would have more to contend with than the invariable antipathy of established landowners to parvenu interlopers, due to a prevalent anti-semitism, which, if not as pronounced as it was to become in the later nineteenth and twentieth centuries, was nevertheless something to be considered. Thirty years after, Baroness Mayer recalled this for Lady Eastlake: 'I should think their residence here is a great benefit to the neighbourhood, though she says laughingly, that she was at first accused of "trying to unchristianise the district."' There had clearly been some unpleasantness.[5] James advised the Rothschilds that if they wished to make themselves a power in the neighbourhood, and in the State, by which he meant building up political influence and obtaining social acceptance, they should concentrate their capital in or about one spot. This they did, to great effect, becoming known not only as sportsmen, but as model landlords to their tenant farmers, as philanthropists in their improvements to their labourers' housing, and as agressive agricultural improvers using the latest machinery for the reclamation of unpromising land.[6] Within twenty years there were Rothschilds appointed to the Bench, sitting on the local authority and finally representing the county in Parliament.

Baron Mayer continued to build up his holding, but it was not until 1850 that he bought the Manor and Advowson of Mentmore for the sum of £12,400. The plan attached to this conveyance shows that he already owned much of the adjoining land.[7] He was to continue his purchases with such vigour that at his death in 1877 he owned all the land between Cheddington, Wingrave and Wing, with a few very minor exceptions. Creating an estate piecemeal took time. Sir Anthony no doubt infuriated the Duke of Buckingham when he bought the Aston Clinton estate from him in 1851; the mansion here was a long low stucco building in an unconvincing renaissance manner. Two years later Lionel acquired the Halton estate from the financially embarrased Sir George Dashwood. This completed the first period of Rothschild colonisation, which was to be followed by a second, corresponding with yet another period of agricultural depression in the 1870s, caused this time by foul weather and competition from Prairie wheat, Australian lamb and Argentinian beef, the latter brought in by the new refridgerated steamships. At this time, Lionel bought Tring, Mayer bought Ascott, and Ferdinand James, of the Vienna branch of the family, who had settled in England, acquired Waddesdon. His sister Alice, who joined him after his wife had died of a miscarriage following a railway accident, bought Eythrope. Devey was to work for them all.

Sir Anthony was the first to employ him. He may have been given his name by a fellow Liberal, or possibly have seen the lodges which Devey had designed for Cliveden, but there were examples of his work nearer at hand. The Revd Edward Bonus had become Rector of All Saints' Hulcott and All Saints' Buckland in 1860, and in 1863 he commissioned Devey to build a new village school and attached master's house at Buckland. Sir Anthony gave the land on which it was built. It contained a classroom and a schoolroom and is typical of a number of village schools which Devey was to build in the neighbourhood, of diapered red brick with stone dressings with a rough-cast second storey and tall red brick diagonally set chimney stacks. A good light was provided by two three-light and one four-light transomed windows of a rudimentary Early English design. The building was not only picturesque but had the ecclesiastical details appropriate to a church school. (Fig.27) The following year Devey made equally attractive additions to the school at Hulcott which had been built to the designs of John Durley, a local builder, in 1859, and also carried out some alterations at Hulcott Rectory. Sir Anthony paid Devey's account for 'Plans and superintendance of the School and parsonage' which amounted to £100.

Sir Anthony had embarked upon extensive additions to Aston Clinton which began in 1856 and continued until his death in 1876. He began by employing George Henry Stokes as his architect; Stokes had been a pupil of Gilbert Scott, was employed by Sir Joseph Paxton as his architectural assistant, and as such had been responsible for the construction of Mentmore. Devey was first employed on estate work in 1864, paid for 'Plans for various cottages' in 1867, which may have included the West Lodge, and in 1872 designed the park gates, a very grand arrangement of gate piers and balustrades which incorporated a new stable block. Judging by the amounts shown as paid to him in the Aston Clinton estate accounts he also took over from Stokes the continuing works of improvement to the mansion.[8]

At Mentmore he again replaced Stokes, who had completed the house and was beginning on the estate work. There are designs by Stokes for a pair of cottages, for the village school, and also his preliminary design and contract drawing for the Dairy, a charming brick building in the *cottage orné* manner, with jutting eaves supported on plain triangular brackets and a veranda of rustic woodwork. Attractive though this is, even with its present unfortunate coat of white paint, it is comparable to many designs for rural buildings drawn by the amateurs and relatively unknown architects who produced the architectural pattern books refered to previously, and looks very out-dated when compared with Devey's work on the estate. He designed the stables and riding school, and three lodges in differing styles all in 1868-70. The stables and the Crafton Lodge are in his expected Wealden manner, the Wing Lodge, which has been subjected to monstrous additions, was simple, half timbered on a brick plinth with a tiled roof. The South Lodge is one of his most charming creations. (Fig.28) It is triangular in plan, again built on a brick plinth with half-timbering and rough cast above, and with a most complicated thatched roof. He continued to work for Hannah, Mayer's only child, who inherited Mentmore after his death in 1877, and married Lord Rosebery the following year, designing for her the Rosebery Arms at Cheddington Station, a group of three cottages nearby, now called Mentmore End, and the School Master's House in Cheddington.

Lionel de Rothschild, as we have seen, first bought the Halton estate and then in 1872, Tring Park. In 1873 he paid Devey £100 for '5 cottages' which were probably on the Halton estate, and there are a pair that look of this date in the Halton Road. What is more interesting is that Devey's cashbook records substantial payments which cover the period 1874 to 1878 and it seems probable that these relate to the rebuilding of Tring Park. This house had been designed by Sir Christopher Wren in c.1670 for Henry Guy, Gentleman of the Privy Chamber to Charles II. It was greatly extended and recased by Lionel in a *dix-huitième* style using red brick with stone dressings and a slate Mansard roof. The name of the architect employed cannot be discovered as the considerable archive that was kept at Tring, which covered not only the estate, but also the natural history collections, was destroyed during World War II, but the house as rebuilt is sufficiently close to the mansion which Devey was to build in Lennox Gardens for the Hon. Mrs Hunloke to allow at least the suggestion that he was responsible for rebuilding Tring.

So far as Ferdinand James de Rothschild is concerned, he went to G.H. Destailleur (who seems to have been already a Rothschild architect and was putting up the Palais Rothschild on the Prinz-Eugen-Strasse in Vienna) for the building of Waddesdon, and to W.F. Taylor of Bierton, a partner of John Durley, the builder, for the estate buildings. Waddesdon was, according to the *Red Book*, in which Ferdinand recorded his building works, modelled on the *châteaux* of the Touraine and exceeded Mentmore in grandeur. Taylor's cottages are elaborate to a fault. Ferdinand did, however, obtain from Devey a design for a model farm to be built on the family estate in Silesia, for which a charming aerial perspective survives. (Fig.29) This makes no concessions to Austrian vernacular architecture and would have looked quite in place in the home counties; it is doubtful if it was built. A cashbook entry enables this to be dated to 1868, and another records more work for Ferdinand which was billed in 1879, but is not identifiable, and may have been for some alterations to his Town house. However, his sister Alice went to Devey for the designs of the Water Pavilion she built on the Eythrope estate, which she had bought in 1876. This building is unique in Devey's work, a fanciful confection combining his version of Jacobean with French Renaissance details borrowed from Waddesdon, such as the tower with a concave conical roof and the large gable on the garden front which is a recasting of the dormers of the larger house. (Fig.30) What Miss Alice required was an elaborate summer house with two reception rooms

Fig.29 Design for a farm in Silesia

only and no bedrooms as she had been advised that the low-lying position by the River Thame was unhealthy. Guests set out in their carriages from Waddesdon, to take tea at Eythrope, and perhaps a cruise on the river. Some of her guests found the proceedings a little strange. Mary Gladstone was one 'After luncheon drove to Alice de Rothschild's place 4 miles off for tea. This is quite small, but a model of comfort and everything in it a gem of its kind, the garden beautifully arranged, all the farm buildings and stables etc. perfect, but she never sleeps there and it felt a waste. In a steam launch, rather absurd, to see the tea house, up a wee stream widened by her to hold the boat.'[9]

The last Rothschild mansion with which Devey was connected began as a very humble affair. Ascott was a two-storey four-roomed cottage with a single-storey extension at the east end. In 1874 it was acquired by Leopold and a new parlour, staircase and porch were built on the west, and the ground floor of the old house turned into the hall and kitchen. (Fig.31) There were four bedrooms above. (Fig.32) A year later the offices were extended, a new hall was built and more bedrooms provided. In 1878 the offices were extended again and in 1879 work began on a billiard room and conservatory, yet further extensions to the offices and the building of an archway connecting the house and the stable block. (Fig.33) Still further additions were put in hand in 1884, and building work continued after Devey's death when James Williams took over the job, first as head of a short lived partnership Williams, West and Slade, and then on his own. The original cottage was half-timbered with a tiled roof, to which Devey added red brick on the ground floor and in the chimney breasts. The later rambling extensions were in close set studding with pretty woodwork detail, but attempts to keep the building unpretentious were finally thwarted by its size. (Fig. 34) Mary Gladstone aptly described it as 'a palace-like cottage'.[9]

Fig.30 Eythrope

Fig.31 Ascott, sketch perspective

Fig.32 Ascott, c.1878

When Lionel died, his son Nathaniel, later to become the 1st Baron Rothschild, inherited Tring, and his second son, Alfred came into the Halton estate and rebuilt the house in a Second Empire style using an obscure architect named William R. Rogers or Rodriguez, and William Cubitt & Co. as builders. Alfred showed little interest in the lives of his tenants and his estate building work seems to have been restricted to the Weston Lodge, and the addition of sgraffito panels showing rural pusuits such as hunting and wood cutting to a number of the village houses. This is a strange aberration in an English village and the idea is borrowed from the Continent. Nathaniel employed a local architect called William Huckvale for a number of buildings in Tring such as the Museum, the Louisa almshouses, the Rose and Crown and two blocks of commercial premises flanking the entrance to the park, but he did employ Devey on two buildings in Aylesbury. His father had bought the King's Head, an inn dating from the fifteenth century, and some adjoining houses in Temple Street which he intended to demolish in order to make another entrance into the hostelry. For some reason this scheme was not proceeded with, but Devey was instructed in 1879 to repair the King's Head, a process which involved the demolition of the gable above the gateway and the rebuilding of this with an oriel window. The Temple Street site was presented to the town and The Literary Institute was built at the expense of the family and opened on the 7th May 1880. There is a reading room on the ground floor and a library of 1,600 books in glass-fronted book shelves on the first floor. Devey was unable to be present at the inevitable celebratory lunch but his health was proposed by the Chairman and drunk by the company at table.

Granville George Leveson Gower, 2nd Earl Granville became the Whig member for Morpeth in 1836, and like the Rothschilds, was a firm freetrader; from 1855 he led the Liberal party in the House of Lords, served as Secretary of State for the Colonies in Gladstone's first administration and Foreign Secretary in the second. When Lord Palmerston died in 1865, Lord John Russell offered Granville the Lord Wardenship of the Cinque Ports with a residence in Walmer Castle. 'As you have no place on the sea, perhaps you would like to be Warden of the Cinque Ports. The salary is nil, and the expense something.'[10] Granville had remarried two months before and was to have two sons and three daughters. Once at Walmer he found that his increasing family, friends who were about to or had just endured a Channel crossing and other visitors, became such a crowd, that the accommodation at the Castle which had been

Fig.33 Ascott, the entrance courtyard

Fig.34 Ascott, the conservatory

Fig.35 Sketch elevation of Walmer Castle

previously sufficient if rather spartan, was no longer large enough. There were other problems; kitchen smells penetrated the main rooms, something that Victorians found most offensive, and the drains and the men servants' lavatory added to the atmosphere.[11] A programme of building work was put in hand which began early in 1872 and continued for three years. Devey was almost certainly recommended to Granville by Sir Walter James.

Walmer was the southernmost of 'The Three Castles which keep the Downs', built in 1539-40 at the command of Henry VIII to guard the important anchorage within the Goodwin Sands, the only safe haven between the Medway and Portsmouth. The enemies were the Catholic sovereigns of France and Spain. The other castles were Deal and Sandown, the latter of which was in a ruinous state, and they were more forts, or defensible batteries which would have been commanded by a master-gunner, than castles, concentric in plan and designed to withstand attack by artillery. Devey produced a delightful watercolour elevation showing the proposed addition of nurseries and extra bedrooms in a new storey above the bastions, which illustrates two alternative treatments. (Fig.35) On the left it is built in diapered brickwork with a band of chequered stone and flint flushwork, derived, like the cut flint at Betteshanger, from the Sandwich Fisher Gate. On the right the building is simply of stone. This was what was decided upon, and a ready source was located. 'Under the advice of Mr. Devey, though archaeologists protested, he transferred the old stones of Sandown Castle, which was rapidly crumbling into the sea, and with them erected a new tower.'[10] It is strange that Devey, who had such a respect for old buildings, should advise such a course. Granville also built stables and kennels for his pack of harriers, and had Devey convert the old

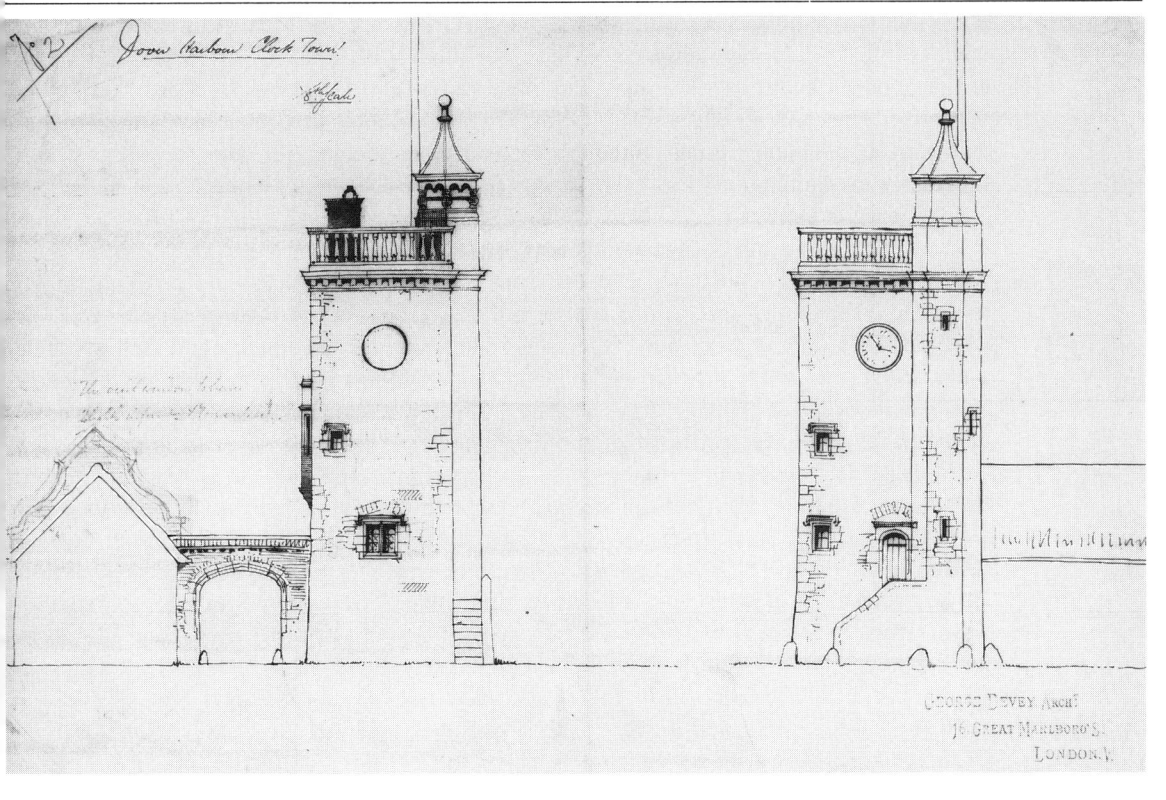

Fig.36 Elevations of Dover Clock Tower

semaphore station at Kingsdown into a summer house with a fine view of the Channel which he named 'Villa Veta' after his daughter, and carry out some work at St. Margaret's Bay, where a small house can be identified as his work. Villa Veta would have had a prospect of constant interest, with every class of sailing vessel from Blackwall frigates to convict hulks sheltering below, and being tended by small craft sailing out from Deal, the famous pilot galleys and Deal luggers. It survives, now called South Foreland House, encumbered with later additions which which have converted a rather frivolous small building into an substantial house. It was decorated with Dutch gables and is most curiously finished on the exterior with broken tiles set as a jigsaw in mortar, similar tiles being used to form the mouldings of the gables. This does not occur elsewhere in Devey's work, and is not a finish peculiar to vernacular buildings in east Kent. It has something of the inconsequential charm of a grotto, that is a building put together from materials which came to hand, sometimes bones and broken china as well as the more expensive shells and mineral specimens, and was perhaps intended to look as if amateurs had taken part in the construction.

Lord Ronald Gower paid the Granvilles a visit in 1874: 'A long and dull railway journey to Deal. Mr. Dasent (Delane's brother-in-law); Devey, the architect; and Miss Blanche Pitt, Granville's neice were all the party. Dasent is an amusing and incessant talker, and prevented the others from going to sleep after dinner. Walmer has been much improved by Lord Granville. Before his time it must have been about as uncomfortable a habitation as a lighthouse or a Martello tower. We visited Lord Clanwilliam's castle at Deal; but he is only there - wise man - during the autumn; and then went with Granville and Devey to see a little house they have built on a desolate hill, which Lord Granville calls "Vetas" (his eldest daughter's name) "Villa".[12] Devey designed a farm for Lord Granville in 1876. He had gained a reputation as a farmer nearly ten years previously: 'Earl Granville and Lord Torrington - the former especially - excel as dairy farmers' a curious hobby for a man brought up in Paris and without a country estate, although he had been looking for one for some years.[13] Previously his farming had had been conducted on the outskirts of London, and he had had a small place at Golders Green. Now Devey designed him a model farm at Cliffs End, which is about ten miles north of Walmer. This consisted of a farm house and dairy, a cow house with standings for twelve cows, two calf pens, piggery, barn, stables and cart and waggon sheds and other storage space.

Granville's interest in country matters led him over the years to try and find a country estate within reasonable distance of London. This continued even after he came to Walmer and eventually some suitable land became available, a map of which survives, but this unfortunately gives no indication of the location. Devey was instructed to prepare designs for a mansion, to be called Maplewood, for which he was paid in 1879, and a model was constructed which was photographed in 1909.[14] For some reason this was not proceeded with. Granville became a great friend as well as a client. 'He would call at the office and walk off arm-in-arm with Mr. Devey, consulting him frequently on a great variety of matters of taste. He had great faith in Mr. Devey's judgment and advice.' Devey also worked on Granville's Town houses, in Bruton Street and at No.18 Carlton House Terrace, and thanks to his influence, for the Ramsgate and Dover Harbour Boards designing for the latter the Clock Tower which still stands in the Western Docks. (Fig.36) This was designed in 1876 and James Williams, newly made a partner, attended a meeting of the Harbour Board in May with a model which was accepted, and the construction of the tower was authorised at a cost not exceeding £1000. Despite the fact that the contractor for the building was the highly competent W.J. Adcock of Dover, who was to carry out such major works for Devey as St Alban's Court, the Board complained in March the following year of 'the unsatisfactory state of the Clock Tower the water driving through the Walls.' Devey recommended that the

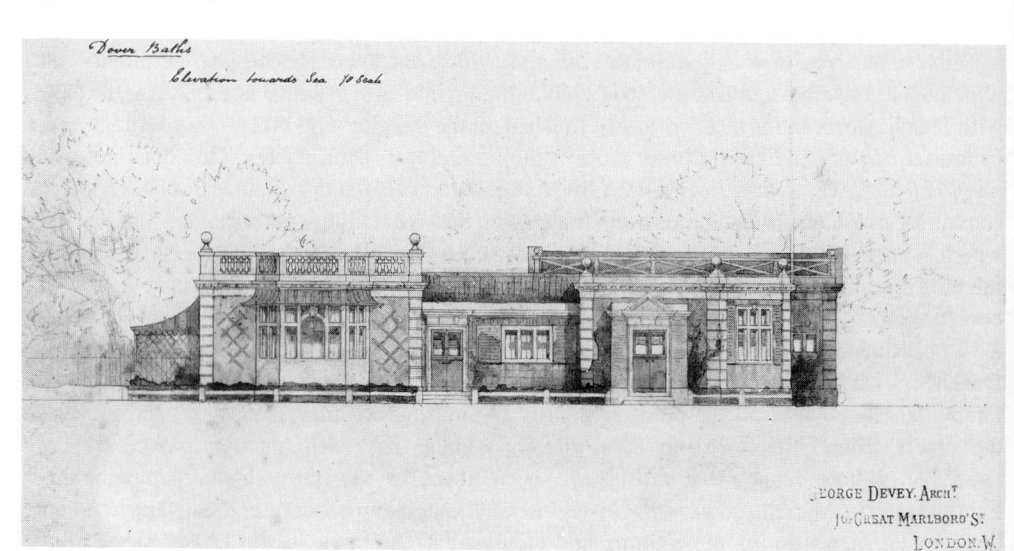

Fig.37 Elevation of Dover Baths

Fig.38 Elevation of cottages at Lullington

stonework should be pointed in cement to which the Board responded with asperity that Mr Devey should be reminded 'that the Tower was erected in accordance with plans and specifications prepared by him and they look to him to take such measures as he may advise to make the Walls of the Tower watertight.'[15] This episode did not sour relations between Board and architect and Devey went on to prepare plans for the laying out of building land in front of Camden Crescent and Granville Gardens. At the same time the lease of the building which had housed Marsh's Royal Baths expired and the land was taken in to extend Marine Parade. Devey designed the new 'Baths and Bathing Establishment and Reading Room' between Camden Crescent and the sea. (Fig.37) This part of the Dover seafront and all Devey's work was demolished by German shells during the War.

Two other small commissions arose through the Granville connection. The first was a drinking fountain at Deal, a most philanthropic and welcome gift to the town in days when pure drinking water was not necessarily available to all. It 'forms an ornamental object at the corner of the Guildhall, Lower-street. So handsome a gift will no doubt be rightly appreciated by the inhabitants.'[16] Sadly, it is no longer in use. The other matter was the problem of the Reporters' Gallery in the House of Lords. On the 14th July 1883 Devey appeared before a Select Committee and produced and explained a plan for enlarging the Gallery by making it continuous across the end of the Chamber. He proposed that the panelled front should be removed and replaced with metal railings to match those of the side galleries. But John Taylor, the Surveyor to the Houses of Parliament objected to the design because the Gallery was lower than those at the sides, and the junction between the two would be difficult to manage. The scheme was not adopted.

During the early 1860s Devey had to continue to make do with small commissions. Indeed, the works for Lord Granville, or obtained through his influence with the Harbour Boards, on which he was entitled to a seat as Lord Warden, were, though no doubt welcome, fairly insignificant. A set of new bedrooms at Walmer Castle, the internal rearrangement of

Fig.39 Whitchurch School

Carlton House Terrace and a design for its small patch of garden were not going to bring fame, although in due course, as we shall see, they did lead to more worthwhile work. There was a steady stream of such things, estate cottages for William Duckworth of Orchardleigh, (Fig.38) and for Alfred Morrison of Fonthill, new stables for Thomas Longman, the publisher, of Farnborough Hill, more cottages and the rebuilding of the Bull Inn, Benenden, for Gathorne Hardy, later Lord Cranbrook of Hemsted Park, minor works for Lord Ducie, Lord Cranworth, Lord Bagot and Lady Ashburton, and also a number of schools such as those at Whitchurch in Buckinghamshire, (Fig.39) at Benenden, Kent (Fig.40) and at Jarrow, Co. Durham, the last of which he designed for Sir Walter James. (Fig.41) And then, at last, came a number of big commissions.

His first large, new country house was designed for Charles Pilgrim and built in 1866-7. Pilgrim had been resident in Buckinghamshire since 1858 at the very latest, the year he joined the 2nd Royal Bucks Regiment of Yeomanry Cavalry, becoming the commander of the Artillery Troop, which seems to have kept its equipment at Stowe. The Akeley Wood estate adjoined that of Stowe, and here he had built a house described by *Kelly's Post Office Directory* in 1895 as a 'half-timbered Elizabethan cottage standing in about 200 acres.' The house, lodge and stables were indeed half-timbered, but the Wealden style of wooden framing is replaced here by that of Lancastrian houses such as Smithills Hall, where Devey was later to work on a restoration and substantial additions. He does, however, use his broad chimney breasts with diagonally set chimney stacks, which are built in the ginger-coloured local sandstone, with a rather curious effect. (Fig.42) The house was enlarged in 1911-12 when Ernest George was called in to add nurseries, a new dining room and to extend the offices.

This job was followed by several commissions to make additions to old houses which he did in a sympathetic manner. The first was Wilcote House in Oxfordshire for Charles Sartoris, originally a seventeenth century farmhouse. Here Devey added new rooms on the south and converted the old part into offices. Wilcote is almost certainly the house which was the subject of another of Williams' anecdotes: 'When the Earl (Granville) was Foreign Minister, Devey would often dine with them at Carlton House Terrace ... It was at one of these banquets, sitting between

Working for the Whigs 65

Fig.40 Benenden School

Fig.41 Jarrow School

Fig.42 Akeley Wood

Sir William Harcourt and the late Bishop of Oxford, that Sir William began talking to Devey of a wonderful house being built for a friend of his, in Oxfordshire, where the architect, an ingenious and clever man, by using old stonework and tiles, had managed to make a most charming old-looking mansion. Sir William was afterwards very much amused to find he had been talking to the architect.' Similarly large additions including a tower were made to Lion House, Newport for George Hooper, and to Zeals House in Wiltshire, which was much enlarged for William Chaffyn-Grove, as was Rochetts in Essex for O.E. Coope. However the most important of such works was that carried out at Brantingham Thorpe for Christopher Sykes, the younger son of Sir Tatton Sykes of Sledmere.

Fig.43 Brantingham Thorpe, before the alterations

Fig.44 Brantingham Thorpe

Brantingham was bought for Sykes by his father for use as a hunting box, and the survey drawings show that it was an eighteenth-century, two-storey Gothick villa with pointed doors and windows under thick hood moulds, and a hipped slate roof and crenellated eaves. (Fig.43) It was not sufficiently grand as it was, for the use to which Sykes intended to put it, namely the entertainment of the Prince of Wales when he attended the newly established Doncaster races. Devey retained the original fabric including the canted bays on the entrance front, adding hybrid Dutch and shaped gables to these, replacing the battlements with a balustrade and putting in new windows with simple mullions and transomes. (Fig.44) The interiors were panelled and the woodwork carefully designed to accord with a chimney piece of c.1715 brought to the house from 66 High Street, Hull. This work was carried out in 1868-71, and further alterations were proposed a year or so later when Devey prepared a number of designs for new polygonal bays flanking the entrance. (Fig.45) Sykes also consulted Devey about stained glass, which was obtained from the Whitefriars Glass Company for the four light transomed window on the staircase. The lower lights were filled with mantling and the coats of arms of Sykes, Foulis, Tatton and Kirby, and the upper with scenes from the life of the client's namesake, St Christopher. An even more remakable window in the hall, no doubt made by the same company, has similar heraldic glass and a series of gold stained oval panels imitating Flemish seventeenth century glass and showing scenes from ancient local history.[17] Christopher Sykes was another Liberal M.P., though a rather inactive one, and the next group of houses to be described were built for persons of similar political views; three friends, all Liberals and staunch admirers of Gladstone; all were bankers and all bought country properties at Coombe near Kingston-upon-Thames from the Duke of Cambridge, sixty minutes by carriage, we are told, from Lombard Street in the City of London.

Fig.45 Brantingham Thorpe, design for the new bays

Edward Baring, later created Lord Revelstoke, was a partner in Baring Brothers, Bertram Wodehouse Currie and George Grenfell Glyn, who had sat as a Liberal M.P. from 1857 until he succeeded his father as 2nd Baron Wolverton, were partners in Glyn, Mills, Currie & Co. Currie and Baring bought two small houses, Coombe Warren and Coombe Cottage in the 1860s and employed Devey on large extensions and estate buildings. Wolverton bought the nearby Warren House in 1880 and also employed Devey on extensive building works.

Work on Coombe Warren I began in the summer of 1869 and was visited by Currie on the 11th October 'At Coombe I arrived 3.45, and found the tower dismantled of its ivy and with a hole in its middle, the back-yard blocked up with carts, and a yawning gulf lined with brickwork ... Hadler, the foreman was on the premises, and showed me the elevation of the new buildings, which is well enough. Devey, the incorrigible, has introduced a great deal of timber in the gables ...'[18] The reference to a tower is rather mystifying, other evidence seems to indicate that what Currie had bought was an old farmouse and a new wing was built on in a matching style, which was clearly one which included a number of Devey's half-timbered gables. Even with the addition it remained a small house with only a drawing room, dining room and study besides the kitchen offices and the bedrooms. (Fig.46) It was the first house in which Devey employed the device of setting the offices off at an angle to the main block, which lends itself to picturesque grouping, but also has the added benefit that the service ranges of houses may be built to the same height as the rest, but their impact is diminished by perspective. The older part, which contained the kitchen, burnt down in January 1870, when the new part can have been barely completed, and Mrs Currie noted later 'With his accustomed promptitude, Bertram at once entrusted to Mr. Devey the task of erecting a new house. The wing had been built to match the old house. I requested that the new house should not be built to match the wing. We had seen what an easy prey timber beams become to fire; nor do their old fashioned and picturesque appearance compensate for the loss of comfort which they entail. A stone or brick building offers much more substantial resistance to the cold of winter or the heat of summer.'[19] For Coombe Warren II Devey returns to the east Kent manner of Betteshanger, building a substantial three-storey house of ragstone and diapered red brick with two-storey bays of large mullioned windows, one lighting each of the main rooms, the drawing room, library, saloon and dining room. A stone-built conservatory led off, and similarly lit an inner hall. (Fig.47) These bays were on the east and west fronts of the house, that on the south had no such projections. This had three gables, that on the right flanked by a pair of chimney breasts corbelled out of the wall some feet above the ground and both cutting into the gable above. This is a feature found in the early sixteenth century

Fig.46 Coombe Warren I

Fig.47 Coombe Warren II, the entrance courtyard

buildings like the entrance range at Sissinghurst Castle, and is one which Devey used often, even in comparatively plain houses such as Kelsall Lodge, Tunbridge Wells, which he designed for the builder James Haward, who was the contractor for Coombe Warren I. (Fig.48) At Coombe Warren the former kitchen was converted into a chapel for Mrs Currie, who was a Roman Catholic, and the offices greatly extended; in fact, Currie's country house became a mansion. The tops of the bay windows were crenellated and together with Dutch gables with triangular and segmental pediments, and with the angled chimney stacks they gave the house a very lively skyline. (Fig.49) There was a certain amount of sculpture on the house, a figure and two urns are placed in niches on the south front and a number of tondos containing potrait busts of Shakespeare, Sir Philip Sidney and other literary characters modelled by the architectural sculptors C.H. and J. Mabey. Stained glass for the chapel and a bay window on the stairs was ordered from Whitefriars by Devey.[20] The final extension to the house was undertaken in 1881, when the kitchen was rebuilt in the style of the main part, in stone and brick, with a tower above which contained rooms for the Currie's eldest son Isaac, who was to die of tuberculosis at the age of twenty four. A family friend wrote of poor Zak 'He now has two rooms in a tower lately added to the house, partly to carry a water-cistern but more to satisfy Grevy, the chef, who demanded a new kitchen because the chefs of Monsieur Baring and Lord Wolverton mocked themselves of his inferior accommodation.'[20] Zak was sent to Scotland rather than to Italy in an attempt to cure his tuberculosis, and after his death Devey designed a monument with the boy's reclining effigy for the chapel, and a *prie- dieu* for his mother.

The interiors at Coombe Warren II were singularly lavish, more so than in the earlier building which, so far as can be made out from the few remaining photographs, had lower ceilings with thin

Fig.48 Kelsall Lodge

ceilings with thin plasterwork and Jacobean panelling below. One room, the staircase hall, had between at the cornice level a plaster frieze carved by the Mabeys representing the months, with the labours and delights being carried out by, or enjoyed by *putti*. Since the house has been demolished, photographs by Bedford Lemere & Co. and Walter Godfrey's description must sufffice

> The central hall or saloon is entirely panelled in oak, with great refinement of detail. The arches which screen the staircase, their pilasters, and the fine carved chimney-piece ... are worthy of comparison with the best of Jacobean work...The ceiling is divided by moulded oak ribs into square panels of plaster, relieved only by modelled fleurs-de-lys and roses. The panelling in the drawing room is divided into bays by fluted and decorated pilasters, reaching to the full height of the room, and contains elaborate framing for pictures ... The woodwork is coloured an ivory-white, some of the panels being "brushed in" with a hard brush to produce a rough texture in the paint. Above the carved frieze and cornice a ceiling of moulded plaster ribs arranged in a flowing pattern gives an excellent finish ... The circular bay-window, in close proximity to the fireplace, was a favourite device of Mr. Devey's.[22]

Devey was also responsible for the design of the gardens at Coombe Warren, building terrace walls and steps, an Italian garden, a small circular 'Temple' with a lead-covered domed roof, garden walls and gateways and an orangery. This lay to the north of the house, as did the stables, and the north lodge, an attractive red brick building with an octagonal battlemented tower, which some person of little taste has cut down in height and painted white. Despite this the major part, together with a small lodge on the other side of the stable entrance make an attractive group on the corner of Beverley Lane, which divides Currie's land from that of Baring. There were also a number of cottages for gardeners and another

Fig.49 Coombe Warren II, the south front

lodge, with Dutch gables, at the extreme western end of the estate. One of the last of B.W. Currie's embellishments, the building work was continued by his son Laurence after his death, was the Bay House, a small octagonal baroque building in the manner of Wren at Hampton Court, which was partly a summer house and partly a fane devoted to Mr Gladstone. (Fig.50) His bust by C.H. Mabey was displayed there.

Coombe Warren was sold by Laurence Currie in 1926. The mansion was demolished, the grounds broken up into building plots, the orangery turned into a house and the smaller estate cottages enlarged into gentlemen's residences.

Edward Baring began building work on his property before Currie, although improvements to the house itself came later. The stables have a tablet dating them to 1863 and are in Devey's Wealden style, built of ragstone with yellow stock brick above, with stone blocks rising at random into the brickwork, and some red brick used as dressings. They are entered through an arch with a hood-mould in brick, to the left of this is a typical gable with roughcast in the apex and a chimney breast impinging on it on the left. There is a ventilator with an ogee-leaded roof and weather vane. To the north of this Baring built a dairy with a pair of half-timbered gables and a veranda and balcony with a wooden balustrade. (Fig.51)

Coombe Cottage itself became an ideal 'ivy-covered, red-brick house, with a tower at one end, a cool oak hall and staircase, a drawing-room full of water-colours, a room next to it full of books, with a drawing-table and painting materials ready, and a long dining-room, of which the narrow end was a sitting-room, and had a verandah looking out on to the garden.'[23] The original very plain house was on the south near the road. Devey's new range, built in 1869-72, ran to the north, the junction between the two being marked by a three-storey brick tower, in which he placed the porch, topped by a wooden balustrade. Beyond this Devey built a series of gables of different heights and materials terminating in another tower, all of which give a rather chaotic impression of a sequence of additions made over some period of time. (Fig.52) The builders were again Haward Brothers. Finally Devey built Coombe Wood, now Hopping Wood Farm, with three small ranges round a courtyard and an imposing dovecote which looks more likely to have been designed by the young James Williams than by Devey himself.

Baring sold out in 1885. The London and South Western Railway wanted part of the land for a new line, which was in fact not built. He insisted that they buy the whole estate and from then on divided his time between 37 Charles Street, Westminster, and Membland near Noss Mayo, where he had Devey build him large additions onto his new country house. Currie also employed Devey elsewhere, at No.1 Richmond Terrace in 1877 where he raised the southeast wing to form a tower. The sumptuous redecoration of the principal rooms was designed by him and carried out by William Turner Lord, whose firm also worked for Baring at 37 Charles Street. The carving in the oak room and the library was executed by Messrs. Mellier, who were to carry out the woodwork at Minley Manor, Currie's house in Hampshire where Devey began a programme of extension and decorations which was continued by Arthur Castings after his death.

Devey worked at Warren House during the last two years of his life, 1884-86. It was a large red brick in an unimaginative Gothic revival style which had been built by the banker Hugh Hammersley, and bought by Wolverton in 1880. Devey made some large additions on the east front which are dated 1884, and he was careful to match his new work with what was already there. Alterations to the offices on the west enabled him to add a gable in rough-cast with a curly bargeboard, which is tucked into an awkward angle. There are also terraces, walls and garden steps to the rear of the house where the ground falls away which look very much like the work of Devey.

Fig.50 Elevation of the Bay House, Coombe Warren

Fig.51 The Dairy, Coombe Cottage

Other commissions for prominent Liberals followed later; the major item was the building of Hall Place and other work in and around Leigh for Samuel Morley in 1871-4, Send Holme for William Hargreaves in c.1871, and Oldbury Place for G.J. Shaw-Lefevre in 1878-81.

Samuel Morley was another prodigious entrepreneurial figure of his day. He was a Liberal Member of Parliament from 1865, and a most succesful hosiery manufacturer who ran the business of I. & R. Morley, founded by his family in Nottingham, and he was, like Currie, a member of the Temperance movement, signing the pledge of Total Abstinence in 1882. He bought the Hall Place estate in 1870 from Thomas Bailey, who had already employed Devey on Park House and some unidentified work, perhaps attempting repairs to the Elizabethan manor which 'had, however, been very badly built, and required considerable alteration to meet modern requirements'.[24] Morley also attempted to make the old house habitable and spent nearly a thousand pounds on this, but eventually decided that only a new one would answer. Fortunately a summary of the accounts rendered by George Myers and Sons, the contractors employed, has been preserved in the estate office, from which we learn that a total of £70,913 was spent, of which £54,364 was for the new mansion and £8,551 for the stables. It was the most expensive building Devey ever designed.

At the time it was begun it was also the biggest he had undertaken and here he introduces what was to become a favourite plan. The front porch led into a rather cramped anteroom from which the visitor turned first sharp left and then right into a central saloon. Off this lay on the left, the library and drawing room, with the Oak parlour and the principal stairs straight ahead. The dining room was to the right of the entrance, and to the right of the stairs lay Morley's own room and a room for his secretary, with another business room beyond the servants' stairs. The materials are what are now becoming standard for Devey's larger houses, red brick diapered with vitrified headers, sandstone dressings, and in this case a Westmoreland slate roof. It had a range of seven gables of varying sizes on the entrance front, with a tower above the porch, and another tall slender octagonal stair turret rising above the offices. (Fig.53) These, the kitchen, scullery and pantries are set forward at an angle of 15 degrees, and screened from the entrance drive by a two-storey quadrant wall terminating in the bakehouse. The garden front has a run of six gables and four bays ending on the north with the five-storey tower rising above the servants' hall. Nearly all the gables have two-storey bay windows, mullioned and transomed, with a particularly attractive arrrangement, a small sun room opening off the drawing room. Some windows have arched lights, some bays are battlemented and some have balustrades and substantial moulded brick chimney stacks and pinnacles provide decoration at roof level. It must, however, be confessed that the design is a touch mechanical, and like Coombe Cottage demonstrates that Devey was not at his happiest when dealing with larger buildings. At Coombe Cottage the length of varied gables appears too disorganised, at Hall Place they are perhaps too regimented. It was a problem he was not to overcome, the felicity with which he could arrange the features of smaller houses did not translate into the mansions. The stables are altogether a happier piece of design (Fig.54) and the boathouse by the lake is a typically Devey arrangement of roof levels and gables. (Fig.55)

Fig.52 Coombe Cottage

76 *George Devey*

Fig.53 Hall Place, the entrance front under construction

Fig.54 Hall Place stables

Fig.55 Hall Place boathouse

Send Holme, on the other hand, is a medium-sized country house and is of the type in which Devey was to make his major contribution to English domestic architecture, the middle-class house which relied on vernacular models rather than a foreign or revivalist style. Hargreaves was a friend of John Bright, the Radical, who was invited to join Gladstone's administration in 1868. He had never been in office and consulted Hargreaves before committing himself to government, a step which he felt inevitable as Gladstone was pushing through so many of the reforms advocated by him, but one which effectively removed him from the forefront of public life. Send Holme is of three storeys with high rising local stone footings and red brick above, in a restrained Tudor style. The entrance front is given interest by an arrangement of no less than seven gables of different shapes and sizes, but the garden front is symmetrical, diversified by bay windows, verandas, chimney stacks and small gables. (Fig.56) It had a lodge, with a porch entered through a pair of arches; Devey suggested 'It is assumed that Flowers might be kept in this Porch and would be seen through the openings.'

Oldbury Place was a plain eighteenth-century block of a house built of rubble with galleting; G.J. Shaw-Lefevre, later Baron Eversley and founder of the Commons Preservation Society and thus to a great extent the saviour of Hampstead Heath, Wimbledon Common and Epping Forest, was another man who served with Gladstone, and he called in Devey in 1878 to make an addition to the east end of the house containing a library and drawing room, to build a new porch and inner hall, to convert the dining room into a room for Shaw-Lefevre's own use, and to add an L shaped range of offices. The new work was carried out in stone and Devey placed Dutch gables with pediments on the north, east and south of the new range. Here again he proposed a pair of chimney stacks corbelled out at first floor level impaling the gable on the entrance front, but these were not built.

Fig.56 Send Holme

There seems little doubt that Devey was himself a Liberal, and possibly one with radical views. James Williams remembered 'He always liked to call himself a working man, and often regretted that there was no badge for us to wear in common with all workmen, showing the sympathy he had with all honest labour. One reason he gave was that when out driving, on business, workpeople along the road might see that we were not out merely for pleasure.'[25] Whatever his own political views might have been, it was the Liberal connection which launched him into the most prosperous period in his career.

5

The Use of Photography

Light is that silent artist
Which without the aid of man
Designs on silver bright
Daguerre's immortal plan.[1]

One of the curious coincidences of the nineteenth century was that two alternative methods of photography became available to the public in one month, in January 1839. These were the Photogenic Drawings which William Henry Fox Talbot exhibited at the Royal Institution on the 25th of January, having been precipitated into a contest for the honour of being the 'inventor' of the art by the announcement of Louis Jaques Mandé Daguerre's discovery at the Academie des Sciences on the 7th January. Needless to say both men had been working for a number of years towards the goal of developing a latent image obtained by exposing a suitably prepared surface to light and thereafter fixing this by chemical means, and the events of January 1839 were simply the publicising of their achievements. They had been preceded by numbers of other persons who had tried to preserve the images obtained with the camera obscura and other devices by mechanical rather than manual means, and many different methods had been tried without much success. At the time Fox Talbot certainly thought their processes were the same, and he was wrong. He was making prints on sensitized paper, taken from negatives capable of being used more than once. Daguerre made use of silvered copper plates, on which a direct positive print was made showing the subject in reverse, and from which more copies could not obtained. What followed was a rather unsavoury flurry of patents and litigation, with Daguerre selling his invention to the French Government (who generously donated it to the world by publishing at least thirty editions of his manual in eight different languages) but taking out a patent in England five days before, and selling licenses to English practitioners.[2] This species of sharp practice was echoed by the behaviour of Fox Talbot, who consistently protected his rights in the Courts even maintaining that his calotype patent covered the collodion process invented by Frederick Scott Archer. Fortunately sufficient photographers were prepared to defy him, and sufficient pressure brought to bear by distinguished men, Sir Charles Eastlake, President of the Royal Academy, and the Earl of Rosse, President of the Royal Society, to oblige him to relax his attempts to protect what he mistakenly regarded as his own.[3]

As is now well known, painters put this new art to use with little delay, with varying degrees of discretion as to what they were about. Photographs, as employed by J.-A.-D. Ingres, could do much to decrease the number of tedious sittings for portraits, and they could provide accurate likenesses of eminent persons for history paintings such as Edouard Manet's

The Execution of the Emperor Maximilian. Carefully posed and lit models in a chosen setting were used by Theodore Robinson, for whom, in a work such as *The Layette*, they took the place of the preliminary designs and sketches, studies of the figure and the worked up *modello* which had previously been the painterly approach to composition. They were used by Courbet, Delacroix, Degas, and Corot, in whose studio 300 were found after his death; they were eventually to settle once and for all the question of how a horse galloped, a man walked, or an eagle flew.[4] The flying gallop of horses in old sporting paintings and prints immediately became quaint and unacceptable. Finally they were used in a completely mechanical way by Thomas Sidney Cooper, who filled his sketches of the countryside round Canterbury with carefully trimmed photographs of cows and sheep, creating through these *montages* the models for his oil paintings.[5] The help they could give to architects was equally obvious, but a matter which they did not generally ackowledge, nor has it been explored yet by architectural historians.

When G. E. Street wrote the preface to his travel book *Brick and Marble in the Middle Ages*, he explained that he had restricted the number of illustrations for reasons of cost and refers his readers to the works of Mr Gally Knight, and for Venice, to 'Mr. Ruskin's engravings and to the photographs which have rendered her features so well known to almost all students of architecture.' But Street never admits to using photographs himself, although four years later at a meeting of the Architectural Photographic Association he asserted that they were 'singularly well adapted to serve as the foundations on which to build our nineteenth-century style of domestic architecture for cities as this.'[6] Ruskin was one of the first to use them, for two reasons. The first was that he had had intermittent trouble with his eyesight since before October 1840 which he records in his diaries, writing for example,in Naples on the 11th March 1841 '... sketching, till the sun got too intense for my eyes;'[7] The second was his alarm at the destructive restoration of old buildings which came particularly to his attention when he arrived in Venice in September 1845 with J.D. Harding, who had taught him painting some years before. His reaction to this was to attempt to record the ruinous beauty of Venetian Gothic with all the 'cracks and stains' that he had learnt to appreciate, but only with difficulty to record on paper. Harding had realised the help the daguerreotypes could afford and had written about them in his book *The Principles and Practice of Art*, published that same year, but took care to point out their artistic disavantages; 'By this most ingenious discovery, identical imitation is carried out to the utmost degree; and its effects in informing the eye are truly wonderful; but together with those objects which we esteem beautiful, others are also presented which the moment has brought together in ill assortment; and in the midst of beauties, we also perceive much which is either offensive to the mind, or which in a picture would be better omitted.'[8] The upshot of it was that in early October Ruskin bought twenty daguerreotypes from 'a poor Frenchman' and wrote home to his father 'certainly Daguerreotypes taken by this vivid sunlight are glorious things. It is very nearly the same thing as carrying off the palace itself; every chip of stone and stain is there, and of course there is no mistake about proportions. I am very much delighted with these, and am going to have some more made of pet bits. It is a noble invention — say what they will of it — and anyone who has worked and blundered and stammered as I have done for four days, and then sees the thing he has been trying to do so long in vain, done perfectly and faultlessly in half a minute, won't abuse it afterwards.'[9]

The point is fairly made that all artists, and for that matter architects, are pressed for time, and that a photograph will accurately record in seconds what it might take a day to draw, with only the easily corrected defect of perspective distortion which varied according to the lens used. Photographs can also be made of places and things that only the most dedicated and intrepid student might see. H. de Lacretelle wrote in 1852: 'The young artist has recorded, stone by stone, the cathedrals of Strasbourg and Rheims in over a hundred different prints. Thanks to him we have climbed all the steeples ... what we never could have discovered through our own eyes, he has seen for us ... one might think the saintly artists of the Middle Ages had foreseen the daguerreotype in placing their statues and stone carvings where birds alone circling the spires could marvel at their detail and perfection. ... M. Le Secq, too, has built his monument.'[10]

But Ruskin was to change his mind in later life, and the architectural profession as a whole seems to have been singularly slow and shy about admitting the help that photographs could afford them in the study of old buildings. There was a cherished tradition of the architect filling sketchbooks with useful details on tours such as the one made through Sussex and Kent by Richard Norman Shaw and W.E. Nesfield in 1860, taking in Penshurst, where they came face to face with Devey's work, and the later 'scrambles' of the students of the Architectural Association, which took them to the old and the picturesque within easy reach of London. Still, the fact that this help was actively sought by some at least of the younger generation of Victorian architects, is revealed by the diaries of Charles Barry Junior, who had been assisting his father on the works at the Palace of Westminster, and who was planning a European tour in early 1847.[11]

His interest in photography was stimulated by a lecture 'from Mr Hunt the Photographer', most probably Robert Hunt who had published *Researches on Light* in 1844, at the Royal Institution on the 13th February 1846. Just eleven days later he went to a Mr. Catherwood and was 'occupied with him for some hours passing through the process of preparing taking & fixing Daguerreotype pictures'; on the 1st March, bearing a letter of introduction from Michael Faraday, he called on Antoine Claudet, who had dealt in glassware and subsequently become one of Daguerre's first licensees in England, but was discouraged by the difficulties then explained to him.

Claudet was not one to let a useful introduction slip and the following day young Barry was taking him over the New Palace and positions were selected from which daguerreotypes could best be taken. After further visits to Claudet and Catherwood and experiments with borrowed cameras, he 'found its field (of the Daguerreotype aparatus) too contracted for taking views of buildings unless at great distances and the focal length so short that the long vertical lines sensibly converge.' He then began to learn Fox Talbot's calotype process which he did up to the 3rd April 'My preparations for departure have been going on with clothes & Calotype apparatus'. And here to the intense irritation of the reader, the diaries cease abruptly in the middle of the entry for the 15th April 1847 so we never discover how he got on.

A considerable number of Devey's collection of photographs survive. They fall into four categories: photographs taken of his houses under construction, photographs of the houses when completed and newly furnished; an archive of photographs of old buildings which he used as exemplars of the styles which he was to adapt and make his own, and photographs of buildings put up by a few of his contemporaries. But clearly quite a number of losses have occured in the hundred years since he died and only deductions can be made from what we have now.

The idea of recording building works in progress was unusual but not new. Sir John Soane, for example sent his pupils, George Basevi, Robert Chantrell, Charles Tyrrell and others to make 'constructional' drawings recording the progress of building work where he could, that is, when the building in question was within convenient distance of London. 'By attending the progress of buildings and by making Drawings of them in their different stages the Student will not only attain great skill in the mechanism of Buildings, but at the same time discover many effects of light and shade ... the young Artist must not stop with making such Drawings; he must at the same time consider and make his remarks on every part of the Construction.' The National Debt Redemption and Life Annuities Office in Old Jewry, the Consols Office of the Bank of England, Chelsea Hospital and the Dulwich Art Gallery were all visited and in the case of the last, a series of watercolours was bound up as *Dulwich College. Sketches of the Picture Gallery, the Mausoleum and the Sisters' Apartments made by the pupils of Sir John Soane during the progress of the works 1812*. His purpose as stated in his Lecture XII delivered to the students at the Royal Academy was to teach his young men the mechanics of construction, but it does seem that he shared with Devey a simple pleasure in seeing his designs being built. But it was certainly not common practice at this or any other time.[12]

Devey seems to have been the next architect to record his houses as they went up, as has already been mentioned. Godfrey recalled 'Devey loved bricks and mortar, and to his delight in seeing a building photographed in the process of erection we owe the possession of many interesting representations of houses, still roofless and surrounded by scaffold poles.'[13] This

Fig.57 Cottage at Fonthill

Fig.58 Retaining walls at the Fonthill Arch under construction

we have already seen in the pictures of work on the Buckingham Building at Penshurst (Fig.18) and the second phase at Betteshanger where the workmen are building the Dutch gables on the garden front, both of which date from about 1861. (Fig.19) The next to survive, in chronological order are a couple of photographs of work in progress on the new retaining walls on the north side of the monumental Fonthill Arch, which Devey built for Alfred Morrison, having already designed a number of cottages for him on the estate. (Fig.57) Morrison had inherited the property from his father James in 1857. James was a self-made man whose fortune arose from his partnership in the drapery business which became known as Morrison, Dillon & Co., the first to rely on a fast turnover for successful trading, hence his motto 'small profits and quick returns'. He also was a Liberal Member of Parliament, and had bought part of the Fonthill estate, employing J. B. Papworth to turn the surviving portion of Fonthill Splendens into an acceptable Italianate villa. The Fonthill Arch is erroneously ascribed by Rutter to Inigo Jones on the strength of local tradition, but more sensibly by others to the time of Alderman Beckford, in which case it may be by his architect, Mr Hoare.[14] Whether it is seventeenth or eighteenth century in date, it forms a massive and unexpected entrance to the park. No park walls abut it, and it must have seemed isolated and the setting

Fig.59 The Chafyn-Grove Almshouses

probably rather untidy before Devey built the splendid baroque retaining walls to either side each bearing five urns and terminating in massive piers topped by more urns of a different design. (Fig.58) It is his first work in the classical style. Flanking archways give access to a pair of lodges and the whole conception has a presence and scale which must have delighted Devey, whose work at this time, the mid 1860s, was mostly confined to buildings on a small scale.

At about the same time he had been called in to design just such a small thing. This was a terrace of almshouses which were built and endowed by William Chafyn-Grove of Zeals House in memory of his mother, and dedicated in 1865. (Fig.59) They are a pleasant row of cottages on the main road, built of red brick with stone dressings and the usual diaper patterning, and the photograph shows them almost complete. This commission led to a considerable enlargement of Zeals House itself, perhaps begun for William who died the year the almshouses were completed, at the age of 25, but completed by his sister Julia Chafyn-Grove. Here again the house was photographed while work was in progress, and there is a nice picture of a couple of masons, carefully posed, carving the mouldings of the new porch; this was probably taken in about 1867. (Fig.60) At very much the same time photographs were taken of Coombe Warren I, with its roof on, but still encased in wooden scaffolding poles, but these are now too faint to be reproduced here.

Hall Place was also recorded before it was quite completed, and the last of this small remaining group of photographs of building in progress is that of the Evangelical Free Chapel at Leigh, which has in the background the village hall, with the scaffolding still up. (Fig. 61) This is dated 1871, and represents just one of the improvements made to the village by Samuel Morley which he began before work on the mansion had been completed. His family were strongly non-conformist, and the chapel was built at the wish of his daughter, who had joined the Associated Methodists, who held mission services in a tent until this 'undenominational chapel' was built. The village hall was used for the Sunday School. After this was completed Devey designed the village school, the infants' part of which was subsidised by Morley to the tune of £300, and the waterworks, a pair of octagonal buildings which housed a new well, 12 feet in diameter at the top, going down to 60 feet, and the pump and filter which fed a 13,000 gallon reservoir and had a daily output of 25,000 gallons of pure water to Hall Place and the estate buildings alone, besides that used by the village.[15]

Any publication of Devey's work occured in spite of him and his clients, and such must have been the case with the article on Coombe Warren which appeared in *The Building News*. The facts of the matter were that in his early professional career when helpful notices in the building press or professional journals might have been welcome, his buildings went generally un-noticed, except when men like Shaw and Nesfield, who like Devey were rejecting the revivalist styles popular at the mid-century, saw them and recognised that the solution to a new domestic architecture lay in a recourse to old English buildings. Both these younger architects resorted to self-publicising to get themselves under way, both produced splendid volumes illustrating continental architecture, mostly ecclesiastical, and both prepared lively perspectives of their early work for publication, such as Shaw's drawings of Leyswood which were published in *The Building News* in March 1871.[16] There is little doubt that the development of the processes available for reproducing architectural drawings had a great effect on the way architects presented their designs.

Wood, copper and steel engravings were the standard methods, all of which had been in use for some time; mezzotints were invented in the middle of the seventeenth century and aquatints in 1768. These were used by Auguste Pugin to illustrate his book on the Royal Pavilion at Brighton. Lithography dates from 1798; it is a convenient method of reproducing drawings made in chalk, crayon or ink on stone or a zinc plate, which has the advantage that it did not require the intervention of a craftsman as the artist could make the drawings himself. The use of a number of different stones or plates enabled colour to be introduced but this was more effectively achieved by chromolithography. The real breakthrough so far as it concerned architects producing drawings of their own works for reproduction and the resulting publicity came with photolithography, which

Fig.60 New entrance porch at Zeals House

enabled his own drawings to be photographed and transferred to a plate. But the drawings had to be restricted to pen, washes showed up as black smudges, as did the finer varieties of cross-hatching. A generation of architects took to photolithography with enthusiasm, with the result that the architectural room at the Royal Academy exhibitions became an area of black or sepia and white.

Devey had nothing to do with this new technology, and what is more, he does not seem to have made seductive but possibly misleading presentation drawings for his clients, relying after an initial freely rendered sketch upon models to show what the finished work would look like. John Brandon Jones now qualifies what he wrote thirty years ago as being intended to be more amusing than a real complaint: 'Voysey said that, "When asked by his client to join a house-party, Devey would make the most facinating catch-penny sketches while dressing for dinner and present them during desert, charming everyone but getting them worked out by his clerks who had to make all the details on the traditional lines of a bastard Jacobean period!" '[17]

Architects practising earlier in the century, such as Anthony Salvin, sometimes took the trouble to have attractive lithographic pictures made of their completed buildings, which were useful as presents to potential clients, like that of Arley Hall chapel which he gave, with others, to Edward Hussey of Scotney Castle, and proposed buildings such as new churches, might also be shown in lithographs which could be used to entice possible subscribers. Almost

Fig.61 Evangelical Free Chapel, Leigh

Fig 62 Design for an unidentified Station Hotel

all the leading architects resorted to large perspectives, usually in watercolour and gouache, prepared by men who specialised in this kind of painting, both for exhibition, preferably at the Royal Academy, and to whet the appetites of their clients. Devey did not do this, and neither, oddly enough did he make his own perspective sketches of his buildings, although with his talent as a watercolourist, these would have been a most attractive, and indeed, an obvious thing to do. The paintings of Penshurst before and after the additions to Leicester Square now at Penshurst Place, the aerial perspective of the farm in Silesia made for Ferdinand de Rothschild (Fig.29) and the sketch for a hotel near a station, so far unidentified (Fig.62) are rare examples of this sort of thing. What he did do, was to present his elevations decorated with attractive but not obstructive shrubberies and often with a carriage and horses coming up to the front door at a spanking trot as in the elevation of Macharioch House. (Fig.63) Percy Stone had an interesting recollection of Devey's way of working: 'during the whole time I was in his office I never saw a drawing pen or a stick of Indian ink. All his drawings were executed in pencil, and weights were used to keep the paper in its place on the board.'

But something to show a possible client was useful, and it was no doubt partly for this reason, that Devey began to have his houses photographed upon completion. He seems to have started systematically in the early 1860s, and the new laundry at Penshurst Place appears to be one of the earliest examples. (Fig.64) Culver Lodge was recorded shortly after it was built, and he had photographs taken of Leicester Square and other work in the neighbourhood. Betteshanger was recorded stage by stage and small works for the Sutherlands at Cliveden and Trentham were recorded, as were the South and Wing Lodges at Mentmore, Buckland and Whitchurch schools, and Wickwar and Chearsley parsonages. Even a house so small and cheap as Grasshome, Dinton, built for a Miss Bland in 1871-2 and for which Devey's commission and travelling expenses amounted to a mere £43.7.0d., was photographed. (Fig.65) Then come the first more substantial commissions, Akeley Wood, taken both when just completed, (Fig.42) and again, some years later covered in creepers. Wilcote, the Lion House, Ash Lawn, Brantingham Thorpe, Calverley Grange, Lillies, and then Coombe Warren and Coombe Cottage. It is most likely that there were more photographs of other works, and that more than the few, or indeed single specimens which we now have of the buildings listed above once existed; we know that with Currie, Baring and Robert Smith, the recording of their houses was conducted on a scale consistent with the large sums of money which had been spent on them, and in one of these instances we know how much the client paid. Baring Brothers English Client Ledgers record the payments to Haward Bros as Coombe Cottage was built, and also those to Cubitt & Co., who were responsible for Membland. There are two payments to Bedford Lemere & Co., for £34.13.0d. in 1876, which is no doubt for recording Coombe Cottage, and for £70.2.0d. in 1879 for the series of pictures of Membland.[18]

All the above named clients employed Harry Bedford Lemere, one of the foremost photographers of the day, with premises at No.147 Strand, London, who was extensively employed by the rich to record their houses and interior decorations. Client, architect and decorators all had an interest in recording the results of much earnest consultation and the spending of a good deal of money, and it has been calculated that Bedford Lemere produced as many as 1,000 photographs a year and perhaps 35,000 in all.[19] Unfortunately few negatives survive from the period before 1889 so Devey's own copies of the photographs of Coombe Warren, Richmond Terrace, Coombe Cottage and Membland, although faded, are of particular interest, the more so as two of the buildings have been demolished and the others gutted. The interiors carried out for Currie are shown to have been particularly grand, whether the Jacobean panelling put into the saloon at Coombe Warren or the plasterwork of the drawing room there and in the dining room at Richmond Terrace.

Finally, topographical photographs were used by architects for study. In view of the long exposure times required in the early days of the art, which required human sitters to be

Fig.63 Elevation of Macharioch House

Fig.64 New laundry, Penshurst Place

clamped into position, buildings as subjects had much to recommend them. Volume 202 of *The Quarterly Review* surveyed the progress of photography, stating that the *London Directory* showed a single daguerrotypist by the name of Beard was in business in 1842, and that by 1857 the number of photographers had risen to 147.[20] Their principal trade was in portraits, but they offered topographic views as well, first general studies of buildings and then details, produced chiefly with the tourist in mind. So, by the middle of the century a folio of useful architectural photographs could be assembled with little trouble. The trouble with these however, was that the professional photographer was more interested in the picturesque than in the sort of detail that an architect would find valuable, a point which was commented on in reviews of the exhibitions of the short-lived Architectural Photographic Association. These began in 1857 but were discontinued after 1861 when the Association confined itself to offering copies of specially commissioned photographs to its members, even so it gradually faded away in the late 1860s. When in its heyday, its officers were most distinguished; William Tite was President and Trustee, Sidney Smirke and A.J.B. Beresford Hope the other Trustees, and the Committee included William Burges, Benjamin Ferrey, G.G. Scott, G.E. Street and M. Digby Wyatt. The lectures which accompanied the exhibitions, revealed considerable differences of opinion about the value of what was on display and for sale, Burges

Fig.65 Grasshome

in particular decrying both sketching and photographs and advocating measured drawings: 'Measure much, sketch little, and above all keep your fingers out of chemicals.' But Burges in fact, was later to have his own work recorded by Francis Bedford at the instigation of R.P. Pullan.[21]

Devey's collection of topographical photographs include, as might have been expected, examples of some of the most important country houses: Longleat, Hardwick, Parham, Charlton Court, Hever Castle, Fairfax House, Putney, said by Godfrey to have been the inspiration for the gables of Coombe Warren II, Hengrave Hall, Burghley House, Dorfold Hall, Heythrop, Little Morton Hall, Kirby, Speke Hall and Smithills Hall. He had a few examples of work by his contemporaries, 196 Queens Gate and Lowther Lodge by R.N. Shaw, the Red House, Bexley Heath built by Philip Webb for William Morris in 1859-61, and a sequence of photographs of the Pavilion at Pregny near Geneva, designed by G.H. Stokes, showing it under construction in 1861.

Whatever the losses which have occured, it seems at the present time that Devey's photographs are the only collection to survive from the office of an architect working during the nineteenth century, apart from two folios of photographs from the office of William Butterfield.[22] One of these has been kept together, and is simply a collection of pictures of Butterfield's completed ecclesiastical works, many abroad, such as Fredericton Cathedral, sent 'with the Bishop's Kind regards'. In no case are they shown under construction. So, the facts of the matter seem to be, that architectural photographs made for tourists and other interested persons were freely and commercially available from an early date but, if the architects of this period collected them in any quantity as part of the tools of their trade, they were at pains not to advertise the fact.

6

The Flourishing Practice

Devey was fortunate in that at about the time that work for the Rothschilds was tailing off, apart of course, from at Ascott where he worked up to the time of his death, he was taken up by another banking family, perhaps not quite so wealthy, but certainly with ample funds for building works at their disposal. These were the Smiths. Their firm, Smith, Payne & Smiths had been founded by Thomas Smith of Nottingham in about 1688 and his son Abel Smith II established the firm in London, with other branches in Lincoln and Hull. All five of his sons became Members of Parliament before Reform and the bank's offices were manned by members of the family who did not squander their means. A partnership deed drawn up in 1788, forbade them, on pain of being removed from the business, from winning or losing more than £50 a day 'by play or betting at Cards, Dice or any other Game of Chance or by any other species of Gaming whatsoever.' A similarly high-minded attitude motivated their approach to investment; a lady sought from the bank a small and secured advance 'to try her luck in a Railway spec.' only to be informed that 'it is contrary to the rules of the House to lend money with the obvious intention of furthering the mania which now exists for Railroad Speculations.'[1]

It was the grandsons of the Members of Parliament who became Devey's clients, and it is convenient to begin with the eldest branch of the family, the four sons of Abel Smith IV. Abel V inherited Woodhall Park, Hertfordshire which his grandfather Samuel Smith III had bought in 1801. Woodhall Park was built in 1777 to the designs of Thomas Leverton and enlarged in 1794. It seems doubtful if Devey was required to do anything to the house, so the considerable sum of £298 charged by him in 1876 and £66 in 1879 must relate to work on the estate and in the neighbourhood, such as the almshouses in Watton-at-Stone which are clearly by Devey and dated 1873. (Fig.66) They are red brick with timber and pebble dash on the upper floor, with his characteristic chamfered corner and chimney stacks. A single drawing, plans of an unidentified 'Ballards cottage', survives, and a few other buildings look as if they may have been altered by him. One certain work is the large addition to Watkin Hall Farm. An account rendered in May 1874 is for enlarging St Mary's Stapleford by throwing out the west wall twelve feet and adding a porch which was completed that year.

The second son, Robert Smith II, employed Devey upon a much more lavish scale, the building of a large new mansion house, which like Hall Place, was begun in 1871. Robert had inherited Goldings upon his father's death over ten years before, and like Morley, first attempted to put the old house in order. It must here be remarked that the Smith's who settled in Hertfordshire, like the Rothschilds, bought property within the same small area. Goldings is just under three miles south of Woodhall Park, and Sacombe Park, the home of the Samuel George Smiths I and II is a mile and a half to the east. Goldings was an early eighteenth century house of two storeys with a pediment, hipped roof and dormers.[2] It was possibly in poor condition but repair was not considered. Something of much greater consequence was required.

Goldings is the biggest house designed by Devey and is roughly one third as large again as Hall Place, and although there are similarities in plan, this is reversed so that the offices run off at an obtuse angle to the left of the front door rather than the right, but in both cases they flank the principal approach to the house. (Fig.67) Quite apart from being on grander scale, there are rooms not found at Hall Place. What is similar is that the visitor enters through a smallish hall into the saloon, but this time finds the library and drawing room on his right, the latter occupying the whole corner area up to the garden entrance; it also has a well lit bay acting as a sun room. The library has a conservatory attached. The dining room is on the right of the front door with a billiard room next door and opposite these are the morning room, own room and boudoir. Beyond these a corridor proceeds past the butler's pantry and the housekeeper's room to the servants' hall, kitchen and the other offices. At Hall Place the kitchen occupied the ground floor of a cross range of the same height and significance as those of the principal part of the house, and the scullery and larders were reduced to a single storey in order to demonstrate that menial activities were conducted therein. At Goldings the whole of the secondary part of the building is kept at the same height as the rest, but the effect of the set-off is to diminish their impact through perspective; this is helped by restricted decoration. The office range is terminated on the garden front by a four-storey tower, and the north front facing the drive projects and recedes almost at random until that point where the visitor drives under an archway lodge into the terraced forecourt. This is an attractive little building with a shaped gable and an oriel, one of the Mabey's tondos (this time of Inigo Jones and thus suggesting the house to be seventeenth century in date) on the left, and a crenellated

Fig.66 Almshouses, Watton-at-Stone

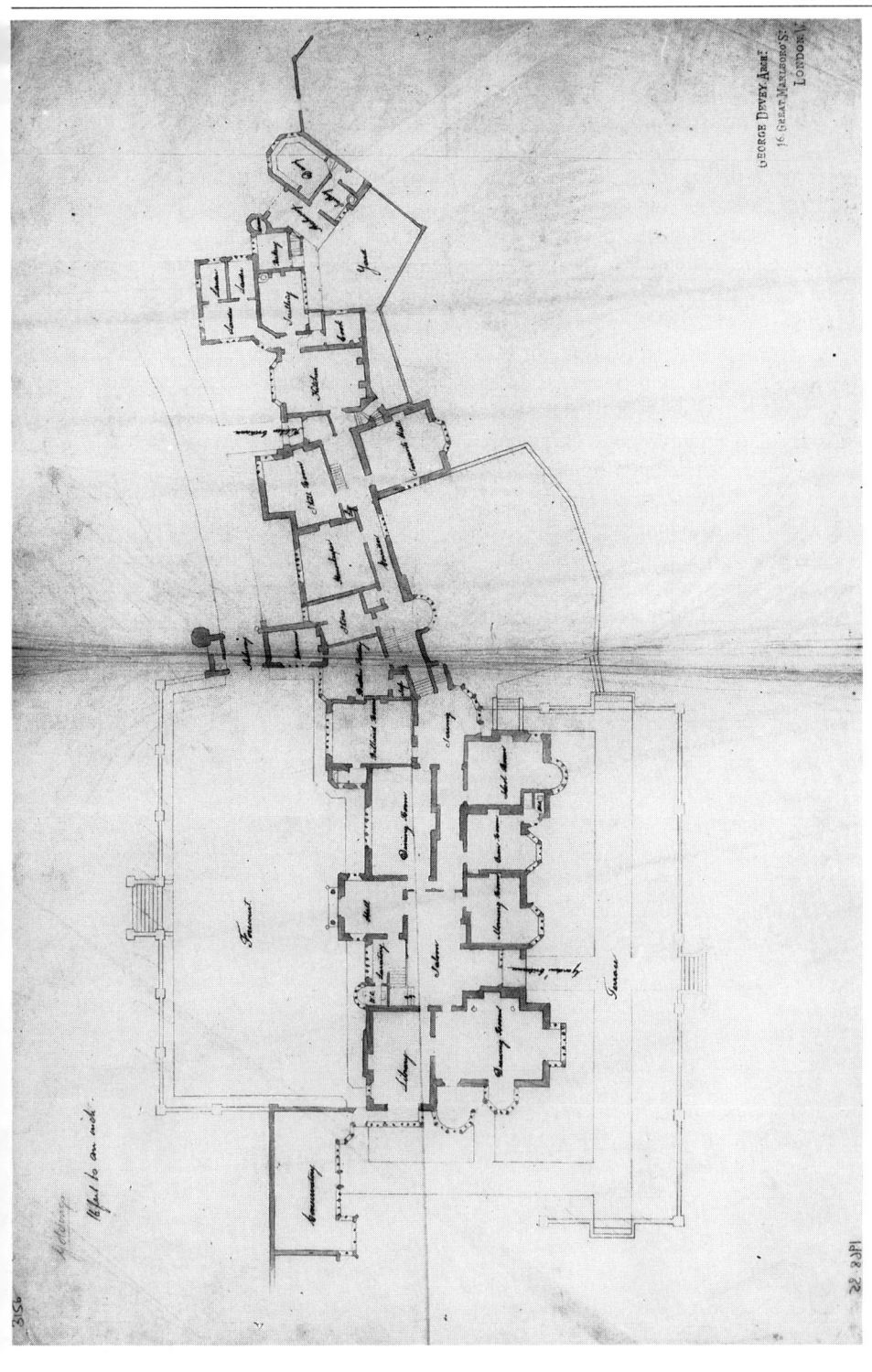

Fig.67 Goldings, ground plan

octagonal stair turret on the right. The butler's quarters are partly in the arch, which would have given him good notice of the arrival of guests. Once through, one is into a narrow forecourt with a retaining wall and steps up into the garden opposite the front door. Devey became fond of enclosed entrance courtyards which recur at St Alban's Court, and did at Killarney and Longwood, both of which were approached through entrance arches. The building is again of red brick, but the diaper pattern is smaller and tighter, and Devey again uses footings of stone, but in a quite different manner to that which he had employed previously. Here stone blocks do not rise at random into the brick wall above, but terminate in an absolutely straight line at mid-ground-floor-window level. In the courtyard the impression is given of an E shaped building, with similar shaped gables above the centrally placed doorway and above a cross range on the left, with a couple of plain gables between. This symmetry is destroyed to the right of the front door where Devey puts two large plain gables, one cut through by a chimney breast, and a two-storey semi-circular bay window. The front door itself is framed by a pair of banded columns on pedestals supporting an entablature and pinnacles above, not unlike those at Doddington Hall in Lincolnshire, attributed to Robert Smythson. Above again, there is an oriel with strapwork decoration. (Fig.68)

The principal garden front consists of three equal-sized gables between a pair of larger shaped gables terminated on the right by a three-storey polygonal bay and an octagonal turret with a cupola which contains the servants' stairs. There are four two-storey bay windows, mullioned and transomed, and with double transoms on the ground floor and a small veranda at the garden entrance with a balcony with pierced stonework above. Inside there are splendid fireplaces, panelling and plasterwork. The doorways between the drawing room and the library and that between the dining room and the saloon, are set in large coffered arches with

Fig.68 Goldings, entrance front

Fig.69 Goldings, drawing room doorway

mouldings and a Gibbsian surround. Within this, a round-headed door is set between rectangular panels with radial fluting above. The design is reminiscent of the panelling in the Pillar Parlour of the Little Castle, Bolsover, from which it would seem that Devey had Smythson very much in mind when he was designing Goldings. (Fig.69)

Two gate lodges, formerly thatched but now tiled, and the laying out of the garden with a terrace and slope down to a great parterre some distance from the house completed the work in the grounds. Robert Smith also employed Devey in the neighbouring village of Waterford, where he restored the church and built a village school.

The next two sons of Abel Smith both employed Devey in Wendover, Buckinghamshire. There was a family connection with this town. Robert Smith I, created Lord Carrington in 1796, had bought the Manor and passed it on to his brother Samuel III; John Smith II had represented it in Parliament in 1802, and had been succeeded by his brother who was its Member in 1806-30. The eldest of these sons, Lieut.Col. Philip Smith had him design Wendover Manor, and his brother, the Revd Albert Smith commissioned a new vicarage. (Fig.70) Both were built in the 1870s, but the sums paid in respect of each cannot be easily distinguished in Devey's cashbook. One is now a special school and the other an old peoples' home, and they have been much altered. Both are rather unsympathetic buildings in harsh red brick, the manor a plain Jacobean design and the vicarage appropriately in a rather attenuated Gothic style.

We now come to Eric Carrington Smith, the grandson of George II who was as important a client as Robert. He commissioned large additions to another country mansion, Ashfold, at Handcross in Sussex, which entirely concealed the original house.

A watercolour sketch of 'Mr. Granger's House, near Slaugham Green, 1787' shows what is clearly a Jacobean manor which had been refaced in the eighteenth century when plain rectangular sash windows of many panes were put in. A pair of dormers in the hipped roof are partly concealed by a parapet and the only surviving feature of interest is a battlemented oriel above the front door.[3] Mr Granger's house was more than doubled in size by red brick additions with what was becoming Devey's usual tight trellis pattern of silver-grey headers, and Dutch gables above. It is difficult to judge the effect of this now that the house has gone, but photographs give the impression of aggressive polychromy and Ashfold seems to have been a classic example of Devey's lack of finesse in the handling of his larger houses. One of the lodges survives relatively unaltered, and this shows that the local stone used in the lower courses of the walls was more finely squared up and cut than was usually the case. The builder employed was again Adcock of Dover.

Before Ashfold had been completed Smith instructed Devey to design his London house, No.19 Lennox Gardens. This was begun in, and is dated on the facade, 1884, and is one of a number of houses designed by Devey for erection on this part of the Smith's Charity estate, which are dealt with in the following chapter.

Devey's last two Smith clients were the Hon. Margaret Louisa Smith the widow of Jervoise Smith who died in 1884, for whom Devey carried out some relatively small unidentified work in 1885, and Martin Ridley Smith of Warren House, Hayes Common. Both men were grandsons of John Smith II of Dale Park.

Martin Ridley Smith bought Warren House in 1885 for the sum of £8,000. The six acres of land on which it was built had been leased in 1882 to Walter Maxmilian de Zoete of the stockbroking family for ninety-nine years and he employed George Somers Clarke to build a large red brick house with stepped gables, and an equally elaborate lodge and stables combined. Smith took a lease of another sixteen acres, in order to enlarge the gardens. Devey worked

Fig.70 Wendover Vicarage

Fig.71 Denne Hill

on the house in 1885-6 and was responsible for building the 'library or billiard room' (as it is described in the sale particulars of 1909) and the adjoining conservatory, both single-storey additions of which the former is linked with the original fabric by a balustrade running at roof level across the front facade and the porch. Devey appears also to have added a two-storey bay to the dining room, and he certainly designed Warren Cottage and a pair of gardeners' cottages, the walled garden and the brick-built arbour near the billiard room. Smith occupied himself at Hayes with hybridising and growing carnations, but he was an active partner in the bank and devised a scheme for combining the various branches of Smith, Payne & Smiths into a public joint stock company, which was not proceeded with. He also had a 'bent for designing new religious systems' and perhaps took an interest in Devey's commitment to the Theistic Church.

The 1870s saw the rapid expansion of Devey's country house practice; during this decade he was to be instructed to build no less than eleven new mansions and to carry out restoration work and to make additions to two important old houses, Smithills Hall, near Bolton in Lancashire, and Sudbury Hall, Derbyshire, besides quantities of smaller commissions, as can be seen in the catalogue. So far as the new houses are concerned, Hall Place and Goldings, both begun in 1871, have already been described; two other, smaller but still imposing houses, Denne Hill in east Kent and Broomford Manor in Devon were begun the same year. Ashfold dates from 1875, as do Blakesware, Hertfordshire and St Alban's Court, again in east Kent. Membland, Devon, was under construction from 1876 and Adderley Hall in Shropshire and Killarney House in Kerry were both begun in 1877. The last was Longwood in Hampshire built in 1879-83. Of these Goldings, Denne Hill, Broomford Manor and St Alban's Court remain pretty much as built, Hall Place has been partly demolished, Blakesware transformed by later additions, and Ashfold, Membland, Adderley, Killarney and Longwood have been demolished. Devey's larger works have been unfortunate in their owners.

Denne Hill, Womenswold was built for Major Edwards Dyson of the 3rd Dragoon Guards. His curious christian name is the surname of his grandmother who was an heiress.

Fig.72 Dutch House, Kew

His family had been mill owners and their seat was Upper Willow Hall, Skircoat near Halifax, which had through improvidence fallen into the hands of trustees but was recovered by Dyson's elder brother, John Daniel, the lieutenant-colonel of the same regiment and the owner of Denne Hill. Edwards had married Caroline Jerdain in 1854, another heiress, the daughter of a barrister of Lincoln's Inn, and grand-daughter of the engraver John Vendramini. He inherited both properties upon his brother's death in 1875.

The design of Denne Hill is more restrained than that of Hall Place and Goldings, as befits a smaller house, and it is stylistically a completely new kettle of fish. (Fig.71) Its putative date is the 1630s and it is in the manner introduced by the bricklayers of the period in their competition with the masons, when they produced houses like Swakeleys and Broome Park, which is less than a mile away. The small, raised pediment on the gable of the service range resembles those at Broome but generally the model followed is the Dutch House at Kew, as becomes obvious when the rear or garden front of that building is compared with the entrance front designed for Dyson. (Fig.72) Denne Hill is of three storeys, and the Dutch House is of four raised on a basement, but both have a symmetrical tripartite division of a central three bays flanked by two bays. Both have three Dutch gables, with triangular pediments to either side and a central segmental pediment, and a central porch of three arches topped by a balustrade. The differences apart from the height are the fenestration, the Dutch House has round-headed and rectangular windows made up of small panes, that of Denne Hill is, apart from three round-headed windows in the dining room, segmental with a keystone and single mullion and transom containing plate glass. The decorative brickwork also differs; Denne Hill lacks the pilasters and denticulated window framing of its model, but has heavy brick quoins, which themselves have a good pedigree in the early seventeenth century, which the single-storey bay windows on either side do not. Mabey's tondos reappear, Inigo Jones again, and a Peter Paul Rubens, taken from the Uffizi self-portrait, wearing a medallion and a slouch hat. The garden front is as symmetrical as the entrance front with the same recessed centre and arrangement of gables, and with two two-storey bay windows. The side elevation is more what one would expect of Devey, assymetrical, with a central single-storey bay flanked on the left by a massive chimney breast and on the right by a two storey canted bay window. The offices are not off-set here, but are simply arranged in two storeys around a courtyard on the west, with a four-storey water tower between them and the main part. Internally the porch leads into a central saloon again and the principal rooms are set around this. Devey was not required here to design overmantels to match the exterior. A number of remarkably good eighteenth century fireplaces were installed.

Colonel Sir Robert White-Thomson KCB bought the Broomford Manor estate in 1863. His great-grandfather is described as a manufacturer of Glasgow, his grandfather as of Camphill in Counties Renfrew and Lanark in the Lowlands, his father is also of Camphill, but married the daughter and heiress of the Revd Thomas White of Lichfield. His younger brother died in the charge of the Light Cavalry at Balaclava. White-Thomson rose to the command of the 4th Battalion of the Devonshire Regiment in 1867-93 and it was presumably for this reason that he wanted a house in the county. Broomford Manor was built in 1871-3 and is the smallest of the country houses to be discussed here. The porch leads into a small hall which leads in turn through a lobby into the staircase hall, off which are the drawing room and library on the left, and the dining room and study on the right. The Butler's pantry, servants' staircase and an L shaped corridor to the offices lie beyond. It is built of local stone, rock-faced up to ground-floor sill level and smoothly cut above. The roof is tiled. Some decorative areas of tile-hanging and half-timbering proposed in the designs were not executed, presumably on account of expense, as it is known that the interiors were not properly completed due to lack of funds. The entrance front has a Dutch gable with a triangular pediment set above a barely projecting gable above the porch, another feature which is found on the garden front of the Dutch House. The side elevation has a two-storey semi-circular bay with a conical roof lighting the library and bedroom above with a chimney breast on the left and french windows into the drawing room on the right, the garden front to the rear consists of a series of three gables linked to the service range by a two storey quadrant bay similar to that at Bettes hanger. (Fig.73) The windows are mullioned and transomed, the chimneys grouped square stacks. Devey amused himself particularly with the kitchen courtyard where there are a series of gables of different size, some superimposed and a combined louvre and dinner bell cote above the kitchen.(Fig.74)

Fig.73 Broomford Manor, garden front

Blakesware, near Ware was another new house of medium size built for Mrs Hadsley Gosselin. Her husband's father was a retired Admiral of the Red who had married the heiress of the Hadsleys of Ware Priory, now the Council Offices, in the town, and Blakesware was bought by him in 1850. The original manor house was a fine brick mansion on the southern part of the estate which had been demolished and was lamented by Charles Lamb who used to stay there with the housekeeper, his aunt, when he was a child. His charming recollection as a small boy given the run of the deserted, but still furnished house is the subject of his essay on 'Blakesmoor'. Gosselin died in 1868 and his wife held a life interest in the property until her death in 1892. Devey's cashbook shows that work at Blakesware began in 1875 and was completed in 1879. Unfortunately the house has been added to, including a Roman Catholic chapel in 1896, damaged by a fire in 1939, and divided into units, so that the original planning appears to be irretrievable. It is of red brick with the same all-over tight diapering seen at Goldings, which is here continued up into the gables. There are battlements, mullioned windows and a square stair tower with a cupola and a three-storey battlemented polygonal bay on the garden front, but it is abundantly clear that much of the architectural decoration has been eliminated rather than restored.

The next mansion to be commenced was St Alban's Court. This was the family home of William Oxenden Hammond, another banker and a partner in Hammond & Co. who had premises at Canterbury, Ramsgate and Whitstable. He was a bachelor, but had once been engaged to Fanny James, and as he grew older he developed certain idiosyncracies and imposed a formality of behaviour on his guests which caused the James family much amusement. Breakfast was taken by the host and his guests together, and all waited in the hall for the last to appear, however late they might be. When they had finished there was an fifteen minute wait before the party made a formal exit. Prayers were read in the evening regardless of what else was going on, and one member of the James family recorded a house party interrupted in the middle of charades and, dressed in various improbable items of clothing, assembling in the library to watch Hammond reading prayers to empty seats, as the servants were not called in on guest nights.[4] Hammond inherited St Alban's Court in 1868 but Devey's cashbook shows that he was already working for him in 1867, and this continued in 1869-72. An account for the considerable sum of £726 was rendered in August 1874, but the contract drawings for the new mansion were only signed by William John Adcock of Dover on the 9th July 1875. It seems likely that Hammond acted as Morley and Robert Smith had done, and at first tried to put the old house in order.

Fig.74 Broomford Manor from the kitchen courtyard

The date of this is unknown, but in its final eighteenth century manifestation the old fabric had been given a nine-bay entrance front with a pediment and balcony above the front door, and a hipped roof, flanked by two-storey polygonal bays with pointed roofs. The principal rooms were arranged along this front, and the offices sprawled to the rear. It was just to the north of the present stables. The new house was built a few hundred yards away up a slight hill to the north of the site of the old one. This achieved two ends, elevation from what the Victorians probably thought to be a low-lying and therefore unhealthy site and pleasant views over the surrounding parkland. The house cannot compare with Hall Place or Goldings in size and it is something of a relief to find that although the building material is again red brick, Devey here largely abandons the use of pattern-forming headers, and reverts to the use of ragstone footings which rise unevenly as at Betteshanger, inviting the belief that what is seen is Tudor on the stone of mediaeval foundations. That this is not so fanciful as it might seem to the architecturally educated, was proved when the writer of this was informed by a Kent County Councillor that St Alban's Court was in fact an old house rebuilt in the nineteenth century.

Fig.75 St Alban's Court, entrance courtyard

The house is, like Denne Hill, strictly rectangular in plan and consists of three ranges set around a walled entrance courtyard on the north, which is entered from the east through a pair of arches. The entrance front, and indeed all the ranges facing onto the courtyard are kept relatively plain. Too much fuss in a constricted space would be overwhelming. Decoration, apart from the stonework which rises and falls intermittently, is restricted to an oriel above the front door and a battlemented octagonal tower in the angle to the right of this. (Fig.75) The main south-facing garden front has two large lateral gables with a run of three smaller examples between, to the west of which rises the semi-circular bay window lighting the hall, which rises the full height of the house. The west front, also overlooking the garden, has similar lateral gables, each of which has a two-storey bay window decorated with strapwork, and a pair of gables between. No Dutch or shaped gables appear here. (Fig.76)

The accommodation reflects Hammond's bachelor state. (Fig.77) The entrance hall is narrow and forms part of a continuous corridor running round the courtyard giving access to the main rooms. A right hand turn from the front door and then a left, led into a two-storey staircase hall with the semi-circular bay window and a fireplace with an elaborate Jacobean overmantel salvaged from the old house. This was panelled, and the family portraits set in the panelling. The stairs were screened off by turned balusters for which Devey made a little sketch on tissue paper; 'A screen like this at Hever Castle has rather a telling effect. It would be repeated on left hand on entering.'[5] The drawing room opened off this hall, beyond which lies the library and Hammond's

Fig.76 St Alban's Court, garden front

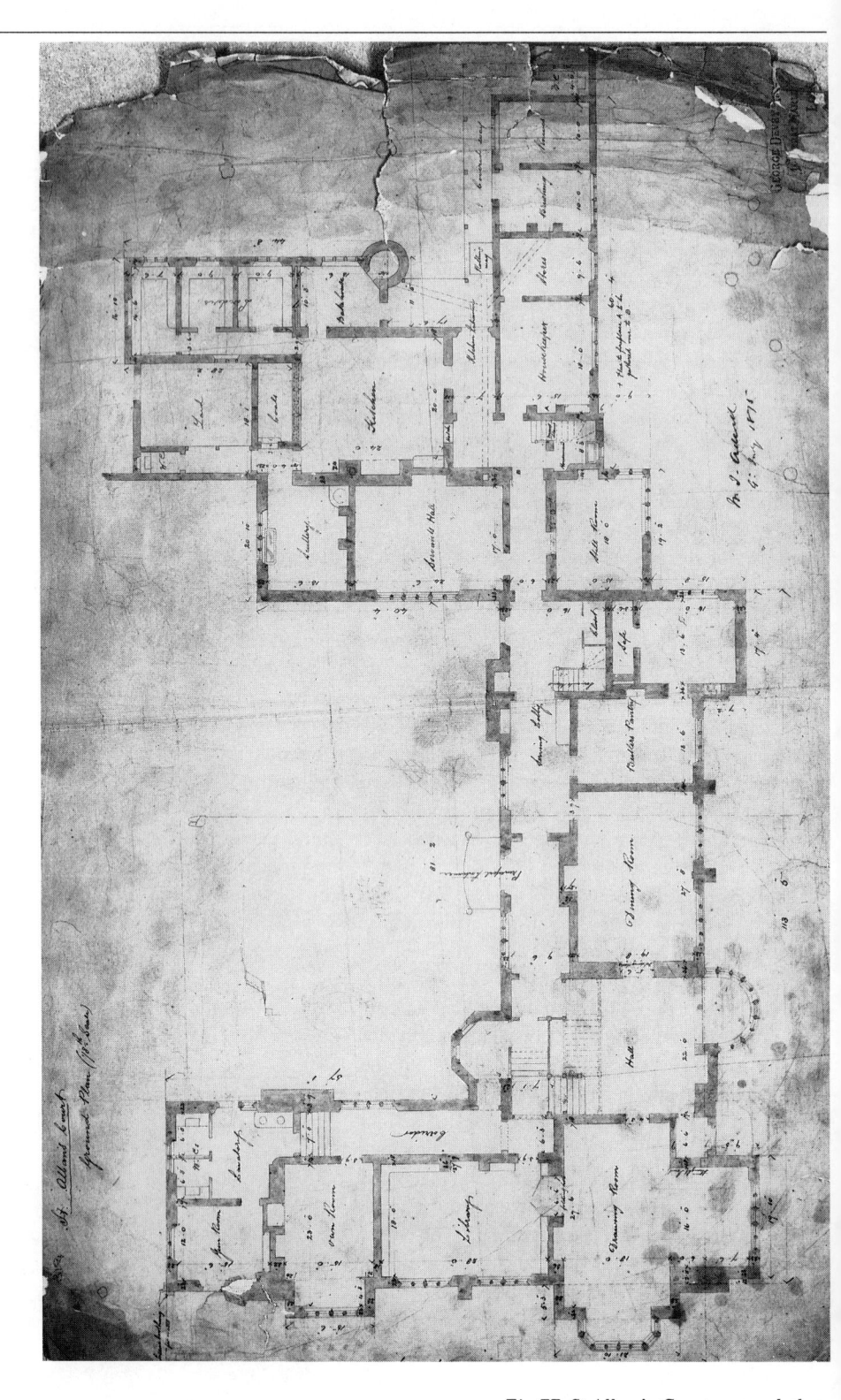

Fig.77 St Alban's Court, ground plan

Fig.78 St Alban's Court, Gardener's House

own set of rooms, the own room, gun room and lavatory, but no billiard room, the house was not that grand. The dining room lay directly opposite the entrance beside which was a particularly large butler's pantry, bedroom and the inevitable plate safe. The usual offices lay beyond. The stables were built adjacent to the site of the old house where a remnant which seems to date from the sixteenth century was incorporated into a gardener's house in half-timbering which with its walled garden formed a picturesque group of buildings when seen from the terraces. (Fig.78)

After, or possibly during the period the house was under construction, no less than nine pairs of estate cottages in and around Nonnington, a Keeper's cottage and a row of four almshouses, were built to Devey's designs. (Fig.79) These were completed by James Williams after Devey's death as the drawings for Mount Ephraim Cottages show. They are in Devey's usual Wealden manner but with the hard finish which always seems to mark Williams' intervention.

Edward Baring, who became the 1st Lord Revelstoke in 1885, purchased the Membland estate which stretched through the parishes of Revelstoke, Newton Ferrers and Holbeton in 1870, and it was sold twenty-five years later. Baring retained Coombe Cottage and 37 Charles Street, Westminster, and kept his 150 ton schooner, the *Waterwitch*, in which he went to Cowes each year, at anchor in the river Yealm. The routine was that the family stayed in London and Kingston from January to August, and then moved down to Devonshire until after Christmas.[6] He was attracted to the neighbourhood when visiting his father-in-law John Crocker Bulteel who had rebuilt Flete in 1835, then sold it and moved to Pamflete. Flete was bought in due course by Henry Bingham Mildmay, Baring's partner in the bank, who married

Fig.79 Double cottage, Nonnington

another of Bulteel's daughters. But there may have been other considerations, similar to those which motivated the Rothschilds to gather together in the Vale of Aylesbury. Some years later the sale particulars claimed 'The Estate, in addition to its many Sporting and Residential Attractions, from its extent and importance confers on its owner considerable Political and Social Position.' The Membland estate was over 4,000 acres and the three estates together formed a sizeable tract of land between the rivers Avon and Yealm. Baring and Mildmay began work on their houses at the same time, the latter employed R.N. Shaw for the protracted reconstruction of Flete, which survives, though somewhat altered. Baring turned to Devey for additions to the mansion, which was pulled down after World War I. However Baring had been obliged to sell it long before; 1890 saw the famous Barings crash when the partners, who had invested heavily in South American railways found themselves faced with liabilities amounting to £21 million. Disaster, which would have seriously prejudiced all English banking houses, was avoided by joint action taken within 24 hours by the Banks of England and France, the Rothschilds and other City firms. Baring was the senior partner in Barings and a director of the Bank of England but without this help he would have been left with an income of £500 a year. As it was things were never the same again.[7]

Membland was a dull but substantial house six bays wide and four storeys in height with two subsidiary blocks, one of which was attached to it by an arcade. It is very much to be regretted that it has gone, as here Devey designed with a frivolity which suited a holiday home by the sea, which was described by Maurice Baring as 'a large square Jacobean house, in white brick, green shutters and ivy, with some modern gabled rough-cast additions and a tower.'(Fig.80) The tower was indeed the most imposing feature of a rather rambling house

Fig.80 Membland, entrance front

which Devey made interesting with his usual Dutch gables. The entrance was on the north side and on the south the lawn sloped down to a ha-ha, 'when you went through the front hall you come into a large billiard-room in which there was a staircase leading to a gallery going round the room and to the bedrooms. The billiard room was high and there were no rooms over the billiard-room proper - but beyond the billiard-table the room extended into a lower section, culminating in a semicircle of windows in which there was a large double writing table.' (Fig.81) What we have here, which can be more clearly seen on the plan, is Devey's favourite arrangement of a low corridor-like entrance hall leading into a two-storey staircase hall or saloon with a sun-room or bay overlooking the view beyond. The drawing room, oddly, could only be reached through this bay, which also led into the dining room, which shared the view. This was separated from a small library and the school room by a narrow corridor leading to the smoking room and the housekeeper's room and offices beyond. What is quite peculiar about Membland is that the accommodation for the butler, his room fitted with cupboards, and the pantry with adjoining strong room, was in the basement with the valets' and housemaids' sitting rooms, where they were convenient for the six cellars and a decanting room, but fairly inconvenient for his other duties, meeting guests, supervising the laying of the tables and serving of meals, and the behaviour of the other male servants. His department was more usually to be found between the offices and the main part of the house where he was strategically placed and in a position to keep an eye on what was going on.

'Later, under the staircase there was an organ, and the pipes of the great organ were on the wall. There was a drawing-room full of chintz chairs, books, pot-pourri, a grand pianoforte and two writing tables; a dining room looking south; a floor of guests' rooms; a bachelors' passage in the wing; a schoolroom on the ground floor looking north, and a little dark room full of rubbish next to it, which was called the *Cabinet Noir*, and there we were sent when we were naughty; and a nursery floor over the guests' rooms.'[6] The organ was manufactured by Hele & Co. of Plymouth and 'worked by hydraulic pressure, with folding mahogany doors, on the inside of which are two well-painted Female Figures with gold background.'[8] Money was not spared on the decorations. William Morris's secretary kept a diary, and the entry for 18th May 1877 recorded 'G.W. (George Wardle) & W.M. talked over Mrs.Baring's house in Devonshire the work we have proposed to do will certainly take two or three years before all completed; we have to get our Lyons silk-weaver at work for one thing.'[9]

Returning to the recollections of Maurice Baring we find, 'Noss Mayo had many white-washed and straw thatched cottages and some new cottages of Devonshire stone built by my father, with slate roofs, but not ugly or aggressive.' These were designed by G.W. Crosbie whose design for the 'Membland Steam Laundry' was published in the *Journal of the Society of Estate Clerks of Works*. Crosbie had acted as clerk of works during the building of the church at Noss Mayo to the designs of J.P. St Aubyn at Baring's expense, and he was thereafter employed on a good deal of estate building. Devey obviously was responsible for the two separate yards of the household stables and the hunting stables, they have his typical Dutch gables but the sequence of small buildings which went up thereafter must on comparison with the laundry be attributed to Crosbie, although he has picked up some of Devey's details which in his hands become more decorative and less vernacular. The arched Wealden chimney on the laundry is a case in point, and the treatment of the roofs at Rowden Farm is another. One curious feature is the design of the louvres ventilating both the laundry and the building housing the electric generator; one is square in plan and the other rectangular, both are built of outwardly splayed weatherboarding with a tiled roof and an airspace at eaves level with wooden dentils.

'Early in February 1877 I engaged Mr. George Devey of 16 Gt. Marlboro Street London, to inspect the old house at Adderley with a view to making it habitable, after thoroughly examining the house he came to the conclusion that any thing that might be carried out would never make it a satisfactory or comfortable house to live in.'[10] Henry Reginald Corbet of Adderley Hall in Shropshire had a problem which was not uncommon in the nineteenth century. He was not to be one of Devey's most satisfied clients. 'An idea of the style of house was given to the Architect, shortly after which a plan was produced, totally unsatisfactory in most respects, especially as regards the servants offices - however Mrs. Corbet thoroughly overcame this ... The elevation was the next difficulty as it was laid out with a succession of gables from end to end all more or less alike and the whole structure looked much like a row of large Alms Houses ... No builder was employed the whole works being carried out by ourselves with a most excellent Clerk of the works.'

This method of proceeding was one which Devey preferred and one which was recalled with approval by James Williams: 'Mr. Devey hated the contract system, with all the endless bickering and compromises so often involved ... and a system (was) adopted whereby the client built on his own account. Of course this new departure entailed more work, for which an additional 2 per cent was charged. Of course, some may question this - especially builders. Everything, however, depends upon the efficiency of the system and the superintendence; given this, and there can be no doubt as to the time and the cost being less and the quality of the work better. Such a system required the confidence of the employer, and that Mr. Devey always commanded.'[11] This was not, in fact, always the case.

Devey versus Drummond, described in *The Building News* as 'A Client his own Builder', was heard in the Queen's Bench Division and lasted for three days, the 15th, 16th and 17th April

Fig.81 Membland, garden front

1886.[12] The matter had already been the subject of a thirty-six day arbitration and their Honours Mr Justice Grove and Mr Justice Stephen did no more than refer the matter back to the arbitrator, whereupon Devey appealed. Drummond was the owner of Swaylands, a large house on the outskirts of Penshurst, and Devey was seeking payment of commission amounting to £1,137. The arrangement had been that, as tenders of £9,000 had been regarded as excessive, Drummond should do the work himself. A curious arrangement was made, that he should authorise the work which was to be executed under the supervision of a clerk of works, but that purchases and contracts should not be made in his name, but in that of the clerk of works. Devey did not adhere to this for some reason, and a contract with Shepherd, (no doubt William Shepherd of Bermondsey who was to build C.H. Wilson's house No. 41 Grosvenor Square) for panelling and parquet flooring, part of the internal finish which it had been agreed should be left to the 'discretion and taste of the architect' was made in Drummond's name. Devey was dismissed. Both the Divisional Court and the Supreme Court of Appeal took a dim view of Drummond's behaviour. He had gone to another builder and the job had finally cost £20,000. Shepherd had sued him, as had Devey. A bill for the panelling had been seen by Drummond 'and if he did not look at it, and preferred going out shooting, it was his own fault.' He 'had unfortunately hit upon the worst possible way of going to work, and if a gentleman chose to be "his own builder" he must at least take care to give enough attention to the business to be cognisant of what was being done.' Lord Esher, the Master of the Rolls, said that he was full of sympathy for the defendant; but he was only suffering as every one would suffer who attempted to build on the terms of being his own builder. The defendant had made alterations from time to time until the cost amounted to nearly £20,000 instead of about £10,000. He had then gone to law with his architect, and, as was usual in such cases, had lost. It would be quite unreasonable to send the case back again to the referee after a trial of 36 days. There would be another hearing of the same length, and, in the result, it was certain the defendant would still lose. There was no rule which enabled the Court to inflict such a frightful injury upon the defendant. He had not taken the trouble to have the contract put into writing, and it was therefore certain that there would be some dispute about it. The question was really one of recollection of the two parties...

Devey may have won, but litigation is an expensive way to resolve disputes. George Drummond was another banker, a partner in Drummond & Co. of Charing Cross and well able to fund massive additions to his house and the cost of legal proceedings. Devey was not, and made a codicil to his will in December 1884:'I desire in view of the vexatious litigation into which I have been compelled to engage that by whatever amount my little fortune may happen to suffer from this or from any other cause the bequests in my will may all be reduced in equal similar ratio And I leave to my Executors judgment the giving away to any of my friends or disposing of my sketches or drawings in anyway they may think best'.

To return to Adderley (Fig.82), it is sometimes folly to pronounce upon a building which has been pulled down in the 1950s and of which few satisfactory photographs seem to survive, but it must be said that it looks to have been a long, gaunt and unexciting house, again in red brick with stone dressings and with a trellis of vitrified headers. The main part was of three storeys, the offices of two and there was a tall, narrow water tower. Plain gables, groups of tall chimneys and an oriel above the front door had all been done better elsewhere. What are most successful, and most fortunately survive with a minimum of alterations, are the north and south lodges which show that when it came to small buildings, Devey had lost none of his power to charm. (Fig.83) What he produced was an L shaped two-storey building formed of intersecting ranges so that a pair of gables abutted each other at the angle nearest the road and drive. This angle was masked by an octagonal tower beside which a chimney breast rose in three steps. The staircase was in a polygonal bay at the rear. The ground floor contained a living room, larder and kitchen and the front door was reached through a wide arch into a porch with stone seats running round. A curved wall swung round towards the road from the stepped chimney breast, concealing a small private garden and the wash house, lavatory and ash hole. Devey also made additions to the Home Farm and designed cottages in the village. Corbet in the end had spent an extraordinary amount of money. Devey's commission at 6 .5 per cent and his travelling expenses came to over £1,950.

Fig.82 Adderley Hall

Fig.83 North Lodge, Adderley

The contract drawings for Killarney House are signed 'John Collen for Self and Brothers 19th December 1877.' The client was Valentine Augustus Browne, 4th Earl of Kenmare, and his splendid new mansion was to stand for only 36 years before going up in flames on the 31st August 1913. (Fig.84) As might be expected in Ireland the tale lost nothing in the telling. The Brownes had received the grant of the estate at Killarney from Queen Elizabeth in 1588 and later the Viscountcy of Castlerosse and the Earldom of Kenmare. They were Catholics. The fire took hold when the 5th Earl and his Countess were visiting an American couple, Mr and Mrs Bowers Bourn who had bought the Herberts' Muckcross Abbey, which had been designed for them by William Burn and built in 1839-43. It was some time before the Kenmares, the principal old established aristocratic landowners in the region would accept an invitation from the newcomers to dinner, and the house burnt down that night. There had been an earlier fire in the butler's pantry which caused some damage, this one finished the house. The local inhabitants said that it was a judgment upon them for associating with the parvenu heathen. [13] The site is said to have been chosen by Queen Victoria, but this seems unlikely as the Queen was last there in 1861, but perhaps might have expressed a view at that time. The old house, which had been built around 1726, down the slope nearer the shore of Lough Leane, was demolished and the new built at a cost of £200,000, paid for out of a rent roll which amounted to £70,000 a year. The estate had, by the time that building began, recovered from the worst effects of the Potato Famine. In 1850 the unhappy position had been that rents received, namely £23,765 were exceeded by the arrears of £27,806, but after this the arrears steadily diminished and by the time building began the rent roll had increased by 25per cent and the arrears reduced to slightly over £1,000.[14]

The plan of Killarney differs from any formerly devised by Devey, in that it was Z shaped and that the main rooms opened off a vestibule or wide corridor that ran across the entrance front. (Fig.85) This is an expansion of the laterally placed halls found at St Alban's Court and Membland. A *porte cochère* led into this, and the visitor was faced by an anteroom, with a large dining room to the right and the drawing room on the left, beyond which the corridor ran into the staircase hall or saloon from which stairs rose to give access to a similar corridor above that on the ground floor. The library opened off the hall, and another corridor making a right angle turn, led on to the private suite of boudoir, own room, small dining room and chapel. Returning to the entrance, the servery was next door to the dining room, and beyond this a small male domain of a smoking room and billiard room, with the butler's pantry, kitchen and

Fig.84 Killarney entrance courtyard

scullery opposite across a continuation of the corridor. The lesser offices lay beyond, with larders, a pastry larder and the dairy in a range flanking the entrance courtyard and set forward at an angle of 18 degrees. The other offices are in an L shaped block projecting forward of the garden front. On this the design is much as one would now expect, a pair of large Dutch gables above the dining room and library with three small gables in between. (Fig.86) Two-storey bays to each of the big gables and another lighting the hall; a three-storey semi-circular bay off the hall on the east front, the chapel with a lead covered cupola and immensely tall wrought iron cross above. The bricks of which it was built are said to have been imported from Switzerland, but this must be another Irish story.

The interiors were finished with the utmost magnificence by London-based craftsmen in particular W.H. Lascelles & Co. Ltd of 12 Bunhill Row, E.C. 'established nearly a century', who used a photograph of the hall and stairs on their advertising leaflet. (Fig.87) They were responsible for the woodwork of the panelling and the stairs, all carried out in oak. Tapestries were hung above the panelling, stamped Spanish leather was used in some rooms and the door handles were decorated with antique enamel watch-cases. The final account, which included some small works on the estate and in the town came to £59,000 on which Devey's commission at 5 per cent amounted to £2,950.

Lord Kenmare employed Devey on the design of a new town hall for Killarney, which survives although much altered. He also designed the fishing pavilion on O'Mahoney's Point, a small rough-cast single-storeyed building with a bay window topped by a shaped gable and stout chimney stack, later to become the golf club house and has now been demolished to make way for better premises. His lodge to the Western Domain survives unaltered, a pretty little building hung with fishscale tiles and fretwork balconies. (Fig.88) An extension to West End House in New Street is clearly by him, but his designs for a Presbyter's House do not seem to have been carried out although returned to his office for alteration by someone called

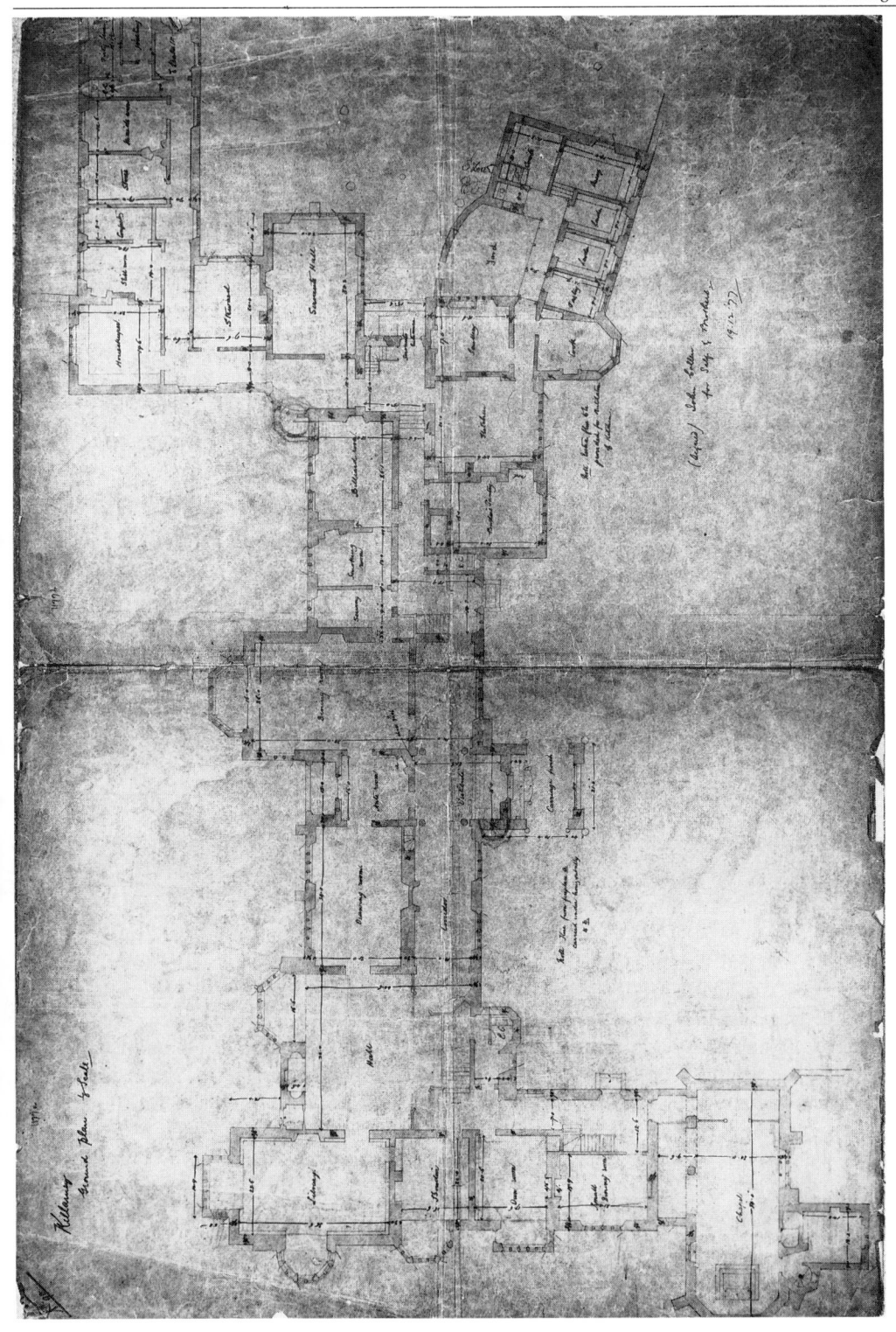

Fig.85 Killarney, ground plan

Fig.86 Killarney, garden front

Stubbs in October 1878. It was to have been attached to the church and is described as being at Killarney, and then at Firies, but is in fact nowhere to be seen.

Devey's accounts for Lord Northesk's new mansion, Longwood near Winchester, show that he was charging '5% on Certificate, Labour & Materials &cs.' and '2 per cent for addtl. attends. & time surveyg.& Checkg. wk & a/cs.', so this is another of the buildings put up without the help of a contractor. The Earl came from a naval family; his father commanded the *Britannia* at Trafalgar after which he was made a knight of the Bath, and his eldest brother was lost in the *Blenheim* less than two years later. His family seat was Ethie Castle, Arbroath and the Hampshire estate came through his mother, the only daughter of William Ricketts Esq. of Longwood. His wife had died in 1874 and he died at the age of 87 in 1881, before Longwood was completed, so the house was obviously always intended for his son, Lord Rosehill. It was the last new mansion that Devey was to build, thereafter he was to be only employed upon adapting and enlarging existing buildings.

The plan, with slight alterations, is that of St Alban's Court, which at some stage in the design, was reversed. A narrow entrance hall leads into a saloon containing the principal stairs, which leads again to a corridor off which lie the drawing room, library and morning

The Flourishing Practice 113

ESTABLISHED NEARLY A CENTURY

TELEGRAMS LASCELLES, LONDON TELEPHONES { 1365 LONDON WALL / 812 EAST.

W. H. LASCELLES & Co., LTD.,
121, BUNHILL ROW,
LONDON, E.C.

Contractors to H.M. War Department and Office of Works, the Admiralty, the Crown Agents for the Colonies, London County Council, &c., &c.

BUILDERS &
CONTRACTORS.
*
MANUFACTURERS
OF
JOINERY,
BANK AND
OFFICE
FITTINGS,
SHOP FRONTS
AND FITTINGS,
PULPITS,
PEWS, ETC.
*
PATENT
"RHOMBUS"
WOOD BLOCK
FLOORING.
*
GREENHOUSES
AND
CONSERVATORIES.
*
WOOD
BUNGALOWS
AND
BUILDINGS.

The Hall, Killarney House, Kilarney, G. DEVEY, ESQ., Architect

Among other works carried out by W. H. LASCELLES & Co. are the following:

Croydon Municipal Buildings	Architect, C. HENMAN Esq
Lowther Lodge, Kensington Gore	„ R. NORMAN SHAW, Esq., R.A
Mary'ebone Parish Church (New Seating)	„ THOS. HARRIS, Esq.
Holy Trinity Church, Marylebone	„ EWAN CHRISTIAN, Esq
St. Mary's, Brighton	„ Sir WM. EMERSON, F.R.I.B.A.
Bovril, Ltd. (Office fittings)	„ H. V. LANCHESTER, ESQ.
Private Chapel, Grimsthorpe Castle	for the RT. HON. THE EARL OF ANCASTER
The Angel Hotel, Islington	Architects, Messrs. EEDLE & MEYERS
The Bishopsgate Institute	Architect, C. HARRISON TOWNSEND, ESQ
London & County Bank (several branches)	
National & Provincial Bank	
London & South Western Bank	

Our works are equipped with the most modern and complete wood working machinery, and we possess facilities for producing the best possible work very expeditiously.

We will willingly give estimates for joinery & wood-work of any description on receipt of particulars.

Fig.87 Killarney, W.H. Lascelles & Co. Ltd. advertisement

Fig.88 Lodge to the Western Domain, Killarney

room, and a boudoir, for which Hammond would have had no use, and a billiard room, which he could not afford. The dining room was again opposite the entrance but only reached from the saloon, and the offices, part of which come forward, forming an enclosed entrance courtyard reached through an arch cut through the base of a tower in the centre of this projecting range.

Longwood was again a very large house and one of Devey's most satisfactory designs. It must again be said that it is difficult to judge from some rather dim photographs, but here Devey appears to have thrown off his tendency to lapse into a rather mechanical succession of gables and well-tried details. The building material is red brick, with diaper and a chequerwork of stone on the entrance tower. The courtyard was sufficiently large to take the five-storey tower with its attached six-storey octagonal staircase turret, and the two garden fronts long enough to allow Devey to give movement to the facades by advancing bay windows and chimney breasts and pushing back the bays in between.

Little need be said about the restoration work and additions which Devey began in 1874 at Smithills Hall and Sudbury Hall, apart from the fact that the former gave rise to two Devey annecdotes. 'The story is told that an artist who was greatly in love with Smithills, being the guest of Mr. Ainsworth, commenced one day to make some sketches, and Mr. Devey found him busily at work on the new parts, in complete oblivion of their comparative youth.'[15] The second is the remarks of A. Needham Wilson during the discussion which followed James Williams' talk at the Architectural Association, seconding the vote of thanks he said that : 'as a young pupil, he visited one of the old halls near Bolton, in Lancashire, where he saw some charming work which had been added by Devey to the place. It came to him then as a revelation, and he hoped it had some influence on his future career.'[16]

Smithills Hall is a stone and timber house dating from the fifteenth and sixteenth centuries which had been bought by Colonel Ainsworth's grandfather Richard in 1801. Richard Ainsworth was a pioneer of chemical bleaching and the first to employ chloride of lime in the process. Richard Henry inherited both the Halliwell Bleachworks and the Hall on the death of his father in 1865.[17] The old house runs around the east, north and west sides of what is now an open court, and Devey was in the first instance employed on the relocation of the offices, the improvement of access to various parts of the building, the provision of extra bedrooms for the staff and the repair and refitting of the chapel which had been damaged by fire in 1856. The stables were removed from the west end of the house to a separate block. He was called back in 1882 to put in yet more staff bedrooms, to design panelling for the hall and dining room and to create a male domain of a billiard room, study and new entrance. He carefully adhered to the original building materials and introduced into his work the quatrefoils found in the old timbering, but his woodwork is more fanciful than the original.

He was equally painstaking in his additions to Sudbury Hall. The 6th Lord Vernon inherited the Hall in 1866 and employed E.M. Barry to prepare designs for a block of new offices between the house and the stables, and to make minor alterations to the Hall such as the addition of balustrades at ground and eaves level; the contract for the latter was signed in 1872. Barry must have been a disaster as Devey was consulted as soon as he had completed this work and produced a series of designs for improving the planning of the offices and their appearance. Barry's plain Tudor gabled range was recast by him in to match the fabric of the Hall, red brick with a tight trellis pattern of headers with stone quoins, basement and balustrade with three handsome two-storey bays on the garden front, all matching the old work in style. His work here led to a useful series of commissions from Lord Vernon, who employed him constantly until he died in 1880. He restored All Saints' Church, adding battlements and pinnacles to the tower. An interesting photograph in his collection shows these constructed in wood and offered up to try out the effect. He made additions to the Curate's house, designed cottages, including the butcher's shop, in the village, built the gas works and enlarged The Boar's Head, which had been a tiny public house at Sudbury Station. He also worked at Poynton Colliery and on Vernon's town house, 34 Grosvenor Street, and obtained through his influence the commission to design the Meynell Hunt stables and kennels, a job which he must have greatly enjoyed.

When one considers the number of Devey's clients who were in high government office or were friends of those who were, it is surprising that no important public commissions came his way. All he obtained in this way were the comparatively small works at Dover and Ramsgate, and the commission to advise about the House of Lords, which he got through Lord Granville. There is more than a suspicion that he liked it this way, and would not have accepted such work if it had been offered, and there is no record of him having ever contemplated entering any of the big competitions, such as those for the Government Offices or the Law Courts. What he must have been pleased with was his one small job for Queen Victoria, though in the event he failed to be presented to her.

James William recalled: 'The introduction to the late Queen came through H.R.H. the Princess Louise and the Duke of Argyll, when Mr. Devey was engaged over a house (Macharioch) for them in Scotland. A letter came one morning from the Princess, asking for some drawings of work to be sent for the Queen to see at Osborne. It was thought of, as more attentive to the royal commands, for the drawings to be taken, so I had the honour of attending, and after luncheon there, of submitting them to Her Majesty and the Royal Family. There were present, in addition to the Queen, the Princesses Louise and Beatrice, the late Duke of Albany, and the Duke of Argyll. It

Fig.89 Barton Manor, model of house and stable yard

Fig.90 Barton Manor, model of entrance to stable

Fig.91 The Ledgers, model of proposed additions

was a family gathering without any state. Her Majesty was pleased with the drawings, especially with a water colour of Mr. Leopold Rothschild's house at Ascott, Buckinghamshire. Mr. Devey was commanded to attend the next day, but although in driving up we caught sight of Her Majesty sitting out under a portico with her attendants, she was, it turned out, a little indisposed, and he never had the honour of a personal interview. This was always a source of regret. We, however, saw that day, the Princess Louise and the Duke of Argyll, who went over the proposed alterations and additions to Barton Manor House on the estate.'[18]

Barton Manor was at that time the house where the equerries lived, and whatever else was proposed, Devey was instructed to build larger stables and to make a new and grander entrance into the stable yard, which was not, in the event, executed. By a great piece of good fortune two models have been preserved at Osborne which illustrate Devey's proposals. One is of the Manor and the attached stableyard, the new gabled entrance, bay window and extension of the cloister. (Fig.89) The other, on a larger scale, is of the entrance, bay window and cupola. (Fig.90) The smaller scale version has been painted to indicate the stone walls, tiled roof and red brick chimney stacks. The larger is left plain deal. Both are stored in stout boxes with brass catches and hinges, stamped on the inside with Devey's name and address. At present there seems to be only one other example of Devey's models in existence, that showing the proposed alterations at Ledgers, which is also preserved in its original box. (Fig.91) We do, however, know that they were made as a matter of course, for the benefit of the clients. The Dover Harbour Board Minutes for the 8th May 1876 record 'The Partner of Mr. Devey attends and produces a Model of a Clock Tower to be erected near the Life Boat

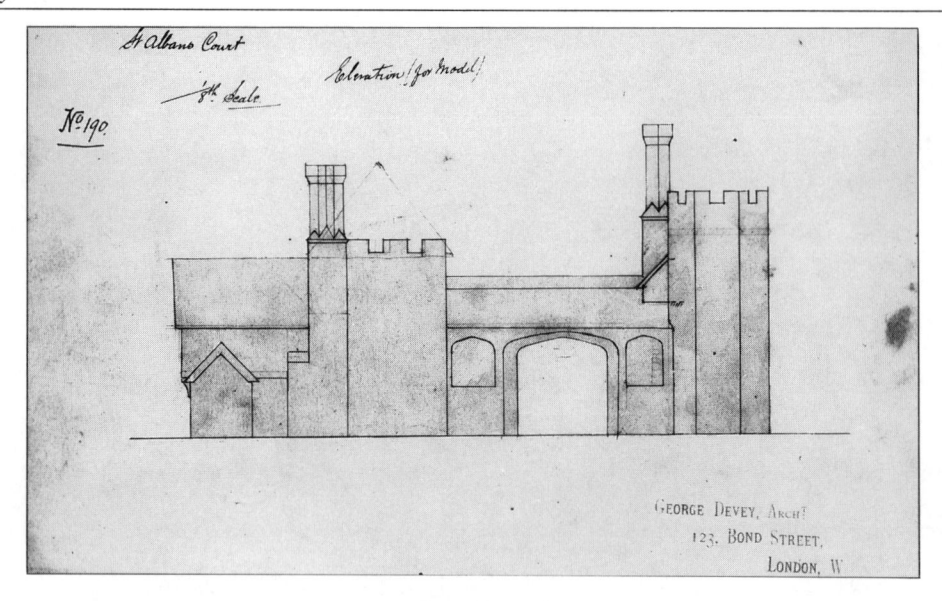

Fig.92 Drawing for a model of a gatehouse, St Alban's Court

Shed and such model is approved'.[19] This has disappeared. The life of architectural models outside the architect's office is disastrously short. They are intrinsically fragile, which is why Devey's are so well boxed, and after they have served their purpose, they attract little regard. A fairly usual fate is for them to be given to children as playthings, and indeed the dolls' house at Greystoke Castle, redecorated and furnished in the 1950s has now been identified as a project for an eighteenth century enlargement of the pele tower.[20]

Devey's consistent use of models was unusual and remarked upon at the time, but their value had been recognised by others. Sir John Soane in his Lecture XII said 'In my own practice I have seldom failed to have a Model of the Work proposed ...I must add that wherever the Model has been dispensed with, I am afraid the building has suffered in consequence thereof, either in solidity or convenience, and perhaps in both.'[21] So far as Devey's office was concerned, James Williams remembered 'one modeller in constant work.'[22] And at a meeting of the Royal Institute of British Architects on the 15th November 1886 Phené Spiers, "refering to the late Mr Devey, suggested that, as the decesed invariably had models made of his works in preference to perspective drawings, the Council would do well, whenever a memoir of his life came to be read, to include an exhibition of such models.'[23] This explains the lack of perspective drawings by Devey, which has already been noted. When James Williams' lecture was printed, a postscript illustrated two photographs for Lord Granville's Maplewood, which was then in the possession of Walter Godfrey, but has now vanished. This is interesting as they show not only the house, but also the layout of garden paths and terraces, and indicate the planting of an avenue of clipped pyramidal yews. Careful drawings were made for these models. One to survive is for the alterations to Melbury House, and a complete set of two plans and four elevations exist for a gateway and lodge which was being considered by Hammond as part of the works at St Alban's Court. (Fig.92) This was not built but shows the care with which Devey proceeded, even when dealing with a comparatively small and inexpensive building.

7

Struck Down in his Prime

John Poyntz Spencer, 5th Earl Spencer, the 'Red Earl', as he was called in Ireland both on account of the colour of his bushy beard, and the measures he was obliged to take to preserve some order after the murder in Phoenix Park of his chief secretary Lord Frederick Cavendish in 1882, was another friend and supporter of Gladstone. He had been the Liberal member for South Northamptonshire for a few months, elected in April 1857, but going to the Lords upon the death of his father in December that same year, and in 1868 had become Lord Lieutenant of Ireland in Gladstone's first administration with Chichester Fortescue, another of Devey's clients, as Chief Secretary. Gladstone's government fell in 1874, and the Liberals were to be in opposition for six years, during which period Spencer occupied himself with estate matters, employing Devey on his building projects, of which the most significant was the proposed development of the Spencer Estate on the outskirts of Northampton.

This was to be on an unpromising piece of land on the west of the London and North Western Railway tracks leading into Castle Station, ominously marked on the 1885 Ordnance Survey as 'Liable to Floods'. Other environmental hazards were a sewage works on the east, a tannery to the south and the Scrap Forge Iron Works on the west. Despite this, the land was developed for housing, but not in the way first intended. What was proposed at the start was a development with five different classes of house arranged on a grid pattern to either side of the Spencer Bridge Road to Dallington. (Fig.93) 'Plots of various sizes' reads the poster, 'Houses built to suit requirements. Plans and full particulars of Messrs. Becke and Green, Solicitors, Northampton. Mr. J.N. Beasley, Chapel Brampton and Northampton. Mr. George Devey, Architect, 123. Bond Street, London. W.'

The designs made by Devey for these houses are in many ways reminiscent of what was being devised by a series of architects for Jonathan Carr's estate at Bedford Park. Both projects appear to have been begun at the same time. Carr's first choice as architect was E.W. Godwin, who was working for him in 1875, but who resigned when his designs were subjected to simplification for financial reasons. He was replaced by R.N.Shaw in 1877, and Shaw gave way to one of his assistants, E.J. May, who he recommended as estate architect in 1880, so the essential character of Bedford Park was settled in the second half of the 1870s. This was also the case with the Spencer Estate. The plans and elevations which Devey made for the houses illustrated on the poster are on Whatman paper watermarked 1876 and Devey's cashbook shows him working for the Earl on unidentified commissions up to 1883. There are also stylistic similarities, both were designed in what had been christened 'Queen Anne' in the early 1870s. 'Angels and ministers of grace! am I dreaming?' wrote Moncure Conway enthusiastically 'Right before me is the apparition of a little red town made up of quaintest Queen Anne houses.' and it seems likely that Devey's little town would have had a similar effect.[1] Five different types of house are shown on the poster, of which the largest is that closest to Devey's habitual style. This is built of red brick on stone footings, with

Fig. 93 Poster advertising the Spencer Estate

half-timbered gables and a two-storey porch. The plans for this house have not survived. The second grandest, could be had in two versions, one, described on the drawings as 'C', in red brick with Dutch gables, and the other, 'D', was to have had a a red brick ground floor decorated with diagonal trellis work, with rough-cast and half-timbered gables above. The accommodation provided was an entrance hall containing the staircase, leading to the dining room, drawing room and library, with a lavatory on the right of the front door. A lobby led to the kitchen from which the servants' stairs ran up to the floor above (wine store under) scullery, stores, coal hole and servants' lavatory. There were five bedrooms, a dressing room, bathroom and lavatory above, and attic bedrooms on the second floor. The next in importance is much closer to what May was doing at Bedford Park and can be compared with houses in Priory Gardens and The Orchard. (Fig.94) These are semi-detached houses presenting to the road a range of Dutch gables, the two inner with triangular pediments, and the outer segmental. Pediments above the front doors are broken so as not to obstruct the fanlights, and each house has a single-storey canted bay with a white wooden balustrade above very like that in Maurice B. Adams' drawing for 12 and 14 Newton Grove.[2] The next to be considered are designs for two types of terraced houses. The first, for the more affluent,

Fig. 94 Design for semi-detached houses, Spencer Estate

are distinguished by pairs of gables. (Fig.95) The accommodation here is more homely: parlour, dining room, kitchen and scullery with four bedrooms above and lavatories on both floors. The simpler version has a continuous bressumer and little bay and oriel windows. (Fig.96) Both have patterned tiled roofs, are of red brick with rough-cast above, and both have, included as part of their design, wooden trellises to support climbing plants. All the houses have gardens furnished with silver birch, ornamental trees and shrubs, clipped hedges and topiary, flowers (including sunflowers) all separated from the road by a low paling in natural wood. It would have surpassed Bedford Park as a garden suburb.

It is perhaps worth noting that the houses for the Spencer Estate share with those at Bedford Park the then unusual distinction of being designed without basements, probably due to the influence of a Dr B.W. Richardson who spoke at the Social Science Association in 1875 in favour of houses with no basements and limited to four storeys in height; his views were published the following year in *Hygeia: A City of Health*.[3] But there were important differences. Bedford Park was designed for an artistic and professional class which scarcely existed in Northampton. The promoters of Bedford Park also put emphasis on their intention that the community should function as a whole, and share the amenities provided by the

Fig. 95 Terrace houses, Spencer Estate

developer, the Club, the Art School, the Stores, the Tabard Inn and the church of St Michael. No such thing was envisaged for the Spencer Estate, and it was probably the lack of the right sort of tenant that caused the project to be abandoned, and run-of-the-mill terrace housing put up instead.

It will be seen from the catalogue that Devey obtained numerous commissions for works of improvement to upper-class houses in London, of which the alterations to No.1 Richmond Terrace for B.W. Currie and to No.18 Carlton House Terrace for Lord Granville were the most important. However it was only in the last five years of his life that he designed entirely new London houses, some for private clients, and also for two speculative builders Samuel Juler Wyand and Messrs Trollopes. He had only done this once before, when he produced the designs for Kelsall Lodge in Tunbridge Wells for the Haward Brothers in 1869. He began in Lennox Gardens.

The will of Alderman Henry Smith, executed in 1627 made *inter alia* two bequests: the first 'for the use of the poore captives being slaves under the Turkish pirate, the some of one thousand poundes, wch some of one thousand my will and meaning is shalbe layed forth and bestowed in the purchase of landes of inheritance to the value of threescore poundes pd annu att the leaste' and second, another £1000 was to be similarly invested 'for the use and reliefe of the poorest of my kindred, such as are not able to worke for theire livinge.' This was the origin of the South Kensington Estate of Henry Smith's Charity.[4] The trustees of the estate

Fig.96 Artisan's terrace housing, Spencer Estate

Fig. 97 No. 8, Lennox Gardens

bought land in the parishes of Kensington, Chelsea and Westminster, all of which had been developed by the beginning of the 1880s apart from two parcels, the Quail Field and Brompton Heath. The former was to be laid out as Lennox Gardens. This and the formation of Cadogan Square, which will be described later, came about after the passing in 1866 of an Act of Parliament for the extension of Pont Street to the west, which caused it to pass over part of the Quail Field. The first house to be built was that which Devey designed for the Hon. Mrs Hunloke.

Mrs Hunloke was Lord De L'Isle's sister. We have already seen that the considerable income she received from her coal mines had enabled her to contribute to building work in Penshurst, and now she decided to build herself. Unlike most of the upper classes who regarded themselves as chiefly resident on their country estates, and made do with comparatively small town houses, often rented, where they resided for the Season, that is the months of May, June and July, she built herself a most imposing mansion at the northern end of Lennox Gardens, and then by way of an investment, a block of three houses between this and Walton Street. Devey's designs were approved by Cluttons, the surveyors to the estate, in March 1882 and they were signed by the contractor, T.J. Messom of Twickenham in May. (Fig.97) The house is of red brick with Portland stone dressings and a slate mansard roof, with four bays on the eastern entrance front, and three bays on the south facing the square. Ornament is restricted to the doorway with its elaborate cartouche above, rather heavy quoining and balustrades above the two bay windows overlooking the square, and at roof level, the latter pierced by pedimented dormers. (Fig.98)The houses for rent are fairly plain, and are treated as a single unit, of four storeys, red brick with diapering and a slate roof above. (Fig.99) There are a pair of Dutch gables with triangular pediments on both the Lennox Gardens and the Walton Street fronts, and three two-storey canted bay windows. The facades presented to the streets are of good quality red brick, to the rear the construction is of stock brick, but even this is made interesting by some diapered in black headers. In the case of all Mrs Hunloke's houses, the style is best described as economical Queen Anne, but without most of the details which define that style.

The houses for letting were begun in 1883, and a house for Eric Carrington Smith of Ashfold was started the same year, and is dated 1884 on a tablet. This is No.19, and is of four storeys on a basement, and three bays wide, again of red brick with Portland stone dressings. The entrance porch is on the right hand side with a door-case supported by a pair of volutes. To the left of this is a two-storey canted bay window and the tripartite division of the rest of the facade is accentuated by a series of three pedimented gables on the roof. In 1884 Devey gained another client, when Major General Stewart employed him to design No.23, which has a two-storey porch decorated with strapwork, windows with arched mullions on the first floor, and a shaped gable with a central triangular pediment above. (Fig.100) No. 43 was begun in 1885 for Lieut. Col. the Hon. Charles Gathorne-Hardy, son of Lord Cranbrook, the overall scheme is the same; three bays, four storeys and a two-storey porch with a shaped gable with strapwork on this and the porch, and a wrought-iron first floor balcony. His initials appear on a tablet between the fourth-floor windows, and the date 1885 in wrought iron. (Fig.101) The builder employed was Samuel Juler Wyand.

Fig.98 No. 8, Lennox Gardens, doorway

Fig. 99 Nos. 2, 4 & 6, Lennox Gardens

Wyand was a speculative builder on a large scale, who began his business taking building leases of houses in St Pancras in 1858. He went on to building houses in Paddington, North Kensington and South Kensington in the 1870s.[5] He employed Devey on four more houses in Lennox Gardens, No. 25, Nos. 13 and 15, and No.41 where Devey also designed interiors for Lieut.Col. Alexander Hamilton. The preliminary design for No.25 was simply a variation on that made for Stewart at No.23, but this was abandoned in favour of a facade in the Franco-Flemish style employed by Ernest George and Peto in Harrington Gardens.(Fig.100) There is a single-storey porch, and the mullioned and transomed windows on the first and second floors have fanlights above. The facade is articulated vertically by brick pilasters and horizontally by bands of stone, widely spaced in the lower part, and close set in the stepped gable which carries a wrought-iron weather vane. Also in wrought iron is the date 1884 carried across the facade and the purely decorative tie plates as found on houses in Amsterdam. It is the most elaborate facade that Devey produced, presumably at the insistence of the first tenant, a Mrs Bold. Nos. 13 and 15 may have been built together but the designs differ; the porches and windows are arranged to balance each other but the detail distinguishes them. They are in no way a pair. So far as No. 41 is concerned, only the floor plans have survived and the facade has been most unfortunately altered. Devey also designed some interiors for houses built by Wyand in Lexham Gardens, but these have all been destroyed.

Fig. 100 Nos. 23 and 25, Lennox Gardens

The 'Specification of Works to be done in the erection of a Mansion, Stables &c. being No.36 Grosvenor Square W. for C.H. Wilson Esqre. M.P. according to Drawings prepared for that purpose by Mr. George Devey' was dated October 1883. Charles Henry Wilson was the joint manager with his brother Arthur of Thomas Wilson Sons and Company, a shipping firm which eventually became the largest private ship-owning company in the world, and operated out of Hull to the Baltic, bringing iron from Russia and Sweden and timber from Norway. Eventually over 100 vessels were sailing to this and other destinations in the Mediterranean, India and America. Wilson represented Hull as a Liberal, from 1874 to 1905, was a free-trader like the Rothschilds, and a supporter of the Temperance movement like Currie and Samuel Morley. His country house was Warter Priory, which he bought from Lord Muncaster in 1871, where Arthur Castings was to be employed on laying out the garden after Devey's death. His first house in Grosvenor Square was No.35, built in the early eighteenth century and which had, what in Victorian times were regarded, as a number of defects, such as low ceilings. No.41, which replaced a house of similar date to No.35 was built with a set of reception rooms for entertaining on a very grand scale. Wilson signed a ninety year lease of the site at £420 a year on 9 August 1883.

Devey's plans were criticised by Thomas Cundy III, the Grosvenor Estate surveyor. The Board minuted 'Mr. Devey, architect attended the Board with the plans. Mr. Cundy thinks the offices very badly arranged, and that there is deficient bedroom accommodation for the family. Mr. Cundy informs the Board that he does not think Mr. Devey can have had any experience in planning a large house. As Mr. Boodle is to arrange for Mr. Devey to meet him at Grosvenor House and submit the plans to the Duke, Mr. Cundy will send a memorandum of his views to be submitted to his Grace.'[6] Cundy's observation was perfectly true of large town houses; as we have seen, Devey had only begun No.8 Lennox

Fig.101 No. 43, Lennox Gardens

Gardens the previous year and all his earlier work in London had been alterations. The usual arrangement of the larger London terrace house was to have the kitchen and the servants' rooms, butler, housekeeper and porter, in the basement, the hall, dining room, study and morning room or parlour on the ground floor, with the stables at the rear, the drawing room and boudoir on the first floor, and bedrooms above. Devey's plan differed, in that although the servants' rooms and the larders remained subterranean, the kitchens were placed next to the dining room on the ground floor, between it and the stables. There was an entrance hall and a central staircase hall, most magnificently cased in marble, off which there was a study overlooking a rear courtyard, and a library with a view of the gardens in the square. (Fig.102) On the first floor an ante room and the drawing room also looked out to the front, and the ball room with an adjoining tea room were placed above the dining room. The servants' bedrooms occupied a mezzanine and the first

Fig.102 No. 41, Grosvenor Square, the staircase hall

floor above the stables, and on the second floor of the house Devey placed the day and night nurseries and a bedroom, with more bedrooms on the third and fourth floors above. The front of the house was chiefly distinguished by a four-storey bay window terminating in a very large triangular pediment, a massive shell niche above the porch, and a balustrade run between obelisks at roof level. (Fig.103) It was of diapered red brick with stone dressings and must have stood out in vivid contrast to the generally stucco fronts of the neighbouring houses. It was pulled down in the early 1960s.

Fig.103 No. 41, Grosvenor Square

Devey did not live to see his last design for a group of London houses built. In the 1770s an area of about ninety acres had been leased by Lord Cadogan to Henry Holland, on which was to be built Hans Town, a new estate of four- and five-storey houses for the upper middle classes and professional men. Holland also built himself a mansion called Sloane Place or The Pavilion, part of the grounds of which were later leased to a Mr Prince who ran a sporting club with its own cricket pitch. The leases all expired in 1874, by which time Holland's houses were in decay and multi-occupation. These were demolished by a builder called North Ritherdon who was replaced as developer by the Cadogan and Hans Place Estate Ltd.

which had Colonel W.T.Makins MP as its chairman. Ritherdon had agreed to rebuild with houses 'not inferior to those in Lowndes Square' built by Thomas Cubitt, with the customary stucco fronts. Makins prefered red brick.[7] He was later to employ J.J. Stevenson to build his own house in Lowther Gardens, and Stevenson was to design houses for Cadogan Square, the show piece of the new estate. Although a few of the houses were designed for specific clients much of the square was sub-leased to developers such as Thomas Pink & Son, Holland & Hannen and Trollope & Sons who played the major part, building the north and east sides. It was for this firm that Devey prepared his designs. (Fig.104) He produced one of his charming sketches on tracing paper, which was then worked up into a finished design. As with the Grosvenor Square house these are five storeys high on a basement, and have the customary three bay division. Although they compose well as a group they are in fact completely interchangeable, and when they were built after his death under the supervision of James Williams, the sequence, which may be indicated as A B C D, was built as A D C B without any ill effect on the overall composition.

Country house work continued to come in during the last few years of Devey's life; much of it is known of only through his cashbook and what was actually done cannot always be distinguished. Only one new house was built in the 1880s, and this was

Fig. 104 Houses in Cadogan Square

Monkshatch, which used to stand on the Hog's Back near Compton. The client here was Andrew Kinsman Hichens, a wealthy young man, a member of the Stock Exchange and partner in Hichens Harrison & Co., who had married Mary Emily Princep, known to her family as May, in 1874. Monkshatch was a large half-timbered country house with the accommodation which might be expected at the time it was built, apart from the fact that a studio 24 by 38 feet in size was placed between the drawing room and the billiard room. Hichens was an amateur painter, but more importantly he had become friendly with G.F. Watts, who had been living with his wife's family at Little Holland House for many years. When Watts was going through one of his periodical bouts of ill health he spent the winter at Monkshatch, despite the fact that his doctor had suggested Brighton, and Lord Leighton, Italy. This was such a success that Watts moved from London to the nearby village of Compton, to a house called whimsically Limnerslease, designed by Ernest George, as Devey was by then dead, and paid for by Hichens.[8] Monkshatch is now demolished, but drawings survive which show a sober building of red brick, half-timbering and rough cast, with a Dutch gable above the big studio window. It was serviceable rather than pretty.

Devey's country house work ended with six big commissions all of which entailed alterations to existing houses. The first was Pitchford Hall, the home of Lady Louisa Cotes. This is one of the best examples of a Shropshire timber-framed building begun in c.1549 when the west range was built, to which north and east ranges were added about thirty years later. A service wing which projects to the west was added before 1682, and this was remodelled in a plain style in the early nineteenth century. Charles Jenkinson, later the 3rd Earl of Liverpool built a service corridor of brick on the east and west side of the courtyard and enclosed this by continuing it across on the south side. Lady Louisa was his daughter and she called in Devey to reorganise what must have been a utilitarian but unattractive jumble of buildings. Devey removed the corridor and renewed the external timbering to match, and moved the main entrance from the south-facing clock tower to the north side, fulfilling a typical Victorian wish for privacy. Visitors, who might not be received, no longer came to the front door through the gardens, thus saving embarrassing meetings. The dining room was turned into a great hall and a new dining room created by knocking together the smoking room and the butler's pantry, the library became Lady Louisa's room and a new one was created south of the drawing room. Eighteenth-century sashes were replaced with oak mullioned casements and the service wing cased in half-timbering to match the rest of the house. It was the sort of combination of restoration and rearrangement by which countless Victorian architects attempted to adapt old and inconvenient houses to modern requirements.

At Melbury House, Devey was dealing with a building more distinguished architecturally than at Pitchford. His client here was the 5th Earl of Ilchester who had already in 1872 employed Anthony Salvin to add a new library, which took the form of a great hall, and was built in Salvin's customary Tudor style to match the original parts of the house, which date from the mid-sixteenth century. Much of this had been obscured by a remodelling carried out in the late seventeenth century, but this did not obstruct the view of the hexagonal prospect tower, and adjacent gables, the details of which formed a model for both Salvin and Devey. Devey's additions doubled the size of the building, and they were carried out in Ham Hill stone to match the original work. He added a range running north and south to the west end of the library. The south end of this ended in a four-storey tower, square in plan, with a stout octagonal stair turret at the north-east corner. (Fig.105) From this, the new range runs back northwards, housing the offices with bedrooms above, and continues round the kitchen courtyard. A new gateway into this was based upon Montacute Priory gatehouse. An attractive little dairy was planned, but not built. (Fig.106)

What is most remarkable about this is the way that Devey has subordinated his usual style in deference to that of the Tudor building. The original house at Melbury was one of a group found in Dorset and Somerset which were the work of masons based at Hamdon Hill, and which are characterised by the use of angle shafts of concave octagonal section, barley sugar pinnacles, crockets running up the gables and arched mullioned and transomed windows. All this Devey uses, and applies the barley sugar twist to the chimney stacks. The most impressive feature in his additions is the tower, which has bay windows on the south and east sides rising its full height. That on the east is based upon the oriel above the gateway of the porch at Forde Abbey. The concave octagonal shafts appear, topped by barley sugar pinnacles, and bands of panels set with quatrefoils and lozenges run round at first-floor level and on the battlements, with additional panels set beneath the windows.

The next two commissions demonstrate usefully the different sorts of job which came Devey's way. At Gaunt's House he was called in by Sir Richard Glyn, one of the banking

Fig.105 New tower, Melbury House

family, but not himself a partner in the bank, to enlarge a house which had been built by his grandfather in 1809, and to provide new stables. The result of this was a large extension and the addition of a battlemented and machicolated tower, all in a curious hybrid style with shaped gables, with sash windows and three Palladian windows preserved from the original house. The result is most unhappy and it may be concluded that the client was trying to both impose his own ideas upon his architect and frugally, to reuse architectural fittings. Another difficult client was encountered in William Robinson. Robinson was one of the most distinguished Victorian gardeners, whose rise from under-gardener at a house in Ireland to fame as the initiator of the revolt against bedding out, and authorship of books such as *The Wild Garden*, and editorship of his own popular periodical *The Garden*, was almost as remarkable as the earlier rise to fame and fortune of Sir Joseph Paxton. Robinson bought Gravetye Manor near West Hoathly in 1884. A former owner had begun to add an east wing and a southern extension to this late Elizabethan house, which had to be partly demolished as they had been built without a damp course. Devey added a new hall with a door set in its north side, and built Robinson's own bedroom above this. New offices were put in the east wing, and a loggia running south from the porch was designed, although this was not built. Robinson kept a ledger in which he recorded both the planting done in the gardens and the work carried out on the house, and certainly in later years he was not satisfied with what had been done, and complained that the plumbing had been found to be defective.[9] 'Tho I employed an architect of highest repute & one of the best firms of builders in London when

building hall and other parts of the house we noticed some unpleasant odours this year (1890)....
Almost everything done by the builders a few years ago was wrongly or carelessly done & had
the house been much inhabited danger must have arisen. Drains were carried under the house,
bath wastes led into soil pipes, drains unventilated & almost every possible mistake made.' The
chimneys also caused trouble, 'Messrs. Devey & Williams had their own way with the fireplace
and chimney in the new hall and failed completely to make the chimney draw & most of the old
fire places are useless and have been the cause of great expense and annoyance in the past.' The
smoke nuisance was solved by bringing over a fumiste from Paris. The work at Gravetye was
most probably incomplete when Devey died. Robinson employed Ernest George on later
extensions and the redecoration of the interiors.

Raikes Currie bought the Minley estate in 1856, having chosen it because 'he was much
concerned with health; and he had a great belief in the efficacy of gravel soil, a high situation
and pure air to preserve that blessing.'[10] Currie's architect was Henry Clutton, who had in the
same year that Raikes bought Minley published *Illustrations of Mediaeval Architecture in
France, from the Accession of Charles VI to the Demise of Louis XII, with Historical and
Professional Remarks*'. The new mansion was put up in 1858-62 in the early French
Rennaisance style and this was to dictate the manner in which subsequent additions were carried
out. 'From 1882 Minley was let to Mr. C. Hoare, the banker. During Mr. Hoare's tenancy I had
added a great part of the Hawley estate to the property at the cost of nearly £30,000. When the
house became vacant in the autumn of 1885, we, that is my wife and my only remaining child,
spent some weeks there in order to decide whether or not we should make it our winter residence.
Having resolved this question in the affirmative, Mr. Devey was called in to advise upon the
necessary alterations and improvements.'[10] Work began with the laying out of terraces and a
parterre, the building of the orangery and its associated cloister leading to the house. The stables
were previously attached to the north-east corner of the house, and these were demolished and
replaced by the kitchen offices arranged around a courtyard, with additional servants bedrooms
above. On the entrance front, Devey added a new porch, the clock tower and the octagonal

Fig.106 Design for a dairy, Melbury House

Fig.107 Dunraven Castle

staircase tower, reorganised the entrance hall, created a new dining room and put in a new servants' staircase. Holland and Hannen were the contractors, and these works cost £55,000. New stables and a lodge were built to the north of the entrance drive. All this was in progress when Devey died, and the Minley commission was taken over by Arthur Castings, who continued with further additions to the house including the chapel, and an extensive building programme of farms, lodges, boat houses and cricket pavilions, to mention but a few, on the estate.

The 4th Earl of Dunraven's principal residence was at Adare in County Limerick, and he also owned Kenry House at Putney and Dunraven Castle in Glamorganshire. This last had come to the Wyndham-Quins from his grandmother, and with it came interests in coal mines and iron foundries. It was not then a castle but a fairly insignificant manor house, which judging from its mullioned windows with square hoodmoulds was probably much rebuilt in the Tudor period. It did, however, occupy a fine site on an exposed headland, and Devey & Williams, as the practice had now become, were instructed to make the building more imposing, by large castellated additions. (Fig.107) These consisted mainly of a tower at the north end of the front facing the sea, extra accommodation and a high wall at the south end giving protection from the south-west gales. Work on designing these began in 1886, but things were not entirely settled when Devey set off on his final trip to Ireland, and the contract drawings were not signed until the 25th May 1887. Dunraven Castle was one of the commissions taken over by James Williams. It was published in *The Builder* of the 26th May 1888 as a work of Williams, West and Slade.

Devey lived with his father until the old man died, their last house being at Ealing Common in a road which later became The Common. This cannot be identified. The 1861 Census shows the household as Frederick Nicholls, now aged 75, solicitor, Ann, aged 76, Frederick William who is described as a gentleman, George, and Sarah Dunn, the cook. Frederick had moved to Hastings by 1882, and Devey lived first at Elm Park House in Chelsea, and moved to Ashley

House, Lavender Hill, which is where he was living at the time of his death, some time between 1881 and 1884. Both of these houses have been demolished.[11] His office had remained at 16 Great Marlborough Street until 1880, when he removed to 123 Bond Street, a more fashionable address. But he was beginning to think about retiring. He had accumulated a comfortable fortune, and probate of his will showed his personal estate as £32,531.1.7d. 'This is a pretty large sum, as times go,' reported The Builder 'for a man to have accumulated by his own exertions in a profession the emoluments of which are not over-liberal.'[12] Although he was only sixty-six years of age we know that he was not strong, and the constant visiting of work in progress all over the kingdom must have been most wearing. His brother, who also never married, was living at Pelham Crescent, Hastings, sharing a house with a Clara Egg, clearly the widow of one of their Egg cousins, and her daughter, another Clara. Devey no doubt visited them from time to time and now decided to join them in Hastings. He bought East Cliff House, No.74, All Saints Street from a Miss Fisk, who had inherited it upon the death of her father in June 1886. It was the house where Prince Augustus Frederick, later the Duke of Sussex, lived after his marriage to Lady Augusta Murray, which was annulled by the Court of Arches a year later under the terms of the Royal Marriage Act. Devey bought it in September. James Williams recalled that it was early Georgian with panelled rooms overlooking the sea, and a paved terrace with a summer house at each end. He had it put in order by an old foreman who had worked on many of his jobs, but did not live to move in.

He probably set off for Ireland as soon as the purchase was completed, on a visit to Lord Kenmare at Killarney, from where he was to journey on to Lord Dunraven's Adare Manor in Limerick, a large Gothic revival mansion built by A.W.N. Pugin for the Catholic 3rd Earl, and altered by P.C. Hardwick, to which the 4th Earl wished to make some alterations. On the journey he caught a bad cold, which turned to pneumonia. The chest infection could not be shaken off, and he died at Hastings of bronchitis on the 4th November 1886, nursed to the end by his cousin Clara Egg.

'An able and accomplished architect, and a chivalrous high-minded gentleman'

Rejected twice by Flora Streatfield, Devey seems to have remained within a web of his family connections, living, like his elder brother, with his father and mother, while they were alive, and nursed by his cousin Clara at the end. But in his professional life also, he is a strangely isolated figure, and clearly not through any lack of the social graces, or he would never have attended receptions at the Foreign Office as the guest of Lord Granville, or have been so lamented by Bertram Currie. He does not seem to have taken any great interest in the Royal Institute of British Architects, and although he was a member and took part in most of the early meetings, he never became one of its officers. Walter Godfrey's story of a party of architects which included Devey, Pearson, Street and Burges making a trip to France, Holland and Belgium is not confirmed by any other source and must be regarded as highly improbable.[1] His election to the Royal Academy was never contemplated. He did not become a Fellow of the Society of Antiquaries or any other learned body, and only joined the Society for the Protection of Ancient Buildings, founded in 1877, the year before his death. It seems more than likely that the work of this Society came to his notice through the interest of its committee in one of the major commissions to do with old houses, such as Melbury, with which he was involved at this time.

He was not a member of the Art Workers Guild, and does not figure as one who attended gatherings of artists and architects, which became formal associations, some only briefly in existence and then dissolved, such as the Hogarth Club. As a result he makes no appearance in the diaries and memoirs of those who joined, and the only information as to what he was like as a man comes from the study of his career and the recollections of Percy Stone, the son of Coutts Stone with whom he served his pupilage with Thomas Little, and James Williams, who, most fortunately, was prevailed upon to give a talk about Devey to the Architectural Association more than twenty years after Devey died.

Percy Stone, speaking at a meeting of the Royal Institute of British Architects a month after Devey's death and burial 'in the charmingly wooded upland cemetery at Ore, overlooking his favourite Hastings,' referred to his father's friendship with Devey, 'and to the fact that he himself was the only pupil now in practice that the deceased had admitted to his office'.[2] But Stone was wrong; perhaps he had not been much in the office during the last years of Devey's life, and so had been unaware that Edmund Livingstone Wratten had been taken on as a pupil and that Percy Morley Horder had joined in 1886, for what was to be a very brief spell. Morley Horder's father was a Congregational minister and his mother was a niece of Samuel Morley, which is no doubt how Devey's office came to be chosen, and it was Morley Horder who sent to the Royal Institute of British Architects the photograph of Devey which forms the frontispiece of this book, with a note saying that it was a good likeness.[3]

The non-conformist background of this family would have been sympathetic with Devey's own commitment to the Theistic Church founded by the Revd Charles Voysey, whose son C.F.A. Voysey spent a couple of years in Devey's office, as 'an improver', in other words he was not a regular employee but someone who was taking advantage of his position to learn his trade, probably without being paid. This was after schooling at Dulwich College and pupilage with J.P. Seddon, who was an architect with a mainly ecclesiastical practice, building churches and vicarages, and the University College of Wales, Aberystwyth, begun in 1864 as the Castle Hotel, in the Venetian manner of the Gothic revival. From Seddon's office he moved to that of Saxon Snell and the design of hospitals and workhouses, which he found dreary. Of his time with Devey, 'Voysey regarded this chance as providential.'[4] He enjoyed the office work and the outside jobs, one of which was being sent to Ireland to prepare a rent roll, perhaps for the Earl of Kenmare, but if so, it does not survive amongst the Kenmare archives. Voysey clearly found this amusing, it was a book two feet long and eight inches wide 'with page after page of water-colour drawings of the Irish shanties and hovels. Street after street, with pigs and peasants going in and out of doors.' It was a curious thing for an architect's office to be involved with. Another story Voysey told about his time with Devey was that in 1881, the architect bought some land adjoining the estate of one of his clients in Northamptonshire, on which he built a pair of cottages, putting Voysey in control and making him prepare the drawings, order the materials, employ the workmen and remain on the spot until all was done, sending in a weekly time sheet. The total cost was to be kept within £500. It was clearly a most helpful exercise in practical building, and it is be regretted that the cottages in question cannot be identified; but it is doubtful that Devey would have been prepared to extend such an opportunity to the son of any but a great friend and his religious adviser. Devey's influence on Voysey as a designer quite outweighed what he had learnt with Seddon, as can be seen in his project for a 'House with an Octagonal Hall'. The materials which he proposed employing, stone footings, diapered brickwork, half-timbered gables, the truncated portion of a shaped gable above the front door, and the gablet where a cross range impinges on the roof ridge are all familiar, and the cupola and weather vane have the broad proportions seen in the dove cote on the roof of Edward Baring's Coombe Wood Farm. Other unexecuted designs such as the Bungalow, Bellagio and an Architect's House, published respectively in *The British Architect* and *The Studio,* again refer back to works by Devey, the continuous close studding of a first floor above rough-cast or stone on the ground floor, this supported on buttresses, and a tower topped with wooden balustrade.

Irritatingly little is known about other members of his office staff, although we know from James Williams that 'At the busiest time there were about ten men in the office, one modeller in constant work, and six clerks of works.' Some surviving paperwork gives a few names, a Henry Owen in the late 1850s and Charles G. Mayland who signed certificates for the Rothschilds' builders in the 1860s. The painter G.P. Boyce began in his office and then moved on to Wyatt and Brandon.[5] This is recorded in Boyce's dairy and he gives the date as 1847, which must be treated with a certain caution as this was the year Devey set up his own office, and it seems doubtful that he was sufficiently well off to employ an assistant, or sufficiently well known to attract a pupil. James Williams had joined him by 1870, although he was not to be made a partner for a number of years. He employed Henry Smith as his surveyor, and Arthur Castings was his chief draughtsman, which he remained, despite being himself a most gifted architect, as he was to show after Devey died.

Devey's death caused the break-up of the office. It can only be assumed that there were some differences in personality between Williams and Castings, as the obvious way out of an unexpected and taxing situation, with the number of incomplete commissions that were in hand, would have been for them to have continued in partnership together. They did not.

The work was divided fairly evenly between them, Williams forming a business carried on as Williams, West and Slade which only lasted a brief while. They moved to 3 Grosvenor Street, and took Ascott, Dunraven Castle, the almshouses at Nonnington, and minor work at Ashfold and other houses. Arthur Castings went to 61 Lincoln's Inn Fields, and continued to work at Minley and St Paul's Walden Bury, as well as picking up other work through the Devey connection such as the laying out of formal gardens at Goldings and Glamis Castle. At this stage, the collection of drawings by Devey which came eventually into the possession of Walter Godfrey, and which were to cause him to write first his prize-winning essay, and then the monograph, must have been divided, and it was only by the greatest good fortune that they were reunited. James Williams had taken on Godfrey as an articled pupil, and he was to become head of the firm. When Castings died in 1913, leaving his wife in a somewhat precarious financial position, she wrote to him reminding him of her husband, 'who cherished his association with Mr. Devey', and asking whether it was possible that some of the drawings she had in her possession might be sold to their old clients, and Godfrey replied that if she would send them to him he would do his best. A note records that Lady Strathmore bought five of Castings' drawings, and perhaps others were sold, but by far the greater part remained in Godfrey's office.[6]

Despite his writings about Devey, Godfrey never met him, and we have to rely upon Percy Stone and James Williams for personal details. Stone tells us of 'a far from robust constitution' and Williams, that when he was ill he occupied himself by drawing, and that he never tired of music. He was fond of animals, particularly his horses whom he visited in stables, and spoilt with carrots. He liked attending horse fairs in Ireland and sometimes bought a horse there 'believing that you should spend some money where you make it.' He had a collection of whips, which he never had cause to use, a hobby which he shared with his lifelong friend George Bentley, for whom he built a house at Upton. 'His "Calls" about town were made in a well-appointed brougham (built under his supervision) and a pair of roan horses, with a coachman who, like his master, looked a gentleman - and was one.' The coachman, who remained with Devey for years, was Jesse East and was left £100, a considerable sum, in his employer's will. Devey's love of horses and a fine carriage can be seen in elevations such as that for Macharioch House, already mentioned, and for Knowle Park and Duncombe Park all of which have sporty equipages at the front door, and however much the tracing of lines and laying on of washes was done by assistants, the horses were affectionately sketched in by Devey himself.

He was unusual in his manner of dress, and disliked the business man's black dress coat wore homespuns and coloured, never white, shirts. Here one is reminded of Voysey who also dressed in an idiosyncratic manner and designed his own suits without lapels or trouser turnups, and favoured clear blue shirts. But Devey, on formal occasions was unexceptionable in his dress, and passed on to Williams an account of an incident at the Foreign Office: 'A noble lord running down the grand staircase came upon a man standing quietly at the bottom, in the same kind of evening dress as himself, and mistaking him for a servant, said sharply : "Are you a waiter?" when the equally quick answer came "No. Are you?"' He had a sense of humour, and handled his workmen well, even when something had gone wrong, but deception was met with anger, and Williams twice remarks upon his sarcasm, giving as an example the foreman who excused some shoddy work by saying it could never be seen, which was countered by, 'What, not seen? I should be ashamed for the birds to see it.' He was considerate to his office staff, and at the time of his death was working out a scheme by which everyone who had worked in the office for more than a year should be entitled to a share in the profits.

Much of his will is taken up with a list of bequests which include gifts to his office staff. Williams, who was co-trustee and executor with Frederick William Devey, was left £1,000,

Arthur Castings had £500 and all his other drawing assistants received £100 each. His brother and sister were left £2,000 each and shared the residue of his estate, cousins and other relatives mostly had £1,000, friends such as the two sons of Boissier, and charities, the Royal Society for the Prevention of Cruelty to Animals and The Institution for the Benefit of Cab and Omnibus Drivers among others, received £100. Isabella James, late of Halton, who one presumes to be the widow of James James was to choose 'any object in remembrance of our friendship' and the Revd Charles Voysey, and the Trustees of the Theistic Church were each given £2,000. Devey had been consistently generous to his chosen church, which taught that there was a kind and forgiving God, and no eternal damnation. At the time it had attracted a large congregation, but not a wealthy one, and Voysey wrote 'Two or three times when funds were well nigh exhausted, he would send his £100. at once to relieve the anxieties of the Hon. Treasurer; and I must add that but for his personal bounty to myself, and the yearly supply to me of alms-money for cases of necessity, I should often have been sorely embarrassed and utterly unable to relieve the poor who came to me ...'

But to return to the office. His immediate successors were not great men and his real legatees were Shaw and and the young men who passed through his office, Nesfield, and Walter Godfrey, who showed in his writings that he appreciated what Devey was about, and in his work, a respect for the fabric of old buildings which led to his appointment as Director of the National Buildings Record in 1941. Devey's contribution to domestic architecture was his observation of what traditional materials and methods of construction could contribute to the comfortable assimilation of a building in the English landscape. And for this he made use of such local expertise as was available. A look at a set of designs for a building such as the Cranbrook Lodge at Hemsted, shows that he produced ground and first floor plans, and four elevations. (Fig.108) Sometimes rafter plans were made, sometimes a detail drawing of a dragon beam or a pendant, often the plan of the chimneys. But the actual particulars of construction were left to the builders, who were frequently local men in a small way of business who had been putting up such cottages all their lives. It is interesting to compare Devey's relaxed approach with that of Philip Webb, a man who was fascinated by traditional building crafts, but who was not prepared to let the traditional builders proceed in their usual manner, and made detailed drawings of every mortise and tenon and insisted that these were adhered to. It is also interesting to note that, unlike Webb or any of the Arts and Crafts architects, Devey seems never to have designed furniture or fittings; the only surviving drawing that shows any is an early elevation of a room at Hall Place where some Jacobean style pieces are shown arranged along the wall. Devey's interest in his interiors appears to have ended with the plasterwork of the ceiling and the wooden panelling. And he had no church practice worth speaking of. The Eastry Workhouse chapel, an unidentified church described as being at Carlton Hill, with no other location, and the cemetery chapel at Pounds Bridge were his sole commissions in this field after he left Thomas Little, but he did carry out eleven church restorations, mostly for clients for whom he had already done domestic work.

In order to fully understand Devey's achievement it is necessary to remember the architectural climate at the mid-century when he began. The work he did in Little's office was in the Gothic Revival style, and this was indeed the time of confrontation between the adherents of the Gothic and Classical styles as represented by the major works of the period, from the Palace of Westminster to the British Museum. It was also the time of the Crystal Palace and the great train sheds, which brought iron construction to general notice, a material that he distrusted. 'He was very much against the use of iron construction, when it could be avoided, and it was amusing to hear him discussing the thickness of web and flange with his surveyor, who always allowed a very ample margin, but Mr. Devey invariably

Fig.108 Cranbrook Lodge, Hemsted

added something, saying we seemed precious afraid of the girder "going up."He prophesied a great day of reckoning, when, one by one they would all collapse about our ears.'[7] Gothic, Classic and the new technology were all rejected. So indeed was what one critic was to call the *bric-a-brac* style of Queen Anne which first came to public notice with Shaw's New Zealand Chambers.[8] Mark Girouard has listed the characteristics of Queen Anne, red brick, white painted sashes with small panes, curly pedimented gables, sunflowers, wooden balconies and fancy oriels.[9] Devey never used sashes and small panes, preferring stone mullions, and certainly never succumbed to the fashion for sunflowers. The other ingredients may be found in his works but with such an admixture of the plain vernacular or grand Jacobean that the result cannot be described as Queen Anne. The closest he ever came to this was in the abortive designs for the Spencer Estate. Devey discovered a style of his own to which he adhered without exception to the end of his life, but although it had a great influence on the next generation of architects, and was through their work to become part of the idiom of English house building, his contribution does not seem to have been generally appreciated.

In the brief obituary written by Percy Stone for the *Journal of Proceedings of the Royal Institute of British Architects* he calls him a pioneer 'followed up' by Shaw, and R. Phené Spiers clearly expected that he would shortly be commemorated with a lecture, which he urged should be illustrated with models and photographs without which 'it would be impossible

140 *George Devey*

Fig. 109 The Devey memorial, Minley

to grasp the wonderful power of design and facility of invention which the works executed under Mr. Devey's direction exhibit.' This did not in fact happen until Williams' lecture, which was given at the Architectural Association, rather than the Royal Institute of British Architects twenty-three years later and illustrated with Devey's sketches. The proposer of the vote of thanks then 'thought some of the younger men present might feel that the designs they had seen possessed no great distinction as compared with what they were accustomed to today, but an artist's work must always be looked at to some extent in the light of the time when it was done, and it must be remembered that these beautiful things were produced at a time when domestic architecture was at a very low ebb.' Another speaker referred to a visit to three Devey houses which had been made a few years ago, and mentioned Minley and

Coombe Warren, 'one of the most delightful houses he had ever known. It was about half an hour's walk from Wimbledon Common, and one could go quite close up to it. Coombe Cottage was quite close to Coombe Warren, and a good deal of that could be seen to.' This makes the point that Devey's work was not generally known because it was accessible neither in publications, nor by visits, to the general public.

It is a fact that those Victorian architects who established themselves in a practice in which the clients were mainly drawn from the upper classes were under constraint not to advertise their work. The clients did not care to have their private business a matter of public discussion, and in any event a man like Devey would not have relished seeing his houses illustrated in *The Builder* or *The Building News*. What is more, Devey did not carry out any public commissions which might have attracted notice. As a result his contribution to domestic architecture was not known to more than a few of his fellow practitioners. He is not mentioned in the 1862, 1873 or the 1891 editions of James Fergusson's *History of the Modern Styles of Architecture*, the last revised by Robert Kerr. Kerr's own *The Gentleman's House*, first published in 1864 ignores him. Charles Lock Eastlake's *A History of the Gothic Revival* which came out in 1872, takes a less restricted view than its title might suggest and lists Nesfield's work at Shipley Hall and Broadlands, described, on the instructions of the architect, as 'Old English Domestic'. Shaw's Farnham Bank and Leyswood are 'Old English', Preen Manor is 'Shropshire half timbered'. Eastlake is cognizant of the development that had taken place in domestic architecture, but he makes no mention of Devey. And neither does Herman Muthesius whose *Das englische Haus* was published in Berlin within twenty years of Devey's death, a book which contained the most thorough analysis of English domestic architecture and an assessment of the contributions of the leading architects, specifically dealing with the rejection of historical styles, the vernacular revival and pursuing the story through to the men who were the heirs of Devey's innovations, the 'Arts and Crafts' architects, Ernest George, E. S. Prior, Ernest Gimson and Edwin Lutyens. So far as the last is concerned, it is instructive to compare Devey's little sepia sketch for Culver Lodge with Lutyens' sketch design for The Hut, made for Gertrude Jekyll in 1892, thirty-five years later.

So Devey passed rapidly into obscurity, though his unacknowledged influence on the progress of domestic architecture persisted. He is buried in plot BE L2 of the cemetery maintained by Hastings Borough Council at Ore. His gravestone stands amidst the elaboration and marble of those of his contemporaries and is a final affirmation of his religious belief. A plain round-topped stone, with his name, date of birth and date of death and no pious texts or the expression of hopes for the occupant's future well-being. After all, he knew there was no such thing as hell.

It is not his only memorial, there are two others. First an architect's work always commemorates the man, and Devey's work is the source of the little thread of sanity in house building that has survived the worst that the twentieth century can do, and which still urges that well-tried and traditional things like bricks and timber are infinitely preferable, in both the country and the town, to fabrications in concrete and glass. (Fig.109) The second was the work of Bertram Currie, who, grieving for his dead friend, had his portrait modelled and placed in the cloister at Minley, beneath which is inscribed :

> *Georgii Devey felicissimo ingenio architecti*
> *amici acceptissimi hanc effigiem in aedibus*
> *ipsius arte amplificatis exornatisque*
> *in memoriam posuit BWC MDCCCLXXXVII*

Notes on Sources

Select bibliography

The following is a list of articles and books, listed in order of publication, which give information or helpful comments about George Devey and his works.

The Building News 12 Nov 1886 p. 721. 'The Late George Devey.'
Royal Institute of British Architects Journal of Proceedings 18 Nov 1886 p. 46. Percy G. Stone 'The Late George Devey, Fellow. Born 1820, Died 1886.'
The Building News 19 Nov 1886 p. 752.
The British Architect 19 Nov 1886 pp. 461, 476.
The Builder 20 Nov 1886 p. 728.
The Times 23 Nov 1886 p. 6.
The British Architect 26 Nov 1886 p. 497.
Royal Institute of British Architects Journal of Proceedings 9 Dec 1886 p. 69.
The Builder 25 Jun 1887 p. 931.
Journal of the Royal Institute of British Architects 19 Sep 1906 p. 501. Walter Hindes Godfrey 'George Devey F.R.I.B.A.' (Godfrey 1906)
The Architectural Review Vol. XXI 1907 pp. 23, 30, 83, 88, 293, 306. W.H. Godfrey 'The Work of George Devey.' Reprinted as a monograph. (Godfrey monog.)
The Architect & Contract Reporter 12 Mar 1909 p. 181, 19 Mar 1909 p. 193.
Architectural Association Journal Vol. XXIV No. 266 April 1909. James Williams 'George Devey and His Work.' (Williams 1909)
Mark Girouard *The Victorian Country House* 1971 II 14. 'Devey in Kent: Betteshanger, St. Alban's Court.'
Andrew Saint *Richard Norman Shaw* New Haven and London 1976.
Mark Girouard *Sweetness and Light* Oxford 1977.

Drawings and other material

The greatest number of Devey's surviving drawings and his photographs (the Devey Collection) were deposited by Mr & Mrs Emil Godfrey with the Drawings Collection of the British Architectural Library in 1968, and have now been purchased by the Royal Institute of British Architects. The whereabouts of others has been given in the catalogue under the name of the building concerned.

Two volumes of his watercolour sketches were presented to the Royal Institute of British Architects by his executors in accordance with the codicil to his will.

His cashbook, recording accounts for commission and expenses, and the payments received, a late volume of fee note counterfoils, a number of specifications, and the index of clients prepared by Walter Godfrey (Godfrey index) are retained in the Godfrey Collection.

The cashbook, which begins in 1867, has enabled most commissions to be dated accurately, but as only the names of clients are given, and not the buildings, a number of works remain unidentified. The clients names are included in the catalogue in the interests of completeness, and in the hope that this will enable more of Devey's works to be located.

The cashbook also shows how Devey's practice expanded, by giving totals of the amounts billed which are as follows :

1867 £1,334
1868 £1,613
1869 £1,221
1870 £2,460
1871 £2,463
1872 £2,813
1873 £4,298
1874 £5,443
1875 £5,623
1876 £9,395
1877 £8,929
1878 £8,045
1879 £3,847
1880 £3,204
1881 £2,723
1882 £2,790
1883 £1,913
1884 £2,715
1885 £2,690
1886 £3,829

The figures reflect in a most interesting way the effect of the agricultural depression which began in 1879 on a practice which was chiefly concerned with country houses and estate works.

Notes

Chapter 1

1. Hyde Park Family History Centre
2. Information from The Law Society Services Ltd, Records and Statistical Department
3. Lewis Winant, *Early Percussion Firearms*, London, 1961, p. 38. A. Aspinall (Ed.), *The Correspondence of George, Prince of Wales, 1770-1812*, Vol I, 57 & 230
4. James Williams, 'George Devey and his Work', *Architectural Association Journal*, vol XXIV, no. 266, April 1909
5. J.E. Hodgson, *The History of Aeronautics in Great Britain*, Oxford and London, 1924, pp. 302-4, Fig. 117
6. For Augustus Egg, see Christopher Wood, *Dictionary of Victorian Painting*, Woodbridge, 1978; *The Burlington Magazine*, April 1983, pp. 202-10
7. Charles Dickens to Sir Edward Bulwer-Lytton, 28 April 1851
8. Walter Hindes Godfrey, 'George Devey FRIBA', *Journal of the Royal Institute of British Architects*, 19 September 1906
9. The river front was still incomplete and subscriptions for this were being solicited. F.N. Devey contributed five guineas. King's College, London, Archives, *Report from the Council to the Annual General Court of Governors and Proprietors, 1933-34*
10. Information from Mr Frank Miles, the Archivist, King's College School
11. Sydney D. Kitson, *The Life of John Sell Cotman*, London, 1937, p.303f
12. W.M. Rosetti, *Dante Gabriel Rosetti: His Family Letters with a Memoir*, London, 1895, p.73
13. A large number of these model drawings, stamped COTMAN, KING'S COLLEGE, LONDON are held by the Norfolk Museums Service at the Castle Museum, Norwich. Cotman did not always use his own work as copying material; he wrote to the College Secretary on 13 July 1838: 'I am now mounting the splendid prints of Le Brun's pictures of Alexander - fine heroic subjects for a public school - and boys should be *early* taught the *virtues* - or they are never understood.' King's College, London, Archives
14. King's College School Archives
15. Williams, 1909, p. 96
16. Godfrey, 1906, p. 502
17. Williams, 1909, p. 95
18. Kent Archives Office: Woodgate Archive, U1050/C 192
19. *The Builder*, 31 December 1859, p. 855
20. Algernon Graves, *Royal Academy Exhibitors, 1769-1904*, London, 1905-6
21. *Catalogue of the Drawings Collection of the Royal Institute of British Architects, L-N*, pp. 35-46
22. *The Builder*, 1 March 1845, p. 107
23. *ibid*. 13 December 1845, p. 597
24. *ibid*. 11 December 1852, p. 786
25. These designs are in the RIBA Drawings Collection
26. Godfrey index of Devey's clients. Godfrey Collection
27. The use of 'Gothick' in this book is intended to distinguish the early fanciful style such as that employed by Horace Walpole from the archaeologically correct Gothic, which was employed from the second quarter of the nineteenth century
28. *The Builder*, 9 June 1849, p. 273

Chapter 2

1. Godfrey index
2. Godfrey, 1906, p. 502
3. Kent Archives Office: Woodgate Archive, U1050/F219. Lambeth Palace Library, MS 1771, *Diary of Lord Northbourne*, 1851
4. For example see Arthur Bryant, *The Triumphant Island*, London, 1950, pp. 135-64
5. William Marshall, *On the appropriation and inclosure of Commonable and Intermixed Lands*, London, 1801
6. William Cobbett, *Rural Rides* ed. G.D.H. and M. Cole, London, 1930, E.T. Cook and Alexander Wedderburn, *The Works of John Ruskin*, London, 1906, Vol. I, *The Poetry of Architecture*, Part I, *The Cottage*, I, p. 12. This was first published in *The Architectural Magazine*, Vol. IV, pp. 555-60
7. *The Gardener's Magazine*, February 1830, p. 140. Loudon quotes G.Z. (whom we know to be a highly respectable man), in the *Farmer's Journal*, 22 February 1830, 'A system has been acted upon for some years of taking the small farms from the occupants, and adding them to the large farms, already too large in many instances; hereby, not merely hundreds, but thousands, of honest, industrial, frugal, and hitherto independent, yeomen, with their families, have been turned adrift, and reduced to absolute beggary'
8. Ibid., January 1827, p. 19
9. Ibid., June 1832, p. 257
10. Ibid., April 1828, p. 43
11. Michael McMordie, 'Picturesque pattern books and Pre-Victorian designers', *Architectural History*, Vol. 18, 1975, pp. 43-59
12. Andrew Saint, *Richard Norman Shaw*, New Haven and London, 1976, Chapter 2
13. Jeremy Maas, *The Victorian Art World in Photographs*, London, 1984. Sir Evan Cotton ed. by Sir Charles Fawcett, *East Indiamen*, London, 1949
14. *The Gardener's Magazine*, July 1839, p. 353
15. Richard Ormond, *Sir Edwin Landseer*, Wisbech, 1982
16. Cook and Wedderburn, op. cit., Vol. XIX, *The Cestus of Aglaia*, p. 50
17. Andrew Greg, *The Cranbrook Colony*, Maidstone, 1981
18. *The Gardener's Magazine*, July 1839, pp. 353-79. The article also describes the features of the garden including the crazy paving, which due to its massive slabs still survives
19. Cook and Wedderburn, op. cit, 'The modern building known in Britain by that name has very long chimneys covered with various exceedingly ingenious devices for the convenient reception and and hospitable entertainment of soot.' Ruskin on the Swiss Cottage
20. James Smith, *Panorama of Science and Art*; James Rickman, 'An Attempt to Discriminate the Styles of English Architecture from the Conquest to the Reformation', Liverpool, 1815. Kenneth Gravett, *Timber and Brick Building in Kent*, London and Chichester, 1971

Chapter 3

1. *The Gardener's Magazine*, October 1831, p. 607
2. *The Gentleman's Magazine*, 1805, II, pp. 1126-8, 'The Pursuit of Architectural Innovation, No. XCI'
3. For an account of this, see the present writer's, *Anthony Salvin*, Cambridge 1988
4. Information from Lord De L'Isle
5. *The Gentleman's Magazine*, August 1863, pp. 178-89
6. *Pinus sylvestris*. The plan is in the Devey Collection
7. Ironically, Betteshanger proved to be in the East Kent coalfield and the countryside here also became punctuated with pit-head gear
8. Lambeth Palace Library, MS 717, Diary of Lord Northbourne 1851. *In Memoriam + Walter Charles, Lord Northbourne of Betteshanger, Kent, and Jarrow Grange, Durham.* Privately printed

9. Godfrey, 1906, p. 516
10. RIBA, *Journal of Proceedings*, III N.S., 18 November 1886, p. 46
11. Kent Archives Office, Minute Books of the Eastry Guardians, G/Ea 19-20
12. For the Sutherland fortune, see Eric Richards, *The Leviathan of Wealth*, London, 1973
13. Devey to Fowler, 22 March 1859; National Library of Scotland, Sutherland deposit; Dep. 313/1566, 1568, 1286, 1294. I have to thank David Murray for a great deal of help in identifying and documenting Devey's work for the Sutherlands in Scotland
14. Loch to Fowler, Dep. 313/1269
15. J.J. Stevenson, *House Architecture*, London, 1880, p. 377
16. Loch to Fowler, 19 April 1858, Dep. 313/1285
17. For the development of Strathpeffer, see Thomas Chalmers Cowan Telfer, *The Architecture of Strathpeffer*, Dissertation for the degree of Master of Architecture, Edinburgh College of Art, Herriot-Watt University, 1981
18. Devey to Fowler, 2 March 1859, Dep. 313/1285
19. Lambeth Palace Library, Tait MSS

Chapter 4

1. Baring Bros & Co., Archives, Baring Scrap Book, 'Halteck - Alnwick Castle'
2. R.S. Surtees, *Ask Mama*, London, 1858, p. 282. Information about the foxhunts from Mr J.N.P. Watson. Jill Allibone, 'The Rothschilds in the Vale of Aylesbury', *Country Life*, 16 & 22 February 1898, pp. 80-3, 110-5. There is a delightful painting at Ascott showing the four brothers in full hunting fig galloping across the country
3. J.K. Fowler, *Recollections of Old Country Life*, London, 1894
4. N.M. Rothschild Archives take the view that all male Rothschilds who bear the name Mayer spelt it with an 'a'. The Marquess of Crewe, however, in his *Lord Rosebery*, London, 1931, Vol. I, p.115, writes, 'In some books of reference, the name is given as Mayer, which may have been the original form in Germany, but he was always known as Baron Meyer.' Lady Eastlake also wrote 'Meyer'
5. C.E. Smith, *Journals and Correspondence of Lady Eastlake*, London, 1895, II, p. 225. Lady Gregory (ed), *Sir William Gregory KCMG, An Autobiography*, London, 1894. Lady Jersey, when asked 'if she knew Baron Lionel Rothschild the head of the firm in England, "I know him by name", she answered, "but of course I could not receive him. I have not allowed him to be presented to me." '
6. *The Gardener's Chronicle*, 1863, pp. 346, 376, 394
7. Buckinghamshire County Record Office, Mentmore Estate Office, D/RO/1-176
8. N.M. Rothschild Archives, Aston Clinton Estate Accounts
9. Lucy Masterson (ed), *Mary Gladstone [Mrs Drew], Her Diaries and Letters*, London, 1930, pp. 360, 196
10. Lord Edward Fitzmaurice, *The Life of Granville George Leveson Gower, Second Earl Granville KG, 1815-1891*, London, 1905
11. PRO Works, 14/82
12. Lord Ronald Gower, *My Reminiscences*, London, 1883, Vol. II, p. 86
13. *The Builder*, 9 March 1867, p. 165
14. Williams, 1909, p. 103
15. Dover Harbour Board Minute Book, Vol. 2; Dover Harbour Board Committee Minutes, 1877-87, HH/A/42
16. *The Builder*, 24 April 1875, p. 379
17. Archive of Art and Design, Powell of Whitefriars window glass order book, AAD 1/5-1977
18. Royal Bank of Scotland, Williams and Glyn's Bank Archives. B.W. Currie, *Memoires*, privately printed
19. Ibid
20. Powell, AAD, 1/3-1977

21. Mary Carberry, *Happy World*, London, 1941
22. Walter Hindes Godfrey, 'The Work of George Devey', *Architectural Review*, Vol. XXI, 1907. Reprinted as a monograph, p. 13
23. Maurice Baring, *The Puppet Show of Memory*, London, 1922, p. 3
24. Williams, 1909, p. 97
25. ibid

Chapter 5

1. By Dr J.P. Simon, written in 1839
2. *The Quarterly Review*, Vol. CI, 1857, No. 202, Art. 5, p. 450. This rankled years after the event: 'We unwillingly recall the fact which rather mars the moral beauty of this interesting proceeding, viz. that by some chicanery a patent for the daguerrotype was actually taken out in England, which for some time rendered this the only country which did not profit by the generosity of the French government. The early history of photography is not so generous in character as that of its maturity'
3. H. & A. Gernsheim, *The History of Photography*, Oxford, 1955
4. For an account of the painters' use of photography, see Aaron Scharf, *Art and Photography*, Harmondsworth, 1983
5. Information from Brian Sewell
6. George Edmund Street, *Brick and Marble in the Middle Ages: Notes of a Tour in the North of Italy*, London, 1855. *The Builder*, Vol. XVII, 1859, p. 171
7. Joan Evans and John Howard Whitehouse, *The Diaries of John Ruskin, 1835-47*, Oxford, 1956, pp. 83, 88, 90, 95, 108, 129, 146, 164, 169, 178, 191, 197, 217, 218, 243, 273, 321
8. Brian Hanson, 'Carrying off the Grand Canal', *Architectural Review*, Vol. 169, February 1981, pp. 104, 109. J.D. Harding, *The Principles and Practice of Art*, London, 1845, p. 19
9. Cook & Wedderburn, op. cit., Vol. III, 210
10. *La Lumière*, 20 March 1852, quoted in Susan Sontag, *On Photography*, Harmondsworth, 1979
11. *The Diaries of Charles Barry Junior, 1846-April 1847* (two volumes), in the possession of Mrs Barbara Stanley-Evans, who has deposited a copy in the Record Office, House of Lords. I have to thank Alexandra Wedgwood for drawing my attention to the younger Barry as a photographer
12. Information from Margaret Richardson. A.T. Bolton, *Lectures on Architecture by Sir John Soane*, London, 1929. Giles Waterfield, *Soane and After*, Lavenham, 1987
13. Godfrey, 1906, p. 516
14. John Rutter, *Delineations of Fonthill and its Abbey*, London, 1823; *The Buildings of England, Wiltshire*, quoting John Harris
15. Edwin Hodder, *The Life of Samuel Morley*, London, 1887
16. R.N. Shaw, *Architectural Sketches from the Continent*, London, 1858; W.E. Nesfield, *Specimens of Mediaeval Architecture*, London, 1862
17. John Brandon Jones, 'C.F.A. Voysey, a Memoir', *Architectural Association Journal*, Vol. LXXII, 1957, pp. 241-62. Information from John Brandon Jones
18. Baring Brothers & Co. Ltd, Archives, English Client ledgers, BK I 71-72
19. Nicholas Cooper, *The Opulent Eye*, London, 1976
20. *The Quarterly Review*, op. cit., p. 443
21. Robert Elwall, 'The foe-to-graphic art: The Rise and fall of the Architectural Photographic Association', *The Photographic Collector*, Vol. V, No. 2, 1985, pp. 142-163
22. Sotheby's, *British Architectural Drawings and Watercolours, 1660-1960*, Sale 25 June 1981, lots 112, 113. Lot 113 is now in the British Architectural Library

Chapter 6

1. J.A.S. Leighton-Boyce, *Smiths the Bankers, 1658-1958*, London, 1958. As the family used the same christian names in each generation, they are numbered as an aid to identification in accordance with the abbreviated family tree in the firm's history
2. East Hertforshire Archaeological Society, *Newsletter*, No. 9, 1958
3. Burrell MSS, British Library, Add MSS 5672, No. 60
4. Information from Lady Katherine Northbourne
5. Drawing in the Devey Collection
6. Maurice Baring, *The Puppet Show of Memory*, London, 1922
7. Diana Hopkinson, 'A Passion for Building: The Barings at Membland', *Country Life*, 29 April 1982, pp. 1236, 1240
8. George Cuitt II watercolour vignette and engraving, Victoria and Albert Museum, E2543-1817, E3077-1980. Baring Brothers & Co. Ltd, Archives, *The Membland Hall Estate, South Devon, 1895*, auction particulars
9. J.W. McKail, *The Life of William Morris*, London, 1899
10. Shropshire Record Office, Corbet of Adderley MSS, Ref. 327, Box 269
11. Williams, 1909
12. *The Building News*, 23 April 1886, p. 684, 25 June 1886, p.1057
13. Leonard Moseley, *Castlerosse*, London, 1956
14. Edward MacLysaght, *The Kenmare Manuscripts*, Dublin, 1942
15. Godfrey, 1906
16. Williams, 1909
17. A.J. Sykes, *Concerning the Bleaching Industry*, Manchester, 1925, pp. 66-69
18. Williams, 1909
19. Dover Harbour Board Minute Book, Vol. II, p. 352
20. Information from Mrs Stafford Howard and John Martin Robinson
21. A.T. Bolton, *Lectures on Architecture by Sir John Soane*, London, 1929, p. 191
22. Williams, 1909
23. RIBA *Journal of Proceedings*, III N.S., 9 December 1886, pp. 69-70

Chapter 7

1. M.D. Conway, *Travels in South Kensington*, London, 1882
2. For illustrations of Bedford Park, see T. Affleck Greeves, *Bedford Park, the first garden suburb*, London, n.d.
3. Mark Girouard, *Sweetness and Light*, Oxford, 1977, Chapter 7
4. Dorothy Stroud, *The South Kensington Estate of Henry Smith's Charity*, London, 1975
5. For more about Wyand, see *Survey of London XLII, Southern Kensington*, London, 1986, p. 292
6. Grosvenor Board Minutes, 21/383-4. *Survey of London, XL, The Grosvenor Estate in Mayfair*, London, 1980, pp.152-3
7. See Girouard, op. cit., pp. 93-7, and Robert Pearman, *The Cadogan Etsate*, London, 1986
8. M.S. Watts, *George Frederick Watts, The Annals of an Artist's Life*, London, 1912, Vol. II, 153
9. Royal Horticultural Society, Lindley Library, *Gravetye Manor Tree and Garden Book and Building Record,; Commenced by Wm Robinson, August 1885*. Mea Allen, *William Robinson, 1838-1935, Father of the English Flower Garden*, London, 1982
10. The Royal Bank of Scotland, Glyn Mills Archives, B.W. Currie's *Notes on Minley*
11. I am grateful to the Local History Librarians of the Boroughs of Ealing and Wandsworth for help in identifying Devey's houses
12. *The Builder*, 25 June 1887, p. 931

Chapter 8

1. Information from Paul Joyce
2. RIBA *Journal of Proceedings,* III N.S., 18 Nov & 9 Dec 1886 pp46-7, 69-70.
3. Clyde Binfield 'Holy Murder at Cheshunt College: The Formation of an English Architect: P R Morley Horder, 1870-1944' *The Journal, United Reform Church History Society* Vol 4, No 2, May 1988 pp103-34
4. John Brandon-Jones 'C F A Voysey 1857-1941' *Architectural Association Journal* 1957 pp241-59
5. Arthur E Street 'George Price Boyce' *The Old Water-colour Society's Club, Nineteenth Annual Volume* London 1941
6. Godfrey Collection
7. Williams 1909
8. James Fergusson *History of the Modern Styles of Architecture* London 1902 II p151
9. Mark Girouard *Sweetness and Light* Oxford 1977

Catalogue Raisonné

Note on the Catalogue

Details already given in the text are not repeated. Dated unidentified schemes are included, as are particulars of executed works which are also unidentified, in order to give a clear idea of the amount of business in hand.

Abbreviations

C: Cost

Cbk: Cashbook, Godfrey Collection

CL: *Country Life*

Com: Commission. Records dates of accounts rendered and cash received. The amounts include travelling and sometimes the clerk of works' wages. They give a good indication of the date at which the work was executed and also the extent of work carried out

DNB: *Dictionary of National Biography*

E: Executed

E?: Possibly not executed

Fee a/c: Fee account counterfoil book, Godfrey Collection

Girouard: Mark Girouard, *The Victorian Country House*, New Haven and London, 1979

Godfrey index: Walter Godfrey's alphabetical index of Devey's clients, Godfrey Collection

Lit: Literature, printed sources

NE: Not executed

PRO: Public Record Office

RIBA: Devey Collection, Drawings Collection, British Architectural Library. The figures in brackets show the number of sheets

S: Documentary sources

Stone 1886: *RIBA Journal of Proceedings* III N.S., 9 Dec 1886 p. 69

Catalogue by Date

Vicarage, South Benfleet (Essex)
New vicarage for the Revd H.R. Lloyd.
E: 1846
S: RIBA plans and sections (3) Godfrey index records an early perspective of South Benfleet vicarage which was rejected by the Royal Academy (Fig. 2).

Oakfield, Smart's Hill, Penshurst (Kent)
Unidentified work for the Revd George Richard Boissier.
E: c.1847
S: Godfrey index *Very early work*; Kent Archive Office: Woodgate Papers U1050/C192; RIBA Sale particulars of *Cottage Residence, Smart's Hill, Penshurst Kent* d.1858.
Mrs Boissier sold Oakfield after her husband died in 1858 and moved to The Grove. It has now been altered and enlarged.

Parsonage?
Design for an unidentified house.
E?: 1848
S: RIBA plan (1)

Penshurst (Kent)
Village and estate improvements for Philip Charles Sidney, 1st Baron De L'Isle and Dudley, and after 1851 for Sir Philip Sidney, 2nd Lord De L'Isle and Dudley.
Leicester Square
E: 1848-51
S: RIBA plans, elevations and photographs (21); Penshurst Place, perspectives (2) (Figs. 4, 5, 6).
Two new cottages were added to the range framing the entrance to the churchyard.
Gateway Lodge
E: c.1858
S: RIBA plans and elevations (6) (Fig. 9)
Butcher's Shop
E: c.1860
S: RIBA elevations (1); Kent Archives Office: De L'Isle U1500 P10/1 (Fig. 12).
Addition of shop window and chimney.
Saddler's Shop
E: c.1860
S: RIBA photograph (1); Kent Archives Office: De L'Isle U1500 P10/3.
Addition of new shop window.
Cottages at Rogues Hill, Ennisfield and Cinder Hill in groups of three, some treated as a Hall house. Cottage at Well Place Farm. Improvements and picturesque additions to other estate cottages.
E: c.1860-77
S: RIBA plans and elevations (7) (Fig. 11).

Ashour Lodge
E: 1861
S: RIBA plans, elevations and perspective sketch (1), (Fig. 10).
Medway Bridge
E: 1873
S: RIBA plans and elevations (5).
Lit: CL: 23 December 1899, p. 814.

A Pair of Cottages
Contract drawing for unidentified cottages
E: 1850
S: RIBA elevation (1), (Fig. 3).
Signed *Thomas Barber February 1850*. Sketch of coat of arms and fleur-de-lis. Barber is not recorded as a builder in the neighbourhood of Penshurst.

House for a Doctor
Preliminary designs for an unidentified house.
E?: 1850
S: RIBA plans and elevations (5).
Two alternative schemes were prepared in the Italian villa and Tudor styles. The house was to have the usual middle class accommodation, a surgery, consulting and waiting rooms. A note refers to a *site adjoining Toll Bar*.

South Park, Penshurst (Kent)
Estate work for Lieut. Gen. Sir Henry Hardinge, later 1st Viscount Hardinge.
Home Farm
New barn, cow sheds and sties
E: 1850
S: RIBA section (1), (Fig. 7, 8).
West Lodge
E: 1853-4
S: RIBA plans and elevations (5).
Lit: DNB VIII p. 1226.
The builder was Richard Collins.

Chafford Arms, Fordcombe (Kent)
New public house for Lieut. Gen. Hardinge.
E: 1851
S: RIBA plans (1).
It had a kitchen, taproom, bar and parlour, four bedrooms, a dressing room above; there were stables and a detached brewhouse containing a bread oven and two coppers; the builder was Henry Constable.

Cottage for Miss Yates
Design for a cottage, possibly to be built at The Birches, Penshurst.
E?: 1851
S: RIBA plans and elevations (1).

Cottage
Design for an unidentified cottage with a two-storey bay window.
E?: 1851
S: RIBA plans, elevations and section (1).

Lodge
Design for an unidentified single-storey lodge.
E?: 1851
S: RIBA plan and elevations (1).

Laundry Cottage
Design for an unidentified cottage with a wash house.
E?: 1851
S: RIBA plans and elevations (2).

Cottage
Design for an unidentified single-storey cottage.
E?: 1851
S: RIBA plan (1).

Church of St Peter, Fordcombe (Kent)
Lych gate for Lieut. Gen. Hardinge.
E: c.1851
S: RIBA elevation (1).
Replaced. It had a simple frame and tiled roof.

Penshurst Place (Kent)
Alterations including the addition of laundry, stabling and outhouses, replanning of drives and formal gardens, and restoration of the Buckingham Building for 2nd Lord De L'Isle and Dudley.
E: 1851-70
S: RIBA plan and elevations (19); Kent Archives Office: De L'Isle U1500 P5/1-2, P6, P10/2 & 7, P12/1, P14/4; Penhurst Place two elevations and photographs; (Figs. 16, 17, 18, 64).
Com: Cbk 1877 Sep £300

Fordcombe Parsonage (Kent)
New parsonage for the Revd Philip Stanhope Dodd.
E: 1852
S: RIBA plans (1); Ecclesiastical Commissioners file 41221.
It was built to a different design.

House
Design for an unidentified house.
E?: 1852
S: RIBA plans (1).

Foreman's House, Lea Bridge Waterworks (London: Hackney)
New house with office and store for Metropolitan Water Board.
E: 1855-6
S: RIBA plans and elevations (6); Metropolitan Water Board Minute Books, vols. 35 and 36.
C: £692
Com: £39
The ground floor was of stone, rough-cast and timbering above, decorative bargeboards and tiled roof. Demolished 1985. O.E. Coope was a director; he employed Devey later at Rochetts.

Cottage
Designs for a cottage adjoining a group of Georgian houses.
E?: 1855
S: RIBA plans and elevations (2).

Garden Cottage, Broomhill, Southborough (Kent)
New cottage for Sir David Salomons.
NE: 1855
S: RIBA plans and elevations (3).
A substantial building of stone with half-timbering above, a polygonal stair turret, cellar, balcony across one gable and scrolled bargeboards. A tablet bears the monogram DS.
Alternative design for a single-storey cottage for Sir David Salomons.
E?: 1855
S: RIBA plans and elevations (2).
Stone built with timbered gables. Monogram DS in gable. The first design was too expensive. Demolished.

Farm
Design for unidentified farmhouse and dairy buildings.
E?: c.1855
S: RIBA plan and sections (1).

Penshurst Cemetery Chapel, Pounds Bridge (Kent)
E: c.1855-7
S: Stone December 1886.
The new cemetery had been consecrated in August 1855 and an Order in Council of May 1857 prohibited further burials in Penshurst Church and churchyard.

Betteshanger House (Kent)
Additions including the James Tower, recasing and alterations to the house, laying out garden terraces for Sir Walter Charles James, later 1st Baron Northbourne.
E: c.1856-81
S: RIBA plans and elevations and photographs (18), (Figs. 19, 20, 21, 22).
Com: Cbk 1867 June £124, 1868 January £75, 1869 January £159, 1874 April £27 June £25, 1877 March £166, 1882 September £67.
Lit: *In Memoriam + Walter Charles, Lord Northbourne, of Betteshanger, Kent and Jarrow Grange, Durham.* Privately printed.
Double cottage
S: RIBA perspectives and plans (3).
C: £240
Cottage now known as The Cloisters
S: RIBA plans and elevations (6), (Fig. 23).
Lit: Girouard

House
Design for an unidentified house.
E?: 1856
S: RIBA elevations (1).

Double Cottage
Design and contract drawing for unidentified cottages near Penshurst.
E: 1856
S: RIBA plans, elevations and details (3).
The builder was Richard Collins, who worked at South Park.

Double Cottage
Design and contract drawing for unidentified cottages near Penshurst.
E: 1856
S: RIBA plans, elevations and sections (2).
The builder was Richard Collins (see above).

Hammerfield and Steam Hammer Lodge, Penshurst, (Kent)
Large addition to house and new lodge for James Nasmyth.
E: 1857-9
S: RIBA elevations (2), (Fig. 13).
Lit: Samuel Smiles ed., *Autobiography of James Nasmyth,* London, 1883, DNB XIV p. 116.

Culver Hill, Penshurst (Kent)
Gardener's cottage for James Nasmyth.
E: 1857-9
S: RIBA plans, elevations and photographs (10), (Figs. 14, 15).

Cliveden (Buckinghamshire)
New lodges, cottages, cow house and additions to Spring Cottage for Harriet, Duchess of Sutherland and George Granville Leveson-Gower, 2nd Duke of Sutherland.
  Woodgate Cottage
  E: 1857
  S: RIBA plan (1).
  C: £400
  Windsor Lodge
  E: c.1857
  S: RIBA plans and elevations (5).
  Ferry Cottage
  S: RIBA plans, section, elevations and photograph (12).
  Spring Cottage
  S: RIBA photograph (1).
  Additions including veranda and balcony above to the octagonal Gothick tearoom designed by Peter Nicholson for the Countess of Orkney in 1813.
  Cow house
  Cliveden estate office: plans, elevations and sections (8).
  This seems to have been incorporated in the buildings now called Dairy Cottages.
Lit: DNB XI p. 1031.
Devey was introduced to the Duke by Lord De L'Isle.

Trentham (Staffordshire)
Cottages, lodge and village school for the Duke of Sutherland.
  Tittensor Cottages
  E: c.1857
  S: Stafford County Record Office plan and elevation D593/H/12/2/193/6, 10, 19; H/12/2/889 (4). RIBA photograph (1).
  This pair are on the east side of the A34.
  Tittensor Cottage
  Design for a large unidentified house.
  NE: 1857
  S: Stafford CRO elevations D593/H/12/2/192/11, 29, 32, 35 (4).
  Possibly for Tittensor Manor which was built to the designs of the agent, Thomas Roberts.
  Bishop's Gate Cottage
  Design for additions to an unidentified cottage.
  E?: c.1857
  S: Stafford County Record Office plans D593/H/12/5/20/17, 18 (2).
  Thatched Barn
  Design for unidentified barn.
  E?: c.1857
  S: Stafford County Record Office elevation D593/H/12/5/20/4 (1).
  Toft Farm
  NE: c.1858
  S: Stafford County Record Office plans and elevations D593/H/12/2/227/1-14 (14).
  A proposal for rebuilding, not carried out.
  Toft Cottages
  E: c.1858
  S: RIBA photograph (1).
  A pair of new cottages.
  Gravel Pit Lodge
  E: 1859
  S: RIBA plan, elevations and photograph (4); Stafford County Record Office elevations D593/H/12/2/211/2, 3 (2) (Fig. 24).
  Tittensor School
  E: 1859
  S: RIBA photographs (2) National Society File.
  A new village school.
  Heath Cottages
  Design for an unidentified double cottage.
  E?: 1860
  S: RIBA plans and elevations (5).
  Hem Heath Cottage
  Design for an unidentified house.
  E?: 1862
  S: RIBA plans and elevations (5).
  Other work continued at Hem Heath up until 1877.
  Com: Cbk 1868 August £37, 1877 March £167.

Altnarynie Lodge, Achferry, by Lairg (Highland Region)
Design for a shooting lodge for Francis, Lord Elcho.
NE: 1858
S: National Library of Scotland: Sutherland Deposit Dep 313/1285 George Loch to William Fowler (1857-59) 1858 bundle, dep 313/1289 Scouri District 1857-59;

Dunrobin Estate Architect's Office plans, elevations (5) and specification.

Evander McIver wrote to Fowler 22 June 1858 to say that the design would *cost double that anticipated,* and would he amend the designs and specification to make them *quite intelligible to the contractors of this country.* The lodge was not built and Lord Elcho gave up his tenancy in 1860.

Dunrobin Estate (Highland Region)
Estate building work for the Duke of Sutherland.
Old Barn Cottages now known as Big Barns
E: 1858-9
S: Dunrobin Estate Architect's Office: plans, elevations and sections (5), RIBA plans (1), National Library of Scotland, Sutherland Deposit Dep 313/1285 Loch to Fowler (1857-59) 1858 bundle 23 February 1858 reference to *the altered Old Barn.*
Big Barns is now ruinous.
Grieve's House, Culmaily Farm and Culmaily Smithy, Golspie
E: 1858-9
S: Loch to Fowler op.cit. Devey *carries with him sketches of Mr Sellar's Grieve's Cottage.*
The site of the Grieve's house was chosen while Devey was at Dunrobin, but both buildings seem to have been designed by Fowler with picturesque additions by Devey.
Tower Lodge, Golspie
E: 1858-60
S: Ian MacKenzie-Kerr perspectives (2); RIBA plans and elevations (5); Dunrobin Estate Architect's Office: plans, elevations and details (8), Devey to Fowler 22 March 1859; Dep 313/1286. 1294, 1566, 1568 (Figs. 25, 26).
Mr Matheson's House, now Rose Cottage, Dunrobin
Preliminary designs for addition of a corner window
E: c.1858
S: Dep 313/1285.
Langdale Farm House, Strathnaver
Design for a new house for Patrick Sellar.
NE: 1858
S: Dunrobin Estate Architect's Office: plans and elevations (2); Dep 313/1285 Loch to Fowler (1857-59) 1858 bundle 2 March, 25 April, 25 June 1858.
Devey was again asked to improve a design *and ask him for any suggestions by which the elevations may be improved, at present it is as ugly as possible.*
Lochinver House
E?: 1859
S: Dep 313/1294 Loch to Fowler 2 February 1859
Devey designed buttresses and roof trusses for a house converted from a row of fish curing houses.
Mr Begg's House, now Moray House, Fountain Road, Golspie
E: 1859-60
S: RIBA plans, elevations and section (1); Dunrobin Estate Architect's Office: elevations and details (1); Dep 313/1285 Loch to Fowler (1857-9) 1858 bundle 19 April 1858, 1286 18 March 1859, 1294 10 January 1860, 10 March 1860.

Begg was a general merchant who submitted plans for his new house to the estate, *You will at once see how entirely inadmissible it is - it is the worst style of suburban villa.* Devey produced alternative designs which were built.
Venison Larder, Dunrobin Farm
E: 1861
S: Dunrobin Estate Architect's Office: plan, elevations and sections (1) Dep 313.1296 Peacock to Fowler April 1861.
Old Dairy, Dunrobin
E: c.1861
Attributed to Devey on stylistic grounds. Now a private house.
Railway station and bridge at Dunrobin.
Preliminary designs incorporating a statue of the 2nd Duke of Sutherland.
NE: c.1865
S: Dunrobin Estate Architect's Office: perspectives (2).

Keeper's Cottage
Preliminary and executed designs for an unidentified cottage with poultry house and run.
E: 1859
S: RIBA plans and elevations (7).

Lilleshall Estate (Shropshire)
Design for an unidentified double cottage for the Duke of Sutherland.
E?: c.1859
S: RIBA plans and elevations (5).

Cottage
Design for an unidentified cottage.
E?: c.1859
S: RIBA elevation and plan of chimney (1).

Orchardleigh Estate, Lullington (Somerset)
Cottages on Lullington Green, Keeper's Cottage, Park Farm and Parsonage for William Duckworth.
Cottages on Green
Preliminary designs in Wealden and the local vernacular styles.
E: 1860
S: RIBA plans and elevations (10), (Fig. 38).
The cottages were built in the local style.
Keeper's Cottage
Cottage adjoining existing shed.
E: 1864
S: RIBA plans and elevations (6).
The cottage was built to this design.
Park Farm
E: 1863
S: Duckworth MSS: contract drawings, plans and elevation (3) and specification.
The builder was Thomas Ashton.
Parsonage and stables
For the Revd William Arthur Duckworth.
E: 1866-7
S: Duckworth MSS: W.A. Duckworth's diary 1866-7
Com: Cbk 1867 January £32, 1869 November £88.

Mentmore Estate (Buckinghamshire)
Lodges, stables and riding school, cottages and farm buildings for Baron Mayer Amschel de Rothschild.
Williamson's Farm
Addition of barn and byre.
E: 1860-1
S: Buckinghamshire Record Office: D/RO/4/34 AR 49/70 (3-4) plan and elevations; N.M. Rothschild Archives: RAL/XII/41/5.
The builders were J. Durley and Son.
Cheddington Road
Advising on change of course of highway.
E: 1865-6
Com: £97
Crafton Lodge
E: c.1868
S: RIBA plans (1).
South Lodge
E: 1868
S: RIBA photograph (1); N.M. Rothschild Archives: RAL/XII/41/6 (Fig. 28).
Stables
E: 1869-70
S: N.M. Rothschild Archives: RAL/XII/41/6
The builder was Edward Dawson.
Riding School
NE: 1869-70
S: RIBA plans and elevations (9).
The early designs were for an expensive thirteen-bay building, a plain version was built.
Wing Lodge
E: 1870
S: RIBA photograph (1); N.M. Rothschild Archives: RAL/XII/41/6
The builders were J. Durley and Sons of Bierton.
Three cottages at Rowden Farm
E: 1870-1
S: RIBA plans and elevations (5); N.M. Rothschild Archives: RAL/XII/41/6
Unidentified and probably demolished.
Two cottages at Ledburn
E: 1870-2
S: N.M. Rothschild Archives: RAL/XII/41/6
The builders were J. Durley and Sons of Bierton.
Classical garden building
NE: c.1870
S: Buckinghamshire Record Office: DRO/4/34 AR 49/70 (6-8).
Three cottages now called Mentmore End, Cheddington Station
E: c.1870
General estate work
S: N.M. Rothschild Archives: I/2/17-22.
Com: Cbk 1867 December £100, 1871 July £300, 1872 October £200, 1875 August £793.

Hulcott (Buckinghamshire)
Village school, additions to the Rectory and improvements to Manor Farm for the Revd Edward Bonus and Sir Anthony de Rothschild.
E: 1860-4

S: Buckinghamshire Record Office: AR 39/65: 27/1-6 plans and elevations of school (6); N.M. Rothschild Archives XIV/13/0 p. 132.
Com: £100 for *Plans and Superintendance of the School and Parsonage*.

Strathpeffer Spa (Highland Region)
Planning of town and additions to the Pump Room for Anne, Countess of Cromartie and 3rd Duchess of Sutherland.
E: 1861-8
S: Cromartie Estate Office, Castle Leod: Print of plan and aerial perspective of town, design for Pump Room (1); Scottish Record Office: Cromartie MSS CM 271, 712, GD 305.1858-60.
Com: Cbk 1868 August £100.
Lit: T.C.C. Telfer, *The Architecture of Strathpeffer* Dissertation, Edinburgh College of Art, Heriot-Watt University, Department of Architecture, 1981.

Lodges, Northiam (East Sussex)
Designs for unidentified lodges.
E?: 1862
S: RIBA plans and elevations (16).

Church of St Mary, Leigh (Kent)
Restoration of the chancel for the Lay Impropriator, Lord De L'Isle and Dudley.
E: 1862
S: Kent Archives Office: Leigh Parish Muniments P223 8/2; Incorporated Church Building Society 3rd series file 5616.
Lit: *The Builder* 8 November 1862, p. 807.

Lodge
Design for an unidentified lodge.
E?: 1862
S: RIBA elevations and section (5).
The monogram RE is shown in the gable.

Ellison Church of England Schools, Jarrow (Tyne and Wear)
New schools for Sir Walter and Lady James.
E: 1862-3
S: RIBA lithograph perspective (1), Durham County Record Office: E/SBP plans, elevations and details (10), (Fig. 41).
C: £945
Lit: *The Builder* 13 June 1863, p. 430.
Demolished. Accommodation for 96 boys and girls, and 100 infants, built of stone in the Tudor style. The master's house was a brick tower, square in plan and three storeys high.

Chelsham Lodge, Chelsham (Surrey)
Design for alterations to the offices for John Henry Daniell.
E: 1863
S: RIBA plan and section (2).
The house cannot be identified.

Moffats
Design for an addition to a country house for Mr Daniell.
E?: c.1863
S: RIBA elevations (2); Godfrey index.
This house cannot be identified.

Ascott Poultry Houses, Wing (Buckinghamshire)
New poultry houses and runs for Baron Mayer Amschel de Rothschild.
E: 1863
S: RIBA plan, elevation and sections (1).

Buckland National School (Buckinghamshire)
Village school and master's house for the Revd Edward Bonus.
E: 1863
S: Buckinghamshire Record Office: N.S. 4552 plans, elevations and details (7); The National Society file; RIBA photographs (2), (Fig. 27).
Lit: *The Builder* 13 February 1864, p. 122; Constance Battersea, *Reminiscences*, London, 1922.

Whitchurch School (Buckinghamshire)
Village school and master's house for the Revd Alfred Turner.
E: 1863-4
S: RIBA perspective and photographs (3), Buckinghamshire Record Office: AR39/65:64/1A-6A plan, elevations and section (6) (Fig. 39).
C. School £510, house £140.
Com: Cbk 1869 January £49.

Crocker's Hatch Lodge and Fordcombe Lodge, Ashurst Park (Kent)
New lodges for George Field.
E: 1864
S: RIBA plan and elevations (5).

Wickwar Parsonage (Gloucestershire)
New parsonage for Henry John Reynolds Moreton, 3rd Earl Ducie and the Revd Ralph Lyon.
E: 1864
S: RIBA elevations and photograph (3).
Com: Cbk 1869 December £12.

Park House and Hall Place Estate, Leigh (Kent)
House for estate agent and other work for Thomas Farmer Bailey.
E: 1864-6
Com: Cbk 1867 February £59.

Crown Point Estate, Norwich (Norfolk)
Lodge, double cottage and other buildings for Sir Robert John Harvey Harvey Bart.
E: 1864-9
S: RIBA plans and elevations (5); Norfolk Record Office: BR 35/2/51/K elevations of lodge and cottage (2).
Com: Cbk 1869 January £229, paid £81 in 1874.
Harvey was a partner in the Norwich Crown Bank who speculated unsuccessfully on the Stock Exchange. He shot himself in July 1870 and Devey only obtained part of the amount due to him from his executors. The North Lodge and Whittingham White House are by Devey.

Chiltern Hills Waterworks, Dancers End (Buckinghamshire)
Waterworks buildings for the Chiltern Hills Spring Water Co.
E: c.1864
S: Godfrey index.
Demolished.

Fonthill Estate (Wiltshire)
Cottages and retaining walls adjoining the Fonthill Arch for Alfred Morrison.
Turnpike Cottages
E: 1864
S: RIBA plans and elevations (4).
Double cottage with central arch at Berwick St Leonard
E: c.1865
S: RIBA plans, elevations and section (6).
Thatched Lodge
E: c.1865
S: RIBA elevation and photograph (2), (Fig. 57).
Unidentified double cottage
E: c.1865
S: RIBA photograph (1).
Retaining wall at Fonthill Arch
E: 1876-7
S: RIBA photographs (3), (Fig. 58).
Com: Cbk 1867 September £133, 1877 March £37

Aston Clinton House and Estate (Buckinghamshire)
Work on the mansion, new stables and lodge for Sir Anthony de Rothschild Bart.
E: 1864-77
Com: Cbk 1875 August £704, 1876 October £533, 1877 January £97 April £77 July £67 November £84 1878 February £321; N.M. Rothschild Archives: XIV 13/0 1864 April £25 for professional charges, I/2/1 1866 February £63, XIV/13/0 1867 December £100 plans for various cottages etc, I/2/19 1871 May £200 on a/c Archts. charges in connection with works at Aston Clinton (stable a/c), XIV/13/0 1875 July £100 on a/c for drawings etc, I/2/22 1876 November £1165, 1877 May £305 August £132 November £152.
Lit: *The Architect* 6 January 1872 p. 17.
Devey took over these works from George Henry Stokes; the builder was George Myers. The mansion is demolished, the West Lodge and the stables survive, the latter converted into offices.

Heathfield Lodge
Designs for an unidentified house.
E?: 1865
S: RIBA plans and elevations (4).

Chafyn-Grove Cottages, Zeals (Wiltshire)
Almshouses for William Chafyn-Grove.
E: 1865
S: RIBA photographs (2), (Fig. 59).
Tudor style. A commemorative plaque reads. *To the*

ear Memory of his Mother These Alms Houses were
rected and Endowed by William Chafyn Grove A.D.
865. Blessed is the man who considereth the poor the
ord will deliver him in time of trouble. Psalm XLI

Church House, Tortworth (Gloucestershire)
New house for Lord Ducie.
E: c.1865
S: RIBA plans and elevation (4).
New vicarage for Lord Ducie.
E: c.1879
Post Office Cottages
Double cottage for Lord Ducie.
E: c.1879
Com: Cbk 1879 November £85.

Conservatory, Frankfurt (West Germany)
Preliminary design for Baroness (Hannah) Matilde wife
of Willy de Rothschild.
E?: c.1865
S: RIBA plans and elevation (1).

Thatched Cottages
Designs for unidentified cottages.
E?: c.1865
S: RIBA perspectives, plans and elevations (9).

Village Cross, Wingerworth (Derbyshire)
For the Hon. Mrs Adelaide Augusta Wilhelmina Hunloke.
E: c.1865
S: RIBA perspective and elevation (2).
Mrs Hunloke was the sister of the 2nd Lord De L'Isle. The
cross has disappeared.

Double Cottage, Eaton estate (Cheshire)
Design for cottages for Hugh Lupus, Earl Grosvenor.
E?: c.1865
S: RIBA plans and elevations (5).

Charters, Sunningdale (Berkshire)
New stables for Edward William Terrick Hamilton MP.
E: 1866-9
S: Godfrey index.
Com: Cbk 1867 January £37, 1868 January £37, 1869
November £56.

Holwood, Keston (London; Bromley)
Unidentified work for Robert Monsey Rolfe, 1st Baron
Cranworth.
E: 1866
Com: Cbk 1867 January £54.
Lit: DNB XVII p. 158.

Akeley Wood, Akeley (Buckinghamshire)
New country house for Charles Pilgrim.
E: 1866-7
S: RIBA photographs (3), (Fig. 42).
Com: Cbk 1867 £461, 1883 £5.

House in France
Design for a house, possibly for Baron James de
Rothschild.
E?: 1866-7
S: RIBA elevation (1).
Com: Cbk 1867 February £52.

Wilcote House, Wilcote (Oxfordshire)
Large addition to a farmhouse for Charles Urban Sartoris.
E: 1866-70, 1874, 1877
S: RIBA elevation, perspective and photograph; Northamptonshire Record Office: S(R) 438 plans.
Com: Cbk 1867 January £80, 1868 January £337 Xmas
£162, 1870 January £304, 1874 October £40, 1877 March
£97.

Unidentified Work
For Louisa, Lady Ashburton.
E: 1866
Com: Cbk 1867 January £41.
Lit: Virginia Surtees, *The Ludovisi Goddess* Salisbury,
1984.
This may have been connected with the development
of her Addiscombe Villa estate.

Unidentified Work
For Mr Cooke.
E: 1866
Com: Cbk 1867 January £5.

Blithfield Estate, Rugeley (Staffordshire)
New house and unidentified work for Sir William
Bagot, 3rd Baron Bagot.
E: 1866, 1874, 1882
S: RIBA plans (1).
Com: Cbk 1867 February £19, 1874 June £83, 1882
January £33.

Unidentified Work
For Mrs Perry.
E: 1866
Com: Cbk 1867 February £5.

Zeals House (Wiltshire)
Large additions for William Chafyn-Grove and his
sister Julia Elizabeth.
E: 1866-72
S: RIBA photographs (2), (Fig. 60).
Com: Cbk 1867 January £361, 1869 August £20
August £15 November £22, 1870 April £20 October £6,
1872 August £16.
The old house was repaired and a drawing room and
study added. New offices and tower.

Rochetts, South Weald (Essex)
Alterations and new wing and tower for Octavius
Edward Coope.
E: 1866-73
S: RIBA elevation (1).
Com: Cbk 1867 January £73, 1868 January £146, 1869
January £6, 1873 October £323.

158 George Devey

Much of the house, including Devey's additions, has been demolished.

Unidentified Work
For Mr Hargreaves.
E: 1867
Com: Cbk 1867 June £15.

Palace House, Newmarket (Suffolk)
Preliminary design for a new dining room for Baron Mayer Amschel de Rothschild.
E: 1867
S: RIBA section.

Hamptworth Lodge Estate (Wiltshire)
Unidentified work for Robert Duncombe Shafto MP.
NE: 1867
Com: Cbk 1868 January £136.

Unidentified Work
For Dr Robert Greenhalgh.
E: 1867, 1885
Com: Cbk 1868 January £10, 1885 November £5.
The Medical Directory for 1868 and 1885 shows Greenhalgh living at 77 Grosvenor Street, and then at 35 Cavendish Square.

Cottage
Design for an unidentified cottage.
E?: c.1867
S: RIBA elevations (3).

Mount Lodge, The Mount, St Leonard's (East Sussex)
New stables and coach house.
E: c.1867
S: RIBA plans and elevation (1).
Signed by Devey's surveyor Henry Owen and the builder William John Rodda. Demolished.

Double Cottage
Design for unidentified cottages.
E?: c.1867
S: RIBA plans, elevation, perspective and details (3).

Unidentified Work
For Mr Shackle.
E: 1867-8
Com: Cbk 1867 March £47, 1868 January £90.

Grateley House, Grateley (Hampshire)
Unidentified work for Emanuel Boutcher.
E: 1867-9
S: Godfrey index.
Com: Cbk 1868 January £70, 1870 January £136.

Lion House, Newport, Berkeley (Gloucestershire)
Large additions including a tower for George Hooper.
E: 1867-70
S: RIBA elevation and photographs (4).
Com: Cbk 1867 July £50 November £50, 1868 February £50 June £50 December £50, 1870 July £50 October £12, 1872 November £308 paid by Exors.
Demolished.

All Saints, Buckland (Buckinghamshire)
Restoration for the Revd Edward Bonus.
E: 1867-9
S: RIBA photographs (2); Incorporated Church Building Society file 6685.
Lit: *The Architect* 4 December 1869, p. 280.
C: £1630
The builder was Chapell of Northampton. New chancel roof and south porch, oak choir stalls and pews; roof releaded. Minton tiles in chancel. Pulpit and reredos by Grimsley of Oxford, the latter painted by Cox and Son of the Strand.

The Friarage, Rickford's Hill, Aylesbury (Buckinghamshire)
Additions for Miss Goodall.
E: 1867-9
Com: Cbk 1868 January £27, 1869 December £25.
An eighteenth century house to which Devey added a pair of two-storey bay windows at the rear and carried out some work on the offices, of which only the chimney survives.

St Alban's Court, Nonnington (Kent)
New mansion house, stables, gardener's cottage, terraces, new lodge, estate cottages and almshouses for William Oxenden Hammond.
St Alban's Court
E: 1875-9
S: RIBA plans and elevations (91), (Figs. 75, 76, 77, 78, 92).
Estate cottages
E: 1872-86
S: RIBA plans and elevations (16).
Almshouses
E: 1886-7
S: RIBA plans, elevations and details (21), specification.
Com: Cbk 1867 December £125, 1869 December £113, 1871 May £37, 1872 November £50, 1874 August £726, 1875 October £75, 1876 January £100 January £84 April £24 July £37 October £75, 1877 January £177 April £50 July £50 November £50, 1878 £150 October £116, 1879 February £198 October £88, 1880 February £93, 1883 October £13, 1884 July £12.
The builder was William John Adcock of Dover, the clerk of works William Hill. There are eight double cottages in Nonnington and Easole Street. (Fig. 79) James Williams continued to work on the estate up to at least 1896 when he designed the pair now called Gooseberry Hall Cottage.

Farnborough Hill (Hampshire)
New laundry, lodges, cottage and garden layout for Thomas Longman.
E: 1867, 1876
Laundry
S: RIBA elevations and section (2).

Demolished.
Cottage
S: RIBA plans and elevations (6).
This cannot be identified.
Single-storey lodge
S: RIBA elevation and details (1).
This cannot be identified
North Lodge
Com: Cbk 1868 January £26, 1876 August £86.

Titsey Place, Oxted (Surrey)
South Lodge and other unidentified work for Granville William Leveson-Gower.
E: 1868, 1873
S: RIBA South Lodge elevations (2).
Com: Cbk 1873 October £139.

Ongar (Essex)
Unidentified work for Mr Lewis.
E: 1868
S: Godfrey index.
Com: Cbk 1868 May £31.

The Deanery, Hereford (Herefordshire)
Unidentified work for the Very Revd the Hon. George Herbert.
E: 1868
Com: Cbk 1869 January £15.
Lit: F.T. Havergal *Fasti Herefordenses* 1869 *The present Dean has expended a considerable sum in enlarging and improving the Decanal residence at his own cost, A.D. 1867-9.*

Model Farm, Silesia (Poland)
Design for Baron Ferdinand de Rothschild.
E?: 1868
S: RIBA perspective (1) (Fig. 29).
Com: Cbk 1868 June £42.
Baron Anselm had a property in Silesia called Schillersdorf and the farm may have been built there. A note on the sketch records that it was to be sent via Messrs Behrens at Hamburg.

Chearsley Vicarage (Buckinghamshire)
New vicarage for the Revd William Gilbert.
E: 1868-9
S: RIBA photographs (2); Commissioners for Queen Anne's Bounty, Bundle PH 1869 E 1617 *Chearsley Oxford* plans, elevations and sections (11) specification.
C: £916, stables £147.
Com: Cbk 1869 August £30, estimated at £55.
The builder was George Cooper.

Farnborough School (Hampshire)
New school for the Revd Robert Francis Scot of St Peter's, Farnborough.
E: 1868-9, 1874
S: Hampshire Record Office 20M65 plans, elevations and section (9); National Society file.
C: £481; additional school room and master's house £477.
Com: Cbk 1869 January £23.
This cannot be identified; probably demolished.

Hemsted Park, Benenden (Kent)
Estate and village buildings for Gathorne Gathorne-Hardy, 1st Earl of Cranbrook.
E: 1868, 1874-7, 1881
Staplehurst Lodge
S: RIBA plans and elevations (20).
Cranbrook Lodge
S: RIBA perspective, plans and elevations (8). (Fig. 108).
Gardener's Cottage
S: RIBA plans and elevation (2).
Toll Cottage, now Beech House
S: RIBA elevation (1).
Bull Inn, Benenden
S: RIBA elevations (1).
Benenden Village School
S: RIBA perspective and elevations (4); Kent Archive Office DE/S 20/1/1-3 plans and elevations (3); National Society file (Fig. 40).
C: £837
Com: £56
Old Manor House
S: RIBA details and elevation of gate (2).
Church Cottage
Additions including chimney stacks.
St George's Club
E: 1882
S: RIBA plans and elevations (5); Stone December 1886; Francis Haslewood *The Parish of Benenden, Kent* Ipswich, 1889.
Com: Cbk 1874 June £107, 1877 April £59, 1881 November £42.
Lit: A.E. Gathorne-Hardy, *Gathorne-Hardy First Earl of Cranbrook*, London, 1910.
When Hardy bought the estate the Jacobean house was in a dangerous condition, and was replaced by a new mansion designed by David Brandon, who also restored the church. Devey was responsible for the small buildings up to his death, when he was replaced by T.S. Cotman of Ipswich.

Ash Lawn, Benenden (Kent)
New house for the Misses Neve.
E: 1868-71
S: RIBA plans (2).
C: £2049
Com: Cbk 1868 December £50, 1871 May £58, 1877 March £2.
The builder was Philip Newnham.

Brantingham Thorpe (Humberside)
Additions to and recasing of eighteenth-century Gothick villa for Christopher Sykes.
E: 1868-71, 1876-8
S: RIBA plans, elevations, perspectives and photographs (18); Archive of Art and Design: Whitefriars Glass Co. *Window Glass Order Book* AAD 1/5-1977, (Figs. 43, 44, 45).
Com: Cbk 1868 December £65, 1870 January £142, 1871 January £39, 1874 January £336, 1878 January £86, 1880 January £114, 1881 August £28, 1882 May £128.

Lit: Christopher Sykes, *Four Studies in Loyalty*, London, 1946.

Lady Mead, Little Kimble (Buckinghamshire)
Additions for Joseph Parrott.
E: 1868, 1877
S: Buckinghamshire Record Office D/WIG/2/4/25 (part.)
A wing was added on the north of the house.

Coombe Warren, Kingston-upon-Thames, (London; Kingston)
Additions to a country house, rebuilding after a fire, stables, lodges, orangery, Bay House and garden buildings for Bertram Wodehouse Currie.
E: Coombe Warren I 1868-9, Coombe Warren II 1870-2
S: RIBA plans, elevations and photographs (56); Godfrey Collection: specification *Specification of the several Materials to be supplied and works to be performed in the erection of New Stable Buildings and the Enclosing wall side of Roadway to Stable Yard at Coombe Warren in the County of Surrey for Bertram Wodehouse Currie Esq. Under the direction and in accordance with the Drawings and Specifications prepared by Mr. George Devey of 123 Bond Street. December 1880*; Archive of Art and Design: Whitefriars Glass Co. *Window Glass Order Book* AAD 1/3-1977 p. 41, (Figs. 46, 47, 49, 50).
Com: Cbk 1870 January £131 February £101, 1877 April £117 July £64 November £150, 1878 October £331, 1879 February £65 October £140, 1881 April £50 August £100 November £68, 1881 April £164 September £110 October £50, 1883 March £57 June £50 October £81, 1884 May £50 July £30, 1885 May £50. (It is not possible to distinguish payments made in respect of Coombe Warren from those made for work on No. 1 Richmond Terrace. Fee note counterfoils record payments to Smith and Co. in October 1878, to Steinitz, Dickson and Jackson in February 1879, Holland and Hannen were paid in 1881-5, C.H. and J. Mabey in May 1885.)
The builder of Coombe Warren I was James Haward; George Myers built Coombe Warren II; Holland and Hannen built the stables.

Ferndale, later Kelsall Lodge, Ferndale Road, Tunbridge Wells (Kent)
Suburban house for Messrs Haward Brothers.
E: 1869
S: Tunbridge Wells Borough Council, Planning Services plans (5).
Lit: *The Architect* 14 February 1890, illustration; James D. Kornwolf, *M.H. Baillie Scott and the Arts and Crafts Movement*, Baltimore and London, 1972, pp. 14-17, (Fig. 48).
Demolished. James Haward was the builder of Coombe Warren I. It was the first speculative building with which Devey was involved.

Coryton Manor Estate, Okehampton (Devon)
Unidentified work for Thomas Holdsworth Newman.
E: 1869
Com: Cbk 1869 November £51.
Probably cottages arranged around a square, a pair on the east and west, a group of four on the south called Lowertown Cottages and another pair, Church Cottages.

34 Grosvenor Place (London; Westminster)
Unidentified work for the Hon. William Warren Vernon.
E: 1869
Com: Cbk 1869 August £162, 1882 May £7.
Lit: W.W. Vernon, *Recollections of Seventy-Two Years*, London, 1917.
Demolished.

Unidentified Work
For the Rt Hon. J. Stuart Wortley.
E: 1869
Com: Cbk 1870 January £58.

Unidentified Work
For Mr Glyn.
E: 1869-70
Com: Cbk 1870 March £317.

Calverley Grange, now Pembury Grange, Sandown Park, Pembury (Kent)
New country house and gardener's cottage for Neville Ward.
E: 1869-71
S: RIBA elevation and photographs (4), (Fig. 110).
Com: Cbk 1870 January £137, 1871 February £150, 1873 October (to Exors.) £639.
Lit: *The Builders Journal* 4 February 1896, pp. 408-10, 18 February p. 27 James Weir claims untruthfully that he designed Calverley Grange and Coombe Warren while employed in Devey's office.

Lillies, Weedon (Buckinghamshire)
New mansion, stables and lodge for Henry Cazenove.
E: 1869-71, 1874
S: RIBA plans, elevations and photographs (19)
Com: Cbk 1869 November £50 December £50, 1870 February £50 March £50 April £50 May £50 June £50 July £50 August £50 September £50 October £50 October £7 November £50, 1871 April £50 July £25 December £120, 1872 October £5, 1874 September £22 (new bay).
Lillies Farm
E: 1870
Alterations.
Double cottages Nos. 2 and 4, Nos. 21 and 23 High Street
E: 1877
Com: Cbk 1877 April £38 July £32, 1878 October £33, 1886 September £31.

Fig.110 Calverley Grange

2 High Street, Thame (Oxfordshire)
New bank building for the Bucks and Oxon Union Bank.
E: 1869-71
S: Lloyds Bank Archives, Bucks and Oxon Bank Minute Books 1869-71
Com: Cbk 1871 June £63.
Still standing, but has lost details such as a wooden balustrade.

Coombe Cottage, Kingston-upon-Thames (London; Kingston)
New stables, large additions to country house and dairy for Edward Charles Baring.
Stables
E: 1863
House and dairy
E: 1869-74
S: RIBA photographs (14), (Figs. 51, 52).
Com: Cbk 1870 January £170, 1871 January £42, 1872 January £305, 1873 July £25, 1874 July £72 October £45; Baring Brothers and Co. Ltd. *English Client Ledgers* BK1.67-9 show payments to Devey 1872 October £300, 1873 January £215, 1874 January £86 November £156.
Lit: Maurice Baring, *The Puppet Show of Memory*, London, 1922.
The builders were Haward Brothers. Morris and Co. worked on the interiors.

Church of St Augustine, Northbourne (Kent)
Restoration for Sir Walter James
E?: c.1870
S: Stone December 1886.

Church of St George, Ham (Kent)
Restoration for Sir Walter James
E?: 1870
S: Stone December 1886.

Parsonage, Ripple, Deal (Kent)
Unidentified work.
E?: c.1870
S: Stone December 1886.

Dinton School (Buckinghamshire)
New boys and girls schools and master's house for the Revd C.H. Burton.
E: 1870-1
S: Buckinghamshire Record Office AR 39/65:16/1-8 Contract drawings: plans and elevations (8); The National Society file
C: £733, fittings £66
Com: Cbk 1871 December £48.

Unidentified Work
For Sydney Kennedy.
E: 1870
Com: Cbk 1871 January £2.

Rowfant, East Grinstead (West Sussex)
Rebuilding of west front, large eastern addition to a late sixteenth-century manor house and new stable block for Sir Curtis Miranda Lampson 1st Bart.
E: 1870-3
Com: Cbk 1871 January £42, 1873 October £228.
Lit: DNB XI p. 473.
Lampson was an American, naturalised in 1849 who was vice chairman of the company responsible for laying the trans-Atlantic telegraph cable.

Swaylands, Penshurst (Kent)
Large extension for Edward Cropper.
E: 1870-4, 1877
S: RIBA elevations and section (11).
Com: Cbk 1870 February £53, 1874 February £110, 1877 March £21.
Edward Cropper was the son of a Lancashire railway engineer. The house was a modest Tudor villa built by William Woodgate in 1851. Devey added a range twice the size of the original and a tower with an ogival lead roof. Further additions were made by Henry Drummond.

High Hall, Bishop Burton (Humberside)
New house and stables for William Watt and Francis Watt.
E: 1871-5
S: Godfrey index.
Com: Cbk (to the exors. of W. and F. Watt and to Pease) 1871 September £364, 1872 May £50 October £200 December £100, 1873 April £100 July £50 October £25, 1874 January £50 April £75, 1875 June £219 July £363.
Demolished. Photographs show a house that bears no resemblance to any other by Devey, and as identification rests with Godfrey only, High Hall can only be attributed with caution. Colonel Pease was agent to Bishop Burton estate.

Hardwick School (Buckinghamshire)
New village school for the Revd W. Bigg Wither and Henry Cazenove.
E: 1871
S: National Society file.
C: £688 and fittings £21.
Com: Cbk 1871 December £40.
The schools are so low I cannot stand upright in them. The residences are under the same roof; Mr. Devey intends to utilize them in his improvements. The plans are now in the hands of the Diocesan Society - George Devey Architect is a guarantee in itself that they are to meet the Government standard.

The Lodge, Avenue Road, Langley Park, Loddon (Norfolk)
New lodge for Sir Thomas William Brograve Proctor Beauchamp Bart.
E?: 1871
S: Canadian Center for Architecture: *Specification of works required to be performed in building a Lodge at Langley Park Norfolk for Sir Thomas Beauchamp Bart.*
Com: Cbk 1871 May £21.

Unidentified Work
For Major, later Colonel Hardinge.
E: 1871
Com: Cbk 1871 May £21

Grasshome, Dinton (Buckinghamshire)
Small house for Miss Bland.
E: 1871-2
S: RIBA photographs (2), (Fig. 65).
Com: Cbk 1871 January £20, 1872 April £23.

Knebworth House (Hertfordshire)
Design for a new library and new offices for Edward George Earle Lytton Bulwer 1st Baron Lytton.
E: 1871-2
S: Knebworth House Estate Office: plans (3).
Com: Cbk 1873 October £72.
The library was to have been built on the southern part of the front terrace, but was not proceeded with; the offices were demolished in the 1950s. Godfrey 1906 records *A certain amount of work - for Lord Lytton, the novelist - not all carried through, as he was one among the people with whom Mr Devey was not in sympathy, or, putting it perhaps in a more correct form, he was not himself able to see all the beauty in his architect's work; a condition which Mr Devey, like all artists, was not slow in perceiving.* He was replaced by Thomas Henry Watson.

Wendover Vicarage (Buckinghamshire)
New house for the Revd Albert Smith.
E: 1871-3
S: RIBA photographs (2), (Fib. 70).
Com: Cbk 1871 October £120 December £50, 1872 March £25 July £25 December £20, 1873 July £60.

107 Piccadilly (London; Westminster)
Alterations to the offices for Baron Mayer Amschel de Rothschild.
E: 1871-3
S: Buckinghamshire Record Office: AR49/70 (2) plan, N.M. Rothschild Archives XII/41/6 accounts from George Myers and Sons for work on porter's room and servants' hall, 1st floor and roof d: December 1871; for model and alterations to this per architect's drawings d: March 1873.

Hall Place, Leigh (Kent)
New mansion, stables and estate works for Samuel Morley MP.
E: 1871-4
S: RIBA plans, elevations and photographs (15), (Figs. 53, 54, 55).
C: Hall Place Estate Office: *A Summary of the account of George Myers and Sons Builders Lambeth*, drawn up by D.J. Brown, Surveyor of 61, Lincoln's Inn Fields 1871-4, lists:

Works in connection with old mansion	£955. 10. 1.
New Mansion	£54,364.15.2.
Stable buildings	£8,551.7. 2.
Terrace and garden walls	£2,290.7. 3.
Tank on mound and fountain	£1,142.13. 3.
Estate and private account	£3,070.14. 1.
Works since occupation	£538.8. 1.
Total	£70,913.15. 1.

Com: Cbk 1872 January £195 April £100 July £250 October £200, 1873 January £187 April £225 July £950 October £150, 1874 January £300 June £15 (lodge), 1875 December £1376.
Lit: Edwin Hodder, *Life of Samuel Morley*, London, 1887; DNB XIII p. 979; CL li p. 80, gardens viii p. 776.
Home Farm
New dairy and improvements.
Lucy's Farm
Cow shed.
E: 1875

Leigh (Kent)
Village improvements for Samuel Morley.
S: National Society file.
Evangelical chapel and village hall
E: c.1875
S: RIBA photograph (1), (Fig. 61).
Leigh Denominational School
E: 1873
Morley supported Non-Conformist interests and this chapel was built for the Associated Methodists.
Leigh Waterworks

Stoneley Grange, Kimbolton (Cambridgeshire)
New country house and stables for Colonel Montresor.
E: 1870-4
Com: Cbk 1871 December £112, 1872 March £50 October £25, 1873 July £17 October £25, 1874 January £71.

Walmer Castle (Kent)
Alterations and addition of extra bedrooms for Granville George Leveson-Gower 2nd Earl Granville.
E: 1871-5
S: RIBA plans, elevation and photograph (26), (Fig. 35).
Com: Cbk 1872 July £25 October £50 December £70, 1873 April £207 July £120 October £127, 1874 January £104 April £108 July £67, 1875 April £114.
Lit: Lord Edmond Fitzmaurice, *The Life of Granville George Leveson-Gower Second Earl Granville K.G. 1815-1891*, London, 1905.

Denne Hill, Womenswold (Kent)
New mansion for Major Edwards Dyson.
E: 1871-3
S: RIBA photograph (1), (Fig. 70).
Com: Cbk 1871 September £50 October £25 December £50, 1872 March £75 May £75 July £50 September £37 December £37, 1873 April £50 July £199.

Send Holme, Send (Surrey)
New house and lodge for Captain and Mrs William Hargreaves.
E: 1871-5
S: RIBA plans and elevations (21), (Fig. 56).
Com: Cbk 1871 May £52, 1877 January £147.

Hargreaves was a friend of John Bright, who took his advice before agreeing to join Gladstone's Cabinet in 1868.

Rawcliffe Hall, Goole (Humberside)
Large additions and garden works for Ralph Creyke.
E: 1871-6
Com: 1871 September £75 November £50, 1872 March £50 July £37 October £37, 1873 July £52, 1876 April £251.

Lynwood, now the Stydd House, Lyndhurst (Hampshire)
New house for Lady Surtees.
E: 1871-7
S: RIBA elevations and photographs (4), (Fig. 111).
Com: Cbk 1871 December £50, 1872 July £50 October £25, 1873 July £25 October £15, 1874 April £20 June £10, 1877 March £174.

Goldings, Hertford (Hertfordshire)
New mansion, lodges and garden works for Robert Smith.
E: 1871-7
S: RIBA plans, elevations and photographs (34), (Figs. 67, 68, 69).
Com: Cbk 1871 May £64, 1873 July £20, 1874 April £333 April £140 (Goldings Old House) April £127 July £183 October £197, 1875 January £174 April £204 July £316 October £268, 1876 January £344 April £201 June £192 October £51 October £81, 1877 January £63 April £180 November £315.

Broomford Manor, Jacobstowe (Devon)
New house and lodge for Colonel Sir Robert Thomas White-Thomson KCB.
E: 1871-7
S: Formerly at Broomford Manor plans, elevations and details (6), (Figs 73, 74).
Com: Cbk 1871 July £100, 1873 May £43, 1877 August £279.
The builder was Courtney Ash of Ridgeway, Sampford Courtney.

Church of St James, Jacobstowe
Restoration for Colonel Sir Robert Thomas White-Thomson.
E: c.1875
S: Stone, 1886

Bourton Estate, Buckingham (Buckinghamshire)
Double cottages for William Oxenden Hammond.
E: c.1872
S: RIBA plans and elevations (8).
C: £748
Com: Fee a/c 1878 September £156.
The builder was Hawkes. The cottages standing beside the road leading to White House differ from those shown in the designs, which may not have been built.

Bruton Street (London; Westminster)
Preliminary design for alterations for Lord Granville.
E?: 1872

S: RIBA plans and elevation (5).
Demolished.

Villa Veta, now South Foreland House, Granville Road, Kingsdown (Kent)
Conversion of old semaphore station into a summer house for Lord Granville.
E: 1872
S: RIBA (under Kingsdown Cottage) plans (4).

Unidentified Work
For the Revd Edward Bonus.
E: 1872
Com: Cbk 1872 August £95
A number of houses in Buckland look as if they may have been improved by Devey; these can be identified by tablets bearing the Bonus arms.

Elstree (Hertfordshire)
Unidentified work for the Revd Lancelot Sanderson.
E: 1872
Com: Cbk 1872 August £11.
Godfrey refers to St Nicholas, Elstree, but as Sanderson was the headmaster of Elstree School the work was most likely done there.

Aylesbury National Schools (Buckinghamshire)
New master's house and infant school for Mr Cooper.
E: 1872-3
S: Buckinghamshire Record Office: AR 39/65:2/1-3 Contract drawings: plans, section and elevations (3).
The builder was Thomas Haddon.

Waterford School (Hertfordshire)
New school house for Robert Smith.
E: 1872-3
S: Stone December 1886; Hertfordshire County Record Office: School log books.

Yewlands
Unidentified work for Mr Robertson.
E: 1872-3
Com: Cbk 1872 July £50, 1873 April £27.

Boughton Hall, Send (Surrey)
Addition of third storey and alterations for Abraham Walter Paulton.
E: 1872-5
Com: Cbk 1872 July £110, 1875 July £66.
Paulton was married to the sister of Mrs Hargreaves of Send Holme.

Meynell Hunt Stables and Kennels, Sudbury (Derbyshire)
New stables, kennels and huntsmens' cottages for Augustus Henry Venables Vernon, 6th Baron Vernon and the joint masters, Sir Henry Anson Cavendish Bart., Baron Waterpark and Sir William Clowes MP.
E: 1872-5
S: RIBA plans and elevations (4).
C: Stables £5095, kennels £2489, cottages £1020, general £1403.

Fig. 111 Lynwood

Com: Cbk 1872 December £37, 1873 April £56 July £42 October £60, 1874 January £37 April £50 June £50 October £37, 1875 January £25 April £35 December £244
Lit: Field Secretary, Meynell and South Staffordshire Hunt, *The History of the Meynell Hounds & Country*, np, nd.

Lord Vernon did not hunt, but offered a lease of land adjoining Sudbury Park as a site for the stables. When the designs and estimates were submitted to him he did not approve of the elevations, or the cheapness of the proposed buildings. He suggested that Devey should be employed and the cost not be less than £5,000. The builders were Slater and Vernon, the clerk of works Mr Agar.

Eastry Workhouse Chapel (Kent)
Free-standing chapel for Sir Walter James and other contributors.
E: 1873
S: Kent Archive Office: Eastry Guardians Minute Books G/Ea AM 19-20; Stone December 1886. Stone built, Early English with double bell-cote. First suggested in 1871 and consecrated by the Archbishop of Canterbury on the 26 November 1873.

All Saints Church, Brantingham (Humberside)
Unidentified work for Christopher Sykes.
E: 1873
Com: Cbk 1874 January £108.
G.E. Street restored the church in 1867 (Borthwick Institute of Historical Research FAC. 1868/5) What Devey did cannot be determined.

Fairchildes, Fickleshole (Surrey)
Addition to mansion, designs for cottages and Broom Lodge Farmhouse for John Henry Daniell.
E: 1873
Broom Lodge
E: 1882
C: £454
Com: Fee a/c 1882 October £27.
The builder was Ward.
The mansion is demolished and the cottages, if built, cannot be identified. The farmhouse survives.

Church of St George, Benenden (Kent)
Churchyard wall for the Misses Neve of Ash Lawn.
E: 1873
Com: Cbk 1873 May £15.

Knighton, Woodford (London; Waltham Forest)
Two lodges for Edward North Buxton.
E: 1873
S: RIBA plans and elevations (15).
Com: Cbk 1873 July £34.
The south lodge is now No.1, The Glade, the west lodge has been demolished. Buxton bought the Knighton estate in 1863 and was for sixty years in the forefront of the fight for the preservation of Epping Forest.

Unidentified Work
For John Poyntz Spencer 5th Earl Spencer.
E: 1873
Com: Cbk 1873 October £21.
Lit: DNB 1901-11 p. 369.

Unidentified Work
For Mr Kent.
E: 1873
Com: Cbk 1873 October £7.

Unidentified Work
For Mr Bailey.
E: 1873
Com: Cbk 1873 October £142.

Seven Gables, Cliveden (Buckinghamshire)
New cottage for Sir Hugh Lupus Grosvenor 3rd Marquess of Westminster.
E: 1873
Com: Cbk 1873 October £21.
Lit: DNB XXII p. 791.

Unidentified Work
For Mrs Egerton.
E: 1873
Com: Cbk 1874 January £45.

Unidentified Work
For George Frederick Samuel Robinson, 1st Marquess of Ripon.
E: 1873
Com: Cbk 1874 January £61.
Lit: DNB 1901-11 p. 216.

Betteshanger Cottage Hospital (Kent)
For Sir Walter James.
E: 1873
S: RIBA plans, elevations and details (14).
Com: Cbk 1874 January £38.

Kimble (Buckinghamshire)
Unidentified work for W. Dell.
E: 1873
Com: Cbk 1874 July £52 to exors. of Dell paid by Mr Parrott.
This is Joseph Parrott of Lady Mead.

Brede Place (East Sussex)
Unidentified work and preparation of sale particulars for Moreton Frewen.
E: 1873, 1880
S: RIBA lithographed sale particulars (1)
Com: Cbk 1874 January £26.

Barton Manor, Osborne (Isle of Wight)
Alterations and extension of stables for H.M. Queen Victoria.
E: 1873-4
S: Osborne House: models for alterations to the stables (2); RIBA photographs (2), (Figs. 89, 90).
Com: Cbk 1874 April £74 paid by Sir T.M. Biddulph.

Brickwall, Northiam (East Sussex)
Additions, alterations and garden works for Edward Frewen.
E: 1873-7
S: East Sussex Record Office: FRE 8098/3, 4, 6, 7, 8: Inclosure Office to James, Curtis and James 7 April 1875, Statement of Account, Certificate by Devey 17 March 1875, E.W. James to Frewen 22 March and 10 April 1875, (Fig. 112).
Com: Cbk 1874 January £40 April £30 June £10 October £62, 1875 July £302, 1880 December £117.

The builder, George Edwin Jones of Hastings, got into financial difficulties and Frewen completed the work himself. Devey stated that his commission was £202 with an extra £52 for work consequent upon the failure of the contractor, his travelling was £50 and clerk of works wages £249. Brickwall is a large timber-framed Jacobean house. Devey added the east wing, a tower with a low wooden balustrade and designed the garden front with a series of five half-timbered gables.

Hodsock Priory (Nottinghamshire)
Alterations and additions for Sir George Mellish.
E: 1873-6
S: RIBA plans and elevations (26), *Articles of Agreement* d. 12 July 1873, *Summary of Specification, Estimate for woodwork* d. 25 December 1873, *Memorandum of Contracts* d. 17 August 1874, Devey to Mrs Leigh Mellish 29 May 1873, J. Williams to same 18 August 1874.
C: £10,044
Com: Cbk 1873 October £25, 1874 January £77 April £150 June £75 October £75, 1875 January £50 April £37 July £50 October £161.

A sixteenth-century manor already enlarged by Ambrose Poynter in 1829-33 was again altered and enlarged, retaining Poynter's sequence of three great rooms *en suite*. Mellish was a Lord Justice of the Court of Appeal in Chancery.

All Saints Church, Sudbury (Derbyshire)
Restoration for Lord Vernon.
E: 1873-7, 1881, 1883
S: Lichfield Joint Record Office, Faculties B/C/5 Sudbury 1873 and 1874; RIBA photographs (2).
Com: Cbk 1875 October £237, 1876 October £50, 1877 May £26, 1879 November £53, 1881 November £5, 1883 October £20.

North, south and west galleries were removed, a north transept replaced by a second north aisle, the Vernon Chantry enlarged into an organ chamber and vestry, the west tower opened into the nave, new south porch, reseated. The tower was raised and given battlements and pinnacles, and the whole reroofed. A photograph shows the new battlements made up in timber and offered up.

Macharioch House, Southend (Strathclyde Region)
Large additions and new lodge for John George Edward Henry Douglas Sutherland Campbell, Marquess of Lorne.
E: 1873-7
S: RIBA plans and elevations (4), (Fig. 63).
Com: Cbk (To the Duke of Argyll) 1873 July £100 October £75, 1874 January £75 April £30 June £25 October £45, 1875 January £45 November £47, 1877 March £223 (To Lord Lorne), 1877 June £47.

Tradition has it that Lord Lorne rebuilt the house for Princess Louise to whom he was married in 1871. However the plan shows a 'Duchess's bedroom', and as the Duke paid, it may have been intended for the whole family. The old part was converted into offices to which at the west end Devey added a saloon and arranged around this a reception room, the Duchess's suite of ante room, dressing, bed and bath rooms, and a dining room. The offices have been demolished. There was a four-storey south-west tower, and all was built in local stone and harled. The lodge, with a round tower and conical roof is also harled.

Halton Estate and Tring Park (Hertfordshire)
Nos. 29-30 Halton Road and unidentified work for Baron Lionel de Rothschild.
E: 1873-8
S: N.M. Rothschild Archives: Lionel de Rothschild Current Account I/2/20 1873 February George Deven £21 paid by Baylis (the land agent at Aston Clinton) August Myers £300, I/2/21, 1874 February Myers £150 March Myers £300 May £500 for Tring Park, 1875 January George Devey £142.
Com: Cbk 1874 February £21 (Baylis - Lionel de R) October £100 (5 cottages), 1876 June £274 October £150, 1877 January £50 April £50 July £100 November £25, 1878 April £304.

Lionel had inherited Gunnersbury Park, bought Halton in 1853 and Tring Park in 1872. This house was designed by Sir Christopher Wren for Henry Guy c.1670. It was enlarged and recased in red brick in a *dix-huitième* style. Devey was employed on some expensive work just after the house was purchased, and as there is no evidence that he ever worked at Gunnersbury, and only on cottages at Halton, it looks as if he and George Myers were employed at Tring.

Woodhall Park, Watton-at-Stone (Hertfordshire)
Estate works for Abel Smith.
E: 1873-9
Ballard's Cottage
S: RIBA plans (1).
Almshouses, Watton-at-Stone (Fig. 66).
E: 1873
85, Stevenage Road
Addition
Watkins Hall Farm
Large addition
Com: 1874 May £64, 1876 April £289, 1879 April £66

Ascott, Wing (Buckinghamshire)
Conversion of farmhouse into a hunting box, subsequent alterations and large additions, stables, hunting stables, kennels, lodges, cottages at Ascott Green and estate works for Leopold de Rothschild.
E: 1873-87
S: RIBA plans, elevations, details and photographs (144), (Figs. 31, 32, 33, 34).

168 *George Devey*

Fig.112 Brickwall

Com: 1874 June £10 October £30, 1875 January £40 April £52 November £50, 1878 April £207, 1879 October £137, 1880 January £140 April £200 December £560.

The builder was first John Durley of Bierton, who was frequently employed by the Rothschilds. He was followed by Cubitt and Co.

Givons Grove, Leatherhead (Surrey)
Unidentified work for Russell Sturgis.
E: 1874
Com: Cbk 1874 May £55; Baring Brothers and Co. Ltd. Archives: *English Client Ledger* BK.1.70 1874 May 7 Geo. Devey £55.

Sturgis was an American partner in Baring Brothers and Co. He leased Givons Grove in 1866, and a wing in red brick with a hipped roof and stone quoins, now demolished, may have been added by him. He employed William Cubitt and Co. and paid them £2043.

Church of St Mary, Stapleford (Hertfordshire)
Restoration for Abel Smith.
E: 1874-5
S: Hertfordshire County Record Office: Draft Petition, Faculty and plan DSA 2/1/267, vestry minute book; Parish records: Faculty.

New north porch with ringing chamber above and stokehole for heating apparatus below, nave extended 12 feet at west end.

Drinking Fountain, Deal (Kent)
For Lord Granville.
E: 1874-5
S: RIBA elevations (2).
Lit: *The Builder*, 24 April 1875, p. 379.

Unidentified Work, possibly at Granston Manor, Ballacola, Abbey Leix (Eire)
For John Wilson Fitzpatrick, 1st Baron Castletown.
E: 1874-5
Com: 1874 October £50, 1875 October £180 October £51.

A plain late-Georgian house, now demolished, had had the hall knocked in with an adjoining room, with a Tudor staircase and panelling in oak, which may have been done by Devey. Information from Mark Bence Jones.

Rangemore, Barton-under-Needwood (Staffordshire)
Alterations, including the addition of a billiard room for Sir Michael Arthur Bass, 1st Baron Burton.
E: 1874-6
S: RIBA billiard room plan and elevations (2).
Com: Cbk 1874 July £26 (paid by Glench), 1876 June £588.

Rangemore was again altered by Robert Edis and Devey's work cannot be identified.

34 Grosvenor Street, (London; Westminster)
Alterations for Lord Vernon.
E: 1874-6
S: Westminster City Library: Grosvenor Board Minutes 18/167; Greater London Record Office, District Surveyors' Returns 1875/224.
Com: Cbk 1874 October £86, 1875 December £43, 1876 October £28.

Smithills Hall, Bolton (Greater Manchester)
Alterations, additions and new stables for Colonel Richard Henry Ainsworth.
E: 1874-8, 1882-6
S: RIBA plans, elevations, details and photographs (46).
Com: Cbk 1874 June £25, 1875 April £47, 1876 October £125, 1877 May £550, 1882 May £25, 1883 October £100, 1884 September £223, 1885 May £233, 1886 May £268.
Lit: A.J. Sykes, *Concerning the Bleaching Industry*, Manchester, 1925.

Sudbury Hall, (Derbyshire)
New offices and internal alterations including designs for the Oak Parlour, billiard room and secondary stairs for Lord Vernon.
E: 1874-9
S: Sudbury Hall: plans, elevations and details (84); RIBA plans, elevation and photograph (22).
Com: Cbk 1874 October £365, 1875 December £550, 1876 October £460, 1877 May £315, 1879 November £52, 1881 November £11, 1883 October £36.

Park House, formerly the Curate's House.
S: Sudbury Estate Office: Drawer 3 elevations and plan; RIBA photograph (1).

The Butcher's Shop
S: Drawer 3 plans and elevation.

West Brougton Farm
Additions to farmhouse.
NE: 1874
S: Drawer 10 plans and elevations (8).

Gas works

Boar's Head, Sudbury Station
Small inn enlarged.
Com: Sudbury estate Cbk 1875 December £157, 1876 October £10, 1877 May £40.

Byram Park, Ferrybridge (North Yorkshire)
Estate works for Sir John William Ramsden Bart.
E: 1875
Com: Cbk 1876 January £329.

Ramsden was a close friend of Christopher Sykes. Devey was employed in landscaping the grounds, putting in formal gateways and constructing a terrace, with balustrades, stone benches and steps leading down to the lake. Mining subsidence has toppled much of this.

Myton Hall, Myton-on-Swale (North Yorkshire)
Unidentified work for Major Henry Miles Stapylton.
E: 1875
Com: Cbk 1876 January £376.

Myton Hall is a seventeenth-century classical house. Stapylton served as High Sheriff in 1876 and Devey's work may have been improvements in anticipation.

Unidentified Lodge
E: c.1875
S: RIBA elevations (2).

100 Cheyne Walk, formerly 5 Lindsey Row, Chelsea (London; Kensington and Chelsea)
Alterations for Algernon Bertram (Best) Mitford.
E: 1875-6
S: Greater London Record Office: Minutes of the Proceedings of the Metropolitan Board of Works: 29 September 1876 application by Devey to erect a balustrade.
Com: Cbk 1875 April £40 July £42 November £20.
Lit: Buildings of England, London, *The entrance and bay window of No. 100 were added by Devey.*

Church of All Saints, Little Kimble (Buckinghamshire)
Restoration.
E: 1875-6
S: Buckinghamshire Record Office: Vestry Minute Book 1863-86 and correspondence; *Kelly's Directory of Buckinghamshire 1899.*
C: £1,300
Restoration of chancel and nave roofs and reseating.

Unidentified Work
For Mr Marriott.
E: 1875-6
S: Godfrey index describes him as being of Hartford, near Liverpool so probably Hartford, Cheshire.
Com: Cbk 1875 July £75 October £75, 1875 January £75 April £50 June £67 October £50, 1877 January £37.

Unidentified Work
For Mr Clayton.
E: 1875-6
Com: Cbk 1875 April £23 July £10, 1876 April £13.

Send Holme, Send (Surrey)
Additions for Sir Joseph Francis Leese Bart.
E: 1875-7
Com: Cbk 1875 November £50, 1877 March £84.
His wife, Mary Constance Hargreaves, inherited Send Holme in 1874. A veranda was added on the garden front.

Poynton Colliery and Estate (Cheshire)
Unidentified work for Lord Vernon.
E: 1875-7
S: Cheshire Record Office: Vernon Estate papers DVE/1983/1-6; H.A. Trippier MSS.
Com: Cbk 1875 December £131 colliery, December £245 estate 1876 October £185, 1877 May £140.
Possibly an addition to Poynton Towers and a new house, Beechfield built for Lord Vernon's colliery agent, both demolished.

Trevagethan, Truro (Devon)
Additions to farmhouse for Major Quintus Vivian.
E: 1875-7
S: RIBA plans (1).
Com: Cbk 1876 May £119.
The design is for a new house which was not built.

Park House, Frant (East Sussex)
Alterations and additions to house and garden works for Sir Stratford Canning, 1st Viscount Stratford de Redcliffe.
E: 1875-7
S: RIBA elevations and details (8).
Com: Cbk 1875 April £75 July £77 October £62, 1876 January £85, 1878 February £167.
Lit: DNB III p. 883.
Later alterations have destroyed most of Devey's work.

Dudbrook House, Kelvedon Hatch (Essex)
Unidentified work for Frances Elizabeth Anne Waldegrave, Countess Waldegrave and Chichester Samuel Fortescue, 1st Baron Carlingford.
E: 1875-8
Com: 1875 July £60 Carlingford, 1876 April £75 Waldegrave, 1878 April £119 Carlingford.
Godfrey index states this work was at Dudbrook, now partly demolished.

Blakesware, Ware (Hertfordshire)
Mansion for Mrs Frances Hadsley Gosselin.
E: 1875-9
Com: Cbk 1875 November £43, 1876 January £39 April £24 July £60 October £84, 1877 January £155 April £126 July £125 November £154, 1878 January £181 April £233 July £236, 1879 March £218.
The builder was Hawkes, other payments were made to W.H. Lascelles and Co., Clerk, Haden, Eastons and Williams. The house has been enlarged, damaged by fire and divided. The stables are dated 1881, garden buildings 1883.

Ashfold, Handcross (West Sussex)
Mansion, lodge and cottages for Eric Carrington Smith.
E: 1875-84
S: RIBA plans and elevations (21).
Com: Cbk 1875 July £47 October £125, 1876 January £104 April £100 June £111 October £158, 1877 January £124 April £170 July £150 November £144, 1878 January £186 April £210 July £93, 1880 January £247, 1881 November £71, 1884 May £200.
The builders were John Adcock of Dover and Wheatland. The mansion has been demolished.

Unidentified Cottages, Laleham (Surrey)
For George Charles Bingham, 3rd Earl of Lucan.
E: 1876
Com: Cbk 1876 August £92, paid £78.
Lit: DNB XXII p. 196.
Godfrey index names Laleham.

35 Grosvenor Square, (London; Westminster)
Alterations for Charles Henry Wilson, 1st Baron Nunburnholme.
E: 1876
Com: Cbk 1876 August £222.
Lit: *Survey of London, The Grosvenor Estate in Mayfair* XL p. 149; DNB 1901-1911 p. 685.
Demolished.

Condover Hall, (Shropshire)
Garden works and parterres for Reginald Cholmondley.
E: c.1876
S: RIBA plans (4).
Some of the parterres survive in an overgrown condition.

Denton Manor, Grantham (Lincolnshire)
Unidentified work for Sir William Earle Welby-Gregory Bart.
E: 1876
Com: Cbk 1876 November £262.
Possibly garden work; the mansion was demolished and replaced by a house by A.W. Blomfield in 1879.

Unidentified Work
For Fitzwilliam.
E: 1876
Com: Cbk 1876 August £115 to Fitzwilliam exors.

The Chestnuts, later The Gatehouse, Whitehill, Aylesbury (Buckinghamshire)
House for Richard Rose.
E: 1876
S: RIBA photographs (2).
Com: Cbk 1876 April £69.
Demolished c.1951. Rose was a solicitor and a director of the Bucks and Oxon Bank.

19 Curzon Street (London; Westminster)
Unidentified work for Charles Augustus Bennet, 6th Earl of Tankerville.
E: 1876
Com: Cbk 1876 May £46.
Godfrey index states work was in Curzon Street.

37 Grosvenor Square, later 42 (London; Westminster)
Unidentified work for Mary, Countess Dowager of Aberdeen.
E: 1876
Com: Cbk 1876 May £5 paid by the Earl.
Lit: Marjorie Pentland, *A Bonnie Fechter*, London, 1952, pp. 17, 27, 75.

Unidentified Work
For Boyle.
E: 1876
Com: Cbk 1876 May £81.

Gladwyns, Bishop's Stortford (Hertfordshire)
Unidentified work for Horace Broke.
E: 1876
Com: Cbk 1876 April £58.

Spencer Estate, Northampton (Northamptonshire)
Planning of the layout of a suburban estate and designs for various classes of house for Lord Spencer.
NE: c.1876
S: RIBA sale poster, perspectives, plans and elevations (22), (Figs. 93, 94, 95, 96).

Orton's Farm, Spencer Estate (Northamptonshire)
Designs for farm buildings for Lord Spencer.
E: c.1876
S: RIBA plans and elevations (6).
Com: Cbk 1885 August £10.

Unidentified Work
For Mr Coke.
E: 1876
Com: Cbk 1877 March £182.

Wendover Manor (Buckinghamshire)
House for Lieut. Gen. Philip Smith.
E: 1876-7
S: RIBA photograph (1).
Com: Cbk 1876 April £171, 1877 April £100, 1878 October £50.

Weedon Village School (Buckinghamshire)
New infants' school for Henry Cazenove.
E: 1876-7
S: National Society file: Cazenove 5 October 1876, he will pay for the school and asks for help with the cost of the fittings *we mean to have an Evening service in it to counteract the Dissenting Chapel close to it*; formal application d. 18 November 1876; RIBA detail (1).

Great Cliffsend Farm, Cliffs End (Kent)
Farmhouse and outbuildings for Lord Granville.
E: 1876-7
S: RIBA plans and elevations (7).
Com: Cbk 1881 November £120.

Ramsgate Harbour (Kent)
Unidentified work for the Board of Trade.
E: 1876-7
Com: Cbk 1877 March £50.

Dover Harbour (Kent)
Clock tower, marine baths and laying out adjoining land for the Dover Harbour Board.
Clock Tower
E: 1876-7
S: RIBA elevations (1), (Fig. 36).
C: £1433
Com: £108
Baths, Camden Crescent and Lawn
E: 1877-8
S: RIBA elevations (5), (Fig. 37).
C: £1300
Com: £100
Granville Gardens
E: 1878
C: £1700
Com: £152
S: Dover Harbour Board: Minute Book Vol. 2, Minute Books HH/A/49 1862-77, HH/A/42 1877-87.
Com: Cbk 1878 February £108 July £65, 1879 March £147.
The builder was W.J. Adcock of Dover. All Devey's work, apart from the clock tower was destroyed by shelling in World War II.

The Pavilion, Eythrope (Buckinghamshire)
Summer house for Miss Alice de Rothschild.
E: 1876-9
S: RIBA elevations, plans and section (26), (Fig. 30).
Com: Cbk 1876 October £100, 1877 January £77 April £60 July £74 November £25, 1879 October £288.

Clandon Park (Surrey)
Addition of *porte cochère*, internal repairs and redecoration for William Hillier Onslow, 4th Earl of Onslow.
E: 1876-9
S: Surrey Record Office, Guildford Muniment Room RB.670 *An account of the succession to, and events which have occurred on the Estates of the Earl of Onslow, from October 1870 to the end of 1883*. RIBA photographs (2).
Com: Cbk 1877 January £74, 1879 March £12.

Membland Hall (Devon)
Large additions to house, stables and estate work for Edward Charles Baring, 1st Baron Revelstoke.
E: 1876-9
S: RIBA elevations and photographs (11); Baring Brothers and Co.: Archives *Sale Particulars of the Membland Hall Estate, South Devon, 1895*, (Figs. 80, 81).
Com: Cbk 1876 £182, 1877 January £217 April £232 July £267 November £239, 1878 January £186, 1879 April £459; Baring Brothers and Co.: Archives *English Client Ledgers* BK I 71-73 Account of Edward Baring, payments to George Devey 1876 January £225 October £492, 1877 January £278 April £295, 1878 February £443 October £459.
Lit: Maurice Baring, *The Puppet Show of Memory*, London, 1922; CL 29 April 1982, p. 1236.
The mansion has been demolished.

The Durdans, Epsom (Surrey)
Alterations and additions to house, new riding house, entrance gates and railings for Archibald Philip Primrose, 5th Earl Rosebery.
E: 1876-84
S: RIBA plans, elevations and details (16); Godfrey Collection. *Estimate New Kitchen and other Works The Durdans Epsom for the Right Honble. The Earl of Rosebery. Geo. Devey Esqr. Architect - 123 Bond Street W May 1883.*
Com: Cbk 1876 April £60 June £200 October £85, 1877 January £69, 1880 £502, 1881 January £65 April £64 April £35, 1883 October £50, 1884 May £45.
Godfrey 1906: *Durdans, a large house of no beauty, of late date, of monotonous appearance, was entirely remodelled in design, and given its present form. The old sash windows were taken out bodily, and casement lights, with stone jambs, mullions and transoms, substituted, the whole aspect being completely transformed.* Most of Devey's additions have been demolished.
The builder was T.J. Messom.

Maresfield Park (East Sussex)
Internal work for Louisa Elizabeth Anne, Dowager Lady Shelley.
E: 1877
S: RIBA plans (5).
Com: Cbk 1877 September £69.
Demolished c.1924.

Church of St Michael, Waterford (Hertfordshire)
Unidentified work for Robert Abel Smith.
E: c.1877
S: Stone December 1886.

Unidentified Work
For Lady Charlotte Ossington.
E: 1877
Com: Cbk 1877 April £10.
Lady Ossington was the widow of J.E. Denison, 1st Viscount and Speaker of the House of Commons 1857-72. She later paid for the Ossington Coffee Tavern, Newark.

Mentmore Estate (Buckinghamshire)
Master's house and rectory, Cheddington, cottages and public house for Hannah de Rothschild and Lord Rosebery.
Master's house, Cheddington
E: 1877
S: National Society file.
Cheddington Rectory
Unidentified work for the Revd Frederick Burn Harvey.
S: Godfrey index.
The Rosebery (formerly the Aylesbury) Arms, Cheddington Station
Three cottages now called Mentmore End Cheddington
Unidentified cottages
S: Buckinghamshire Record Office Ar 49/70 (1) and (5), D/RO.4.34.1 and 5 plans.
A pair of small cottages with shaped pedimented gables.

Castle Ashby (Northamptonshire)
Proposal for remodelling the long gallery and drawing room, and estate work for Charles Douglas Compton, 3rd Marquess of Northampton.
E: 1877
S: RIBA elevations (7).
Com: Cbk 1878 January £112.
The remodelling was not proceeded with and the estate work unidentified.

Wentworth Castle (South Yorkshire)
Proposals for alterations and screen enclosing courtyard for Frederick William Vernon Wentworth.
NE: 1877
S: RIBA plans and elevations (18).

1 Richmond Terrace (London; Westminster)
South-east wing raised to form a tower and alterations to the interior for Bertram Wodehouse Currie.
E: 1877-8
S: RIBA plans, elevations and photographs (33); PRO Crest/62 p. 139 July 1877.
The wing has been demolished. Decorative work in the hall, staircase, landing, boudoir, drawing and dining rooms and garden hall was executed by Turner Lord.

Adderley Hall, Market Drayton (Shropshire)
Mansion, lodges, farm and cottages for Henry Reginald Corbet.
E: 1877-81
S: RIBA plans, elevations and photograph (10); Shropshire Record Office: 327/351 and 37,290 plans, elevations and details (28), 3390/11/1-6 plans and elevations of south lodge (6) Box 269 elevations and details; H.R. Corbet *Memo. Adderley Hall* (Figs. 82, 83).
Com: Cbk 1877 November £102, 1878 January £112 April £150 July £226 October £323, 1879 February £233 April £183 October £291, 1880 April £74 August £76 November £71, 1881 January £50 August £54.

Killarney House, Kerry (Eire)
Mansion and estate buildings for Valentine Augustus Browne, 4th Earl of Kenmare.
E: 1877-83
S: RIBA plans, elevations and photographs (36), (Figs. 84, 85, 86, 87).
Demolished.
Fishing Pavilion on O'Mahoney's Point
S: RIBA elevations(4).
Built to a different design and now demolished.
Unidentified lodge
S: RIBA plans and elevations (5).
Presbyters' House, Firies
S: RIBA plans (3).
Not built
Western Domain Lodge (Fig. 88).
Killarney Town Hall
Now altered
West End House, New Street, Killarney
Additions
C: Fee a/c £59,000 for mansion, lodge, fishing pavilion, town hall and cottages.
Com: Cbk 1877 July £521, 1878 February £541 April £225 July £334 October £275, 1879 February £271 April £260 October £732, 1880 January £612, 1883 February £1623.
The builders were John Collen and Brothers, woodwork by W.H. Lascelles and Co. Ltd., payments also to Steinitz, Healey and Graham.

Unidentified Work
For Fildes.
E: 1878
Com: Cbk 1878 December £72.

Unidentified Work
For Major Meyrick.
E: 1878
Com: Cbk 1879 February £31.

Public Drinking Fountain, All Saints Street, Hastings (East Sussex)
For Francis William Staines.
E: 1878-9
S: RIBA elevation and photograph (2).
Lit: *Hastings News* 4 April 1879; *Hastings Observer* 9 April 1879.
The builders were Cubitt and Co. and local tradesmen.

Betteshanger Rectory (Kent)
Additions for the Revd John Worthington Bliss.
E: 1878-9
S: RIBA plans (1); Ecclesiastical Commissioners file NB/1788.
Com: Cbk 1879 November £49.
New porch and lavatory, a bay window in the drawing room, kitchen, scullery and pantry. The builder was W.J. Adcock of Dover.

Oldbury Place, Ightham (Kent)
Additions for George John Shaw-Lefevre, 1st Baron Eversley.
E: 1878-81
S: RIBA plans and elevations (12).
Com: Cbk 1879 February £93 October £146, 1881 November £38.
Fee a/c 1878 December £102.
Lit: DNB 1922-1930 p. 765.
The builder was Norris of Maidstone. The house was a plain eighteenth-century block to which Devey added on the east library and drawing room, converting the dining room into an own room, building ante room and porch and an L-shaped office range.

Waddesdon (Buckinghamshire)
Unidentified work for Baron Ferdinand James de Rothschild.
E: 1879
Com: Cbk 1879 October £115.

Unidentified Work
For Hugh Henry Rose, 1st Baron Strathnairn.
E: 1879
Com: Cbk 1879 November £132.
Lit: DNB XVII p. 233.

Langston Arms Hotel, Kingham (Oxfordshire.)
Hunting box for Lord Ducie.
E: 1879
Com: Cbk 1881 April £66.

Benenden Rectory (Kent)
Additions for the Revd E.D. Cree.
E: 1879
Com: Cbk 1879 November £59.
Lit: Francis Haslewood, *The Parish of Benenden, Kent*, Ispwich, 1889.
Cree was Rector in 1877-87 *during which period he greatly improved the Glebe House by adding a New Front ... refacing of the vicarage at the cost to himself of £1,000.*

Maplewood
Design for a mansion for Lord Granville.
NE: 1879
S: RIBA map (1); Williams 1909.
Com: Cbk 1879 June £52.

Unidentified Work
For Major Maxwell.
E: 1879
Com: Cbk 1880 March £72.

The King's Head, Aylesbury (Buckinghamshire)
Alterations for Sir Nathaniel Mayer de Rothschild, 1st Baron Rothschild.
E: 1879-80
C: Fee a/c £775 up to September 1879, £2093 to completion.
Com: Cbk 1879 October £73, 1880 April £98.
Lit: RCHM Buckinghamshire I; Robert Gibbs, *A History of Aylesbury*, Aylesbury, 1885.
Gibbs records that the gable above the gateway was rebuilt and the oriel put in at the same time.

The Literary Institute, Temple Street, Aylesbury (Buckinghamshire)
Library and reading room for Lord Rothschild.
E: 1879-80
S: Buckinghamshire Record Office: C.15/4/2 Robert Gibbs' Scrapbook p. 104 clipping from *Bucks Advertiser and Aylesbury News*, 27 March 1880.
C: Fee a/c £1244 up to December 1879, £1414 to March 1880.
Com: Cbk 1880 January £91 August £153.
The Chairman gave the health of the architect (Mr G. Devey) who was unable to be present, and the manager (Mr Corden) who replied. He thanked the Company in the name of Mr Devey and his manager Mr Williams for their kindness in drinking the toast.

Marlborough House, Hawkhurst (Kent)
Addition of south wing for Edward Hardcastle MP.
E: 1879-80
Com: Cbk 1882 September £35.
Hardcastle was a partner in Hardcastle, Cross and Co. of Bolton, otherwise known as the Bolton Commercial Bank. His father had bought the New Lodge estate in 1857, and he succeeded to it in 1879.

Swaylands, Penshurst (Kent)
Alterations and large additions for George James Drummond.
E: 1879-82
S: RIBA details (2).
Com: Cbk 1881 August £191 November £232, 1882 March £345.
Lit: *Building News* 23 April 1886, p. 684.

Longwood, Winchester (Hampshire)
Mansion and estate work for William Hopetoun Carnegie, 8th Earl of Northesk.
E: 1879-83
S: RIBA plans and elevations (41).
Com: Cbk 1881 January £376 April £109 August £198 November £263, 1882 May £384, 1883 February £1052.

Unidentified Lodge
E?: pre-1880
S: RIBA elevations (3).

Unidentified Single-Storey Cottage
E?: pre-1880
S: RIBA elevation (1).

Unidentified Double Cottage
E?: pre-1880
S: RIBA plan and elevations (3).

Cairnbrook Lodge, (probably no.7) Tudor Road, Upper Norwood (London; Croydon)
Addition of bay window and greenhouse for the Misses Louisa and Rosa Devey.
E: 1880
Com: Cbk 1880 July £137.
Lit: Louisa Devey, *Life of Rosina, Lady Lytton*, London, 1887.
The Misses Devey befriended Lady Lytton after her separation from her husband; she left them her estate and made them her literary executors.

11 Belgrave Square (London; Westminster)
Designs for a boudoir for Lord Kenmare.
E: c.1880
S: RIBA elevations (2).

Unidentified Work
For Mr Augenor.
E: 1880
Com: Cbk 1881 January £3.
Godfrey index states that Augenor was a publisher.

Brampton Ash (Northamptonshire)
Farm buildings and alterations to the manor house for Lord Spencer.
E: 1880
S: RIBA plans and elevations (9).

Unidentified Work
For the Duke of Westminster.
E: 1880
Com: Cbk 1881 January £46.

Howletts, Bekesbourne (Kent)
Designs for encasing and enlarging the house for George Bowdler Gipps.
NE: post-1880
Gipps founded the Canterbury bank Gipps, Simmons and Gipps which amalgamated with Hammond and Co. This is a classical house with an Ionic portico built in 1787 to the designs of John Leach. Devey's proposals were in his Jacobean style.

Haddon Estate Farm, Bakewell (Derbyshire)
Unidentified farmhouse and yard for the Estate Trustees.
E?: 1880-1
S: RIBA plans and elevation (2).
Com: Cbk 1882 January £78.

Milburn, Cospen Lane, Esher (Surrey)
Additions and gardener's cottage for the Hon. Henry Lorton Bourke.
E: 1880-1 and 1886
S: RIBA plans and elevations (24).
Further additions were made after Devey worked here

and the house was later gutted and partly demolished. The gardener's cottage survives.

East Villa, Upton Park, Slough (Buckinghamshire)
Unidentified work for George Bentley.
E: 1880-2
C: £394
Com: Cbk 1880 January £21, 1882 October £19.
Lit: DNB XXII p. 180.
The builder was Priestly. George Bentley was the son of the publisher Richard Bentley, who was a client of Devey's father. He was an old friend *Mr. Devey would refer to him as his chief authority regarding those hobbies of his, whips, coaches, horses etc.* He later bought land upon which he built the house now called The Mere, which James Williams published in *The Builder* 15 December 1888.

Unidentified Work
For Lord Spencer.
E: 1880-3
Com: Cbk 1881 August £273 November £276, 1882 April £74, 1883 November £45.

Worth Park, Crawley (West Sussex)
Unidentified work for Mrs Henrietta Franciska Montefiore.
E: 1881
Com: Cbk 1881 November £36.
The mansion has been demolished.

Knebworth House (Hertfordshire)
North lodge for Lord Lytton.
E: 1881-2
S: RIBA elevation (1).
C: £627
Com: Cbk 1882 May £42.
The builder was W. Warren. Of red brick and similar in design to that proposed for St Alban's Court.

Chittenden and Chittenden Lodge, Hawkhurst (Kent)
Both buildings enlarged for Edward Hardcastle.
E: 1881
Com: Cbk 1882 September £35.
Chittenden was a timber-framed Wealden house enlarged for Hardcastle's unmarried daughters.

18 Carlton House Terrace (London; Westminster)
Alterations for Lord Granville.
E: c.1881
S: RIBA perspectives (2), PRO Crest 19/59/£193 and 60/£426.
New porch, kitchens and garden.

Pembury Grange formerly Calverley Grange, Pembury (Kent)
Additions for Robert Bruce Ronald.
E: 1881
Com: Cbk 1881 August £62 November £109.
The builder was W.J. Adcock of Dover.

Bossington (Hampshire)
Estate cottages for William Henry Deverell.
E: 1881-2
S: RIBA plans and elevations (5), *Specification for the erection of a block of cottages at Bossington for W.H. Deverell Esqr.*
Com: Cbk 1882 May £32.
The builder was Robinson. There was a good deal of cottage building here, namely 13-24, George's Cottage, 19-22, 23-24, 25, 38-39 High Street, and 15-17 South End Cottages.

St Margaret's at Cliffe (Kent)
Cottage on Bay Hill and unidentified work for Lord Granville.
E: 1881-5
Com: Cbk 1882 April £44 October £17, 1883 June £37 November £23, 1885 May £23.
The builder was W.J. Adcock of Dover.

8 Lennox Gardens (London; Kensington and Chelsea)
Mansion for the Hon. Mrs Hunloke.
E: 1881-6
S: RIBA plans, elevations and details (67); Godfrey Collection: *Specification of works to be done in the erection of a Mansion in Lennox Gardens, Chelsea on plots nos. 168 and 168 for the Honble Mrs Hunloke according to Drawings prepared for that purpose by Mr George Devey, Architect of 123 Bond Street W. 1882.* (Figs. 97, 98).
Com: Cbk 1882 September £116 October £50, 1883 March £108 June £100 October £48, 1884 May £252 July £117 September £68, 1885 May £112 November £39, 1886 October £52.
Lit: Dorothy Stroud, *The South Kensington Estate of Henry Smith's Charity*, London, 1975.
The builder was T.J. Messom of Twickenham. Work on the interiors began in October 1883 with Jackson and Steinitz; W. Shepherd of Bermondsey was doing woodwork from May 1884.

Furness Cottage, 1 Grange Gardens, Furness Road, Eastbourne (East Sussex)
New porch, trellis work and summer house for Edmund Aubertin.
E: 1882
S: RIBA elevations, plan and details (11).
Demolished c.1940. Aubertin was a publisher and a long standing friend of Devey.

Unidentified Work
For Mr Singleton.
E: 1882
Com: Cbk 1882 October £91.

Lullingstone Castle, Eynsford (Kent)
Unidentified work for Sir William Hart Dyke, 7th Bart.
E: 1882
Com: Cbk 1882 October £81.
Lit: DNB 1931-1940 p. 247.

Wormleighton School (Northamptonshire)
Addition for Lord Spencer
E: 1882
Com: Cbk 1882 September £21.
A new school room was added on the east of the building erected in 1839.

Unidentified Work
For Dr Shepherd.
E: 1882
Com: Cbk 1882 April £10.

Unidentified Work
For Miss Reily.
E: 1882
Com: Cbk 1883 May £5.

Norton Conyers (North Yorkshire)
Proposed addition of bay windows for Sir Reginald Henry Graham, 8th Bart.
NE: c.1882
S: RIBA plans and elevation (2).
Lit: CL 1986 October 9 p. 1094, October 16 p. 1200.
The estate was sold out of the family in 1865 and repurchased by Sir Reginald in 1881; Devey probably produced his design shortly after this.

The Ledgers, Chelsham (Surrey)
Alterations and additions to house and new stables for Henry Averell Daniell.
E: 1882
S: RIBA plans and elevations (10); Roger Daniell: model (Fig. 91).
Com: Cbk 1882 October £128.
Demolished apart from the stable block.

Knowle Park, Cranleigh (Surrey)
Alterations and additions for Sir George Francis Bonham, 2nd Bart.
E: 1882-3
S: RIBA plans and elevations (17).
Com: Cbk 1882 September £78 October £32, 1883 March £66 October £15.
The builders were William Stanton, Goddard and Hellyer. A plain two-storey house with a hipped roof was decorated with shaped gables. It was doubled in size by an addition containing a new entrance, approached through archways, new offices and nurseries. Rough-cast with brick trim, a tower with a large sundial.

Unidentified Work
For Frederick Wragge.
E: 1882-3
Com: Cbk 1882 October £24, 1883 October £31.
The builder was Clark.

Culver House, Amberley (Gloucestershire)
Alterations and additions for the Revd Lord Charles Thynne.
E: 1882-4
Com: Cbk 1882 July £37 October £22, 1883 March £39 October £21, 1884 July £27.
The builder were Drew, and Niblett and Goddard.

Palace of Westminster (London; Westminster)
Proposal for enlarging the Reporters' Gallery in the House of Lords for a Select Committee.
NE: 1883
S: House of Lords Record Office: *Report from the Select Committee of the House of Lords on House of Lords (Constitution and Accommodation): together with the Proceedings of the Committee, Minutes of Evidence, and Appendix. Session 1883.*

Unidentified Work
For Sir Gabriel Goldney, 1st Bart.
E: 1883
Com: 1883 October £77.

Brewster Lodge, Clapham Common North Side (London; Wandsworth)
Dining room panelling for Philip Henry Wodehouse Currie, 1st Baron Currie.
E: 1883
S: RIBA elevations (2).
Com: Cbk 1883 April £43 October £45.
On the site of what is now Stormont Road, demolished c.1890.

Pitchford Hall (Shropshire)
Alterations for Lady Louisa Harriet Cotes.
E: 1883-4
S: RIBA plans and elevations (12).
Com: Cbk 1883 June £45 October £112, 1884 May £77.

Netley Castle (Hampshire)
Additional bedrooms and other work for Colonel the Hon. Sir Henry George Louis Crighton.
E: 1883-4
S: Hampshire Record Office: Top Netley 1/2 Notes of Canon A.J. Beach, Vicar of Hound and Netley Abbey 1942-72.
Com: Cbk 1883 October £25, 1884 December £73.
Crighton bought Netley Abbey in 1881, and after correspondence with George A. Dunnage, who had been architect to the previous owner, and A.W. Blomfield, he employed Devey: *the first additions by me were carried out under Mr Davey (sic) as architect viz. 6 servants' rooms on the top of the house.* This was in 1883-4 as the builder, Chapman of Wollston wrote in 1907 that he had looked at the contract for the bedrooms amounting to £1220 which with additional works came to a total of £1494 rendered to Devey in May 1884.

Harlestone Schools (Northamptonshire)
New school for Lord Spencer.
E: 1883-5
S: RIBA plans and elevations (20).
Com: Cbk 1884 November £23, 1885 August £39.
The builder was Martin. New schoolrooms were added to an old building; burnt and rebuilt in 1978.

Drayton House (Northamptonshire)
Alterations for Mrs Caroline Harriet Stopford Sackville.
E: 1883-5
S: RIBA plans (5).
Com: Cbk 1883 October £27.

Manor House and Manor Farm, Steane (Northamptonshire)
Farmhouse and cottages for Lord Spencer.
E: 1883-5
S: RIBA plans and elevations (29).
Com: 1883 November £62, 1884 November £41, 1885 March £27.
The cottages have been converted into a house.

41 Grosvenor Square (London; Westminster)
Mansion for Charles Henry Wilson, 1st Baron Nunburnholme.
E: 1883-6
S: RIBA plans and elevations (30), (Figs. 102, 103).
Com: Cbk 1884 July £108 November £138, 1885 £196 November £223, 1886 January £69 September £25.
it: *The Builder* 3 November 1883, p. 608, *The Building News* 19 March 1883, p. 431, DNB 1901-19011, p. 685, *Survey of London, The Grosvenor Estate in Mayfair* XI, p. 151-3.
The builder was William Shepherd of Bermondsey, Goddard, and Farmer and Brindley who probably supplied the marble which lined the hall and staircase. The house was demolished in c.1962.

19 Lennox Gardens (London; Kensington and Chelsea)
House and stables for Eric Carrington Smith.
E: 1883-6
S: RIBA plans and elevations (23).
Com: Cbk 1884 May £40 July £116 September £50 December £57, 1885 May £142 November £59, 1886 January £12 October £34.
The builder was J. Simpson and Son of Paddington and Hitch.

2, 4 and 6 Lennox Gardens (London; Kensington and Chelsea)
Three houses and stables for the Hon. Mrs Hunloke.
E: 1883-6
S: RIBA plans and elevations (27); Godfrey Collection. *Three Houses Lennox Gardens and Walton Street Chelsea and Stables in rear for the Honble Mrs Hunloke. Mr George Devey Architect 123 Bond Street W. Specification of Plumbers Work. June 1883*, (Fig. 99).
Com: Cbk 1884 September £68, 1885 May £112 November £39 October £52.

Honey Hill Farm, Elkington (Northamptonshire)
New farmhouse for Mr Pell and Lord Spencer.
E: 1884
S: RIBA plans and specifications (4).
Com: Cbk 1885 August £10 Elkington.

Plaish Hall, Cardington (Shropshire)
Proposal for the conversion of Upper Home Farm into stables for Edward Sayer.
NE: 1884
S: RIBA plans (1); Shropshire Record Office: Stanley Leighton, *Shropshire Houses* np.
Sayer bought Plaish Hall in 1884 which seems a likely date for Devey's design.

23 Lennox Gardens (London; Kensington and Chelsea)
House and stables for Major General Alexander Charles Hector Stewart.
E: 1884-5
S: RIBA Contract drawings, plans and elevations (12); Godfrey Collection: *Specification of Works to be done in the Erection of House and Stables in the rear on Plot No. . . . Lennox Gardens for General Stewart according to Drawings prepared for that purpose by Mr George Devey Architect. 123 Bond Street W. Specification of Plumber's Work March 1884*, (Fig. 100).
Com: Cbk 1884 December £85, 1885 May £55 August £50 November £53.
The builder was William Shepherd of Bermondsey.

Unidentified Work
For Mr Pattenson.
E: 1884-5
Com: Cbk 1884 August (per Stapley) £100, 1885 April Stapley (Pattenson) £150.

Hayes Place, Beckenham (London; Bromley)
Additions to the house and cottages for Sir Everard Alexander Hambro.
E: 1884-6
C: Dining room £900, terrace etc. £750, Crossley £600.
Com: Cbk 1886 October £124.
The builder was Messrs Trollope. Hayes Place has been demolished.
St. Mary's Cottages
2 and 4 West Common Road
21 and 23, 25 and 27 Hayes Lane.
E: 1886-8

25 Lennox Gardens (London; Kensington and Chelsea)
House for Samuel Juler Wyand.
E: 1884-6
S: RIBA elevations and details (8), (Fig. 100).
Com: Cbk 1886 January £150.
Facade in the Franco-Flemish style similar to those of George and Peto in Harrington Gardens.

Melbury House, Melbury Sampford (Dorset)
Alterations and addition of tower and offices for Henry Edward Fox-Strangways, 5th Earl of Ilchester.
E: 1884-6
S: RIBA plans and elevations (62); Melbury Estate Office: plans and elevations (44); letter books of W.H. Wells, November 1884-November 1886; (Figs. 105, 106).
Com: Cbk 1885 January £76 June £67, 1886 January £114 August £87.

Warren House, Warren Road (London; Kingston)
Additions for George Grenfell Glyn, 2nd Baron Wolverton.
E: 1884-6
S: RIBA elevation (1).
Com: Cbk 1884 December £100, 1885 May £219 August £225 November £74, 1886 January £100 January £276 September £53.
Lit: DNB VIII p. 9.

13 and 15 Lennox Gardens (London; Kensington and Chelsea)
A pair of houses for Samuel Juler Wyand.
E: 1885
S: RIBA plans (7).
Com: Cbk 1885 October £160 (No. 13) £80 (No. 15).

43 Lennox Gardens (London; Kensington and Chelsea)
House for Lieut. Colonel the Hon. Charles Gathorne Gathorne-Hardy.
E: 1885
S: RIBA elevation (1), (Fig. 101).
The builder was Samuel Juler Wyand.

Knowsley Hall (Merseyside)
Proposals for alterations and additions for Edward Henry Stanley, 15th Earl of Derby.
NE: 1885
S: RIBA plans (6).
Lit: DNB XVIII p. 948.

Apparently not proceeded with, these alterations do not appear in drawings by Romaine Walker made in 1912 and Claud Phillimore in 1953-4.

65 and 100 Lexham Gardens (London; Kensington and Chelsea)
Interior designs for Samuel Juler Wyand.
E: 1885
S: RIBA elevations (3).
Com: Cbk 1885 June £25.
Lit: *Survey of London, South Kensington: Kensington Square to Earl's Court* XLII pp. 292-3.
Destroyed.

41 Lennox Gardens (London; Kensington and Chelsea)
New house and stables for Samuel Juler Wyand, interior design for Lieut. Colonel Alexander Hamilton.
E: 1885-6
S: RIBA plans and elevations (6).

Gaunt's House, Hinton Martell (Dorset)
Alterations and additions to the house and new stables for Sir Richard George Glyn, 3rd Bart.
E: 1885-6
S: RIBA plans and elevations (20).
Com: Cbk 1886 October £456.

Warren House, Croydon Road, West Wickham (London; Bromley)
Additions including a billiard room and conservatory, three cottages and garden works for Martin Ridley Smith.
E: 1885-6
Com: 1886 January £127 March £141 September £233.

The builders were T.J. Messom of Twickenham, Ormson and Goddard. Warren House was built by Walter Maximilian de Zoete in 1882 to the designs of George Somers Clarke Sen. Smith bought it in 1886; he was a partner in Smith, Payne and Smiths, bankers, of Lombard Street.

Gravetye Manor, West Hoathley (West Sussex)
Alterations and addition of hall for William Robinson.
E: 1885-6
S: RIBA plans, elevations and photographs (23); Godfrey Collection: *Specification of Works required to be done in Alterations and Additions to Gravetye Near Kingscote Sussex for Wm. Robinson Esq. according to Drawings prepared for that purpose by Messrs Devey and Williams Architects - 123 Bond Street London W. November 1885*; Royal Horticultural Society, Lindley Library: *Gravetye Manor Tree and Garden Book and Building Record, Commenced by Wm. Robinson August 1885*.
Com: 1886 March £82 September £120 (the first cancelled and the value of a large table £22 deducted).

Minley Manor (Hampshire)
Alterations to the mansion including new entrance and hall, dining room and offices, new stables, orangery, loggia, lodges and garden works for Bertram Wodehouse Currie.
E: 1885-6
S: RIBA plans, elevations and details (71).
Com: Cbk 1886 September £536.

Devey died while work here was in progress and a considerable programme of estate building work was continued by Arthur Castings.

8 Hertford Street (London; Westminster)
Design for panelling of boudoir for Sir Maurice Fitzgerald, 2nd Bart.
E: 1885-6
S: RIBA elevations (1); Greater London Record Office: B.A. 1885 July-December p. 708 par 70: application by Devey and Williams to the M.B.W. 11 November 1885 for a conservatory addition at the rear of the house, granted conditionally.
Com: Cbk 1886 January £22 September £58.
The builder was Wetherell; heating by Feetham.

Monkshatch, Hog's Back, Compton (Surrey)
House, stables and lodge for Andrew Kinsman Hichens.
E: 1885-6
S: RIBA plans and elevations (24)
Com: Cbk 1885 May £39 Aug £125 Nov £87 1886 Jan £75 Sep £44
Lit.: M.S.Watts *George Frederick Watts, The Annals of an Artist's life* Vol.II London 1912
The house has been demolished.

Unidentified Work
For C.D.Rose.
Com : Cbk 1885 May £30 Nov £35 1886 £22
The builder was Winkworth.

Dale Park, Arundel (West Sussex)
Alterations and additions to the house, and designs for new lodges for Charles John Fletcher.
E: 1885-7
S: RIBA plans and elevations (14); Godfrey Collection: *Estimate. Alterations and Additions, Dale Park near Arundel, Sussex. For C. Fletcher Esq. Messrs Devey and Williams, Architects, 123 Bond Street, W. May 1885. All Trades. Tenders Addressed to the Architects to be delivered at their offices above at or before 11 o'clock on Thursday the 3rd day of June 1886. Henry Smith, Surveyor, 9 John Street, Adelphi: W.C.*
The builder was William Shepherd. The house has been demolished.

Duncombe Park, Helmsley (North Yorkshire)
Design for rebuilding the house and alterations to the Office Court for William Ernest Duncombe, 1st Earl of Feversham.
E: 1886
S: RIBA plans, elevations and photographs (16).
Com: Cbk 1886 October £214.
Duncombe Park was built in 1711-13 to the designs of the amateur William Wakefield; Sir Charles Barry added pavilions containing the Stable Court and Office Court in 1834. Devey was called in after the fire of January 1879 and prepared designs for a restoration and for converting the north pavilion into a separate house.

Raufenberg, near Falkenstein, Frankfurt (West Germany)
Unidentified work, possibly for a member of the Rothschild family.
E?: 1886
S: RIBA block plan (1).

Dunraven Castle, Southerdown (Mid Glamorgan)
Additions for Windham Thomas Wyndham Quin, 4th Earl of Dunraven and Mount-Earl.
E: 1886-8
S: RIBA plans and elevations (20), (Fig. 107).
Lit: *The Builder* 26 May 1888.
The builder was Samuel Shepton and Son.

Unidentified Work
For Mr Ralli.
E: 1886
Com: Cbk 1886 October £19.
This may have been either Pantia Ralli of Ashstead Park, or Pendeli Ralli of Alderbrook, Cranleigh near Guildford, both in Surrey. The later, designed by R.N. Shaw, has been demolished.

30, 32, 34 and 36 Cadogan Square (London; Kensington and Chelsea)
Design for a block of four houses for Messrs Trollopes.
E: 1886
S: RIBA elevations (2), (Fig. 104).
Lit: Mark Girouard *Cadogan Square, Chelsea* CL 16 November 1978, pp. 1602-7, 23 November pp. 1722-5.
The houses were built in 1889-90 to this design, but for the fact that the house on the left and the second from the right are transposed

Unidentified Work
For A.J. Scott.
E: 1886
Com: Cbk 1886 October £50.

Unidentified House (United States of America)
For Allen Thorndike Rice.
E?: 1886
S: RIBA plans and elevation (25).
Com: Cbk 1886 September £210.
Lit: *New York Times* 18 May, 19 May and 14 June 1889.
Rice died on the 16 May 1889. The house may have been built on his mother's estate 'The Plains', Ridgely, Caroline County, Maryland. Rice took a degree at Oxford in 1875 and later read law at the Columbia Law School. He bought the *North American Law Review* in 1876 and a controlling interest in *Le Matin* in 1884. He had been appointed Minister to Russia in 1889 but his diplomatic career was cut short by his death.

Unidentified Work
For the Hon. Mrs Margaret Louisa Jervoise Smith.
E: 1886 Com: Cbk 1886 April £40

Unidentified Work
For Mr Burns.
E: 1886
Com: Cbk 1886 April £53.

Index

Index

Aberdeen, Mary, Countess Dowager 171
Abraham, Robert 18
Acraman, Daniel Wade 26
Adams, Maurice B. 120
Adcock, William John 62, 100, 158, 171, 173, 175
Adderley Hall, Market Drayton, Shropshire 106, 108, 173
Agricultural labourers' housing 23-26
Ainsworth, Colonel Richard Henry 114-115, 169
Akeley Wood, Buckinghamshire 50, 64, 157
Altnarynie Lodge, Achferry, by Lairg, Highland Region 48, 153-4
Archer, John Scott 79
Architectural Association 81, 114, 135
Architectural models 117-118
Architectural Photographic Association 80, 89
Ashburton, Louisa, Lady 64, 158
Ascott, Wing, Buckinghamshire 54, 56, 167
—— —— ———————— Poultry Houses 156
Ash, Courtney 164
Ashfold, Handcross, West Sussex 95-96, 170
Ash Lawn, Benenden, Kent 159
Ashton, Thomas 154
Ashurst Park, Kent 33, 156
Aston Clinton, Buckinghamshire 54, 156
Aubertin, Edmund 175
Augenor, Mr 174
Aylesbury, Buckinghamshire, Chestnuts, Whitehill 171
—————— ———————— Friarage, Rickford's Hill 159
—————— ———————— King's Head 58, 174
—————— ———————— Literary Institute 58, 174
—————— ———————— National School 164

Bagot, Sir William Bagot, 3rd Baron 64, 157
Bailey, Thomas Farmer 74, 156
Bailey, Mr 166
Barber, Thomas 21, 30, 151
Baring, Maurice 104
Barry, Sir Charles 179
Barry, Junior, Charles 81
Barry, Edward Middleton 115
Barton Manor, Osborne, Isle of Wight 117, 166

Bedford, Francis 90
Bedford Lemere & Co. 71, 88
Bedford Park, Hounslow, London 119
Belgrave Square, Westminster, London, No.11 174
Benenden, Kent, Bull Inn 64, 159
————— —— Church Cottage 159
————— —— Church of St George 166
————— —— Old Manor 159
————— —— Rectory 173
————— —— St George's Club 159
————— —— Village School 64, 159
Bently, George 137, 175
Betteshanger, Kent, Betteshanger House 42-45, 152
—————— —— Church of St Mary 42, 44
—————— —— Cottage Hospital 166
—————— —— Rectory 45, 173
Bicknell, Elhanan 26
Bigg Wither, Revd W. 162
Bishop Burton, High Hall, Humberside 162
Blakesware, Ware, Hertfordshire 99-100, 170
Bland, Miss 163
Bliss, Revd John Worthington 173
Blithfield Estate, Rugeley, Staffordshire 157
Blomfield, Sir Arthur William 171, 176
Board of Trade 171
Boissier, Revd George Richard 18, 23, 50, 151
Bold, Mrs 125
Bonham, Sir George Francis 176
Bonus, Revd Edward 54, 155, 156, 158, 164
Bossington, Hampshire 175
Boughton Hall, Send, Surrey 164
Bourke, Henry Lorton 174
Bourton Estate, Buckingham, Buckinghamshire 164
Boutcher, Emanuel 158
Boyle, Mr 171
Brampton Ash, Northamptonshire 174
Brandon Jones, John 86
Brantingham, Humberside, All Saints Church 166
Brantingham Thorpe, Humberside 66-67, 159-160
Brede Place, East Sussex 166
Brewster Lodge, Clapham Common North Side, Wandsworth, London 176
Brickwall, Northiam, East Sussex 167-8

Broke, Horace 171
Broomford Manor, Jacobstowe, Devon 99, 164
Broomhill, Southborough, Kent 152
Bruton Street, Westminster, London 62, 164
Buckland, Buckinghamshire, All Saints Church 158
———— ———————— National School 54, 156
Bucks and Oxon Union Bank 162
Bunning, James 19
Burns, Mr 179
Burton, Revd C.H. 162
Burton, Michael Arthur, 1st Baron 169
Butterfield, William 90
Buxton, Edward North 166
Byram Park, Ferrybridge, North Yorkshire 169

Cadogan and Hans Place Estate Ltd. 128
Cadogan Square, Chelsea, London Nos.30,32,34 and 36 128-129, 179
Cairnbrook Lodge, Tudor Road, Upper Norwood, London 175
Calverley Grange, Pembury, Kent 160, 175
Carlingford, Chichester Samuel Fortescue, 1st Baron 119, 170
Carlton House Terrace, Westminster, London, No.18 62 175
Carter, John 37
Castings, Arthur 73, 126, 133, 136, 137
Castle Ashby, Northamptonshire 172
Castletown, John Wilson Fitzpatrick, 1st Baron 169
Cazenove, Henry 160, 162, 171
Chafyn-Grove, Julia Elizabeth 84, 157
Chafyn-Grove, William 66, 84, 156, 157
Chapell 158
Chapman 176
Chelsham Lodge, Chelsham, Surrey 155
Chesters, Sunningdale, Berkshire 157
Cheyne Walk, Chelsea, London, No.100 170
Chiltern Hills Waterworks, Dancers End, Buckinghamshire 156
Chittenden, Hawkhurst, Kent 175
Cholmondley, Reginald 171
Clandon Park, Surrey 172
Clark 176
Claudet, Antoine 81
Clayton, Mr 170
Clerk 170
Cliveden, Buckinghamshire 46-47, 153
———— ———————— Seven Gables 47, 166
Clutton, Henry 132
Cobbett, William 24
Coke, Mr 171

Collen, John and Brothers 109, 173
Collins, Richard 21, 151, 153
Condover Hall, Shropshire 171
Constable, Henry 38, 151
Cooke, Mr 157
Coombe Cottage, Kingston-upon-Thames, London 68, 72-73, 162
Coombe Warren, Kingston-upon-Thames, London 19, 68-72, 84, 160
Coope, Octavius Edward 66, 152, 157
Cooper, Mr 164
Corbet, Henry Reginald 106, 173
Coryton Manor Estate, Okehampton, Devon 160
Cotes, Lady Louisa Harriet 130, 176
Cotman, John Sell 15, 17, 29
Cranbrook Colony 27
Cranbrook, Gathorne Gathorne-Hardy, 1st Earl 64, 159
Cranworth, Robert Monsey Rolfe, 1st Baron 64, 157
Cree, Revd E.D. 173
Creyke, Ralph 164
Crighton, Col. Sir Henry George Louis 176
Cropper, Edward 33, 162
Crosbie, G.W. 106
Crossley 177
Crown Point Estate, Norwich, Norfolk 156
Cubitt, Thomas 129
Cubitt and Co., William 58, 88, 169, 173
Culver Hill, Penshurst, Kent 36, 153
Culver House, Amberley, Gloucestershire 176
Cundy III, Thomas 126
Currie, Bertram Wodehouse 46, 68, 73, 160, 172
Currie, Laurence 72
Currie, Philip Henry Currie, 1st Baron 176
Currie, Raikes 132
Curzon Street, Westminster, London, No.19 171

Daguerre, Louis Jaques Mandé 79
Dale Park, Arundel, West Sussex 179
Daniell, Mr 156
Daniell, Henry Averell 176
Daniell, John Henry 155, 166
Dawson, Edward 155
Deal, Kent 63, 169
De L'Isle and Dudley, Philip Charles Sidney, 1st Baron 23, 38, 151
De L'Isle and Dudley, Sir Philip Sidney, 2nd Baron 23, 38, 152, 155
Dell, W. 166
Denne Hill, Womenswold, Kent 97-99, 163
Denton Manor, Grantham, Lincolnshire 171
Derby, Edward Henry Stanley, 15th Earl 178

Destailleur, G.H. 55
Deverell, William Henry 175
Devey, Frederick Nicholls 13, 18, 133
Devey, George architectural training 18-19
—— —— character 137
—— —— *Devey versus Drummond* 106-108
—— —— drawing style 87
—— —— education 15-17
—— —— engagement to Flora Hoskins 50-51
—— —— exhibits at Royal Academy 19
—— —— family background 13-15
—— —— F.R.I.B.A. 50
—— —— houses 133-134
—— —— offices 20, 134
—— —— office staff 136
—— —— photographic collection 87, 90
—— —— religious beliefs 51
—— —— Wealden vernacular and design style 23, 138
—— —— will
Devey, Frederick William 13
Devey, the Misses Louisa and Rosa 174
Dinton School, Buckinghamshire 162
Dodd, Revd Philip Stanhope 152
Doctor, design for a house for 151
Dover Harbour, Kent 62-63, 171
Drayton House, Northamptonshire 177
Drew 176
Drummond, George James 33, 106-108, 174
Ducie, Henry John Reynolds Moreton, 3rd Earl 64, 156, 157, 173
Duckworth, William 64, 154
Duckworth, Revd William Arthur 155
Dudbrook House, Kelvedon Hatch, Essex 170
Duncombe Park, Helmsley, North Yorkshire 179
Dunnage, George A. 176
Dunraven Castle, Southerdown, Mid Glamorgan 133, 179
Dunraven, Windham Thomas Wyndham-Quin, 4th Earl 133, 179
Dunrobin Estate, Highland Region 46, 49, 50, 154
Durdans, Epsom, Surrey 172
Durley, John and Sons 54, 155, 169
Dyson, Major Edwards 97-98, 163

Eastlake, Lady 53
Eastons 170
Eastry Union Workhouse Chapel, Kent 45, 166
East Villa, Upton Park, Slough, Buckinghamshire 175
Eaton Estate, Cheshire 157
Egerton, Mrs 166
Egg, Ann 13-15

Egg, Augustus Leopold 15, 17
Egg, Durs 14
Elcho, Francis, Lord 48, 153
Elkington, Northamptonshire 177
Ellison Church of England Schools, Jarrow, Tyne and Wear 64, 155
Ellison, Cuthbert 42, 43
Elstree, Hertfordshire 164
Eversley, George John Shaw-Lefevre, 1st Baron 74, 77, 173
Eythrope, Buckinghamshire, The Pavilion 54, 55, 172

Fairchildes, Fickleshole, Surrey 166
Fairlight, East Sussex, Church of St. Andrew 19
Farmer and Brindley 177
Farnborough Hill, Hampshire 64, 158
Farnborough School, Hampshire 159
Feetham 178
Feversham, William Ernest Duncombe, 1st Earl 179
Field, George 33, 156
Fildes 173
Fitzgerald, Sir Maurice 178
Fitzwilliam 171
Fletcher, Charles John 179
Fonthill Estate, Wiltshire 64, 83, 156
Fordcombe, Kent, Chafford Arms 23, 151
—— —— Church of St. Peter 23, 152
—— —— Parsonage, Kent 23, 152
Fowler, William 47, 153-4
Fox Talbot, William Henry 79, 81
France, house in 157
Frankfurt, Germany, conservatory 157
Frewen, Edward 167
Frewen, Moreton 166
Furness Cottage, Grange Gardens, Furness Road, Eastbourne, East Sussex 175

Gally Knight, Henry 80
Gardener's Magazine 25
Gathorne-Hardy, Lieut Col. Gathorne 124, 178
Gaunt's House, Hinton Martell, Dorset 130, 178
genre painting 26
George and Peto, Ernest 125, 129, 177
Gillot, Joseph 26
Gipps, George Bowdler 174
Givons Grove, Leatherhead, Surrey 179
Gladstone, Mary 56
Gladstone, William Ewart 46, 67, 72, 77, 119
Gladwyns, Bishop's Stortford, Hertfordshire 171
Glyn, Sir Richard George 130, 178
Glyn, Mr 160
Goddard 176, 177, 178

Godfrey, Walter Hindes 20, 23, 43, 51, 71, 82, 118, 135, 137
Godwin, Edward William 119
Goldings, Hertford, Hertfordshire 91-95, 164
Goldney, Sir Gabriel 176
Goodall, Miss 158
Gosselin, Mrs Frances Hadsley 99, 170
Gower, Lord Ronald 61
Graham 173
Granston Manor, Ballacola, Abbey Leix, Eire 169
Grant, Albert 26
Granville, Granville George Leveson-Gower, 2nd Earl 46, 58, 163, 164, 169, 171, 173, 175
Grasshome, Dinton, Buckinghamshire 163
Grateley House, Hampshire 158
Gravetye Manor, West Hoathley, West Sussex 131, 178
Great Cliffsend Farm, Cliffs End, Kent 62, 171
Greenhalgh, Dr Robert 158
Grosvenor Place, Westminster, London, No.34 160
Grosvenor Square, Westminster, London, No.35 170
————— ————— ————— ——— No.37 171
————— ————— ————— ——— No. 36, later No.41 125-127, 177
Grosvenor Street, Westminster, London No.34 115, 169

Haden 170
Haddon, Thomas 164
Haddon Estate Farm 174
Hall Place, Leigh, Kent 74-75, 85, 156, 163
Halton Estate, Buckinghamshire 54, 55, 167
Ham, Kent, Church of St George 44, 162
Hambro, Sir Everard Alexander 177
Hamilton, Lieut. Col. Alexander 125, 178
Hamilton, Edward William Terrick 157
Hammerfield, Penshurst, Kent 33, 153
Hammond, William Oxenden 100, 158, 164
Hamptworth Lodge Estate, Wiltshire 158
Hardcastle, Edward 174, 175
Harding, James Duffield 18, 80
Hardinge, Lieut. Gen. Sir Henry, 1st Viscount 23, 151, 152
Hardinge, Colonel 163
Hardwick, P.C. 134
Hardwick School, Buckinghamshire 162
Hargreaves, Mr 158
Hargreaves, William 74, 77, 163
Harlestone Schools Northamptonshire 176
Hart Dyke, Sir William 175
Harvey, Sir Robert John Harvey 156
Hastings Drinking Fountain, East Sussex 173

Haward & Brothers, James 70, 122, 160, 162
Hawkes 164, 170
Hayes Place, Beckenham, London 177
Healey 173
Heathfield Lodge 156
Hele & Co. 106
Hellyer 176
Hemsted Park, Benenden, Kent 64, 138, 159
Herbert, Very Revd the Hon. George 159
Hereford, Herefordshire, The Deanery 159
Hertford Street, Westminster, London, No.8 178
Hichens, Andrew Kinsman 129, 178
Hitch 177
Hodsock Priory, Nottinghamshire 167
Holland and Hannen 129, 133, 160
Holwood, Keston, Bromley, London 157
Hooper, George 66, 158
Hoskins, later Streatfield, Flora Margaret Elizabeth 50-51
Howletts, Bekesbourne, Kent 174
Huckvale, William 58
Hulcott, Buckinghamshire 54, 155
Hunloke, Adelaide Augusta Wilhelmina 38, 55, 123, 157, 175, 177

Ilchester, Henry Edward Fox-Strangways, 5th Earl 130, 177

Jackson 160, 175
Jacobstowe, Devon, Church of St James 164
James, James 53, 54
Jones, George Edwin 167

Kelsall Lodge, Ferndale Road, Tunbridge Wells, Kent 70, 160
Kenmare, Valentine Augustus Browne, 4th Earl 109, 173, 174
Kennedy, Sydney 162
Kent, Mr 166
Killarney House, Kerry, Eire 19, 109-112, 173
Kimble, Buckinghamshire 166
King's College School 15-17
————— ————— ————— architects educated at 16-17
Knebworth House, Hertfordshire 163, 175
Knighton, Woodford, Waltham Forest, London 166
Knowle Park, Cranleigh, Surrey 176
Knowsley Hall, Merseyside 178

Lady Mead, Little Kimble, Buckinghamshire 160
Laleham, Surrey 170
Lampson, Sir Curtis Miranda 162
Langley Park, Loddon, Norfolk 162

Langston Arms Hotel, Kingham, Oxfordshire 173
Lascelles and Co., W.H. 110, 170, 173
Lea Bridge Waterworks, Hackney, London, 152
Ledgers, Chelsham, Surrey 176
Leese, Sir Joseph Francis 170
Leigh, Kent 85, 163
—— —— Church of St Mary 155
Lennox Gardens, Kensington, London, Nos. 2,4 and 6 123, 177
—— —— —— —— No.8 38, 123, 175
—— —— —— —— Nos. 13 and 15 125, 178
—— —— —— —— No.19 96, 124, 177
—— —— —— —— No.23 124, 177
—— —— —— —— No.25 125, 177
—— —— —— —— No.41 125, 178
—— —— —— —— No.43 124, 178
Leveson-Gower, Granville William 159
Lewis, Mr 159
Lexham Gardens, Kensington, London, Nos. 65 and 100 178
Lilleshall Estate, Shropshire 46-47, 155
Lillies, Weedon, Buckinghamshire 160
Lion House, Newport, Berkeley, Gloucestershire 66, 158
Little, Thomas 18-19, 135
Little Kimble, Buckinghamshire, Church of All Saints 170
Lloyd, Revd H.R. 20, 151
Loch, George 48, 154
Longman, Thomas 64, 158
Longwood, Winchester, Hampshire 112, 174
Lord, William Turner 73
Lorne, John George Edward Henry Douglas Sutherland Campbell, Marquess 167
Loudon, John Claudius 25, 27
Louise, Princess 115
Lugar, Robert 42
Lullingstone Castle, Eynsford, Kent 175
Lynwood, Lyndhurst, Hampshire 164-5
Lyon, Revd Ralph 156
Lytton, Edward George Earle Lytton Bulwer, 1st Baron 163, 175

Mabey, C.H. & J. 44, 70, 72, 92, 98, 160
Macharioch House, Southend, Strathclyde Region 167
Maiano, Giovanni de 44
Maidstone, Kent, Archbishop's stables 30
Maplewood 62, 118, 173
Maresfield Park, East Sussex 172

Marlborough House, Hawkhurst, Kent 174
Marriott, Mr 170
Maxwell, Major 173
May, Edward John 119
Melbury House, Melbury Sampford, Dorset 130, 177
Mellier, Messrs 73
Mellish, Sir George 167
Membland Hall, Noss Mayo, Devon 73, 103-106, 172
Mentmore Estate, Buckinghamshire 54, 55, 155, 172
Messom, T.J. 123, 172, 175, 178
Meynell Hunt Stables, Sudbury, Derbyshire 115, 164
Meyrick, Major 173
Milburn, Cospen Lane, Esher, Syrrey 174
Minley Manor, Hampshire 73, 132-133, 178
Mitford, Algernon Bertram 170
Moffats 156
Monkshatch, Compton, Surrey 129, 178
Montefiore, Mrs Henrietta Franciska 175
Montresor, Colonel 163
Morley, Samuel 74, 85, 165
Morley Horder, Percy 135
Morris & Co. 106, 162
Morrison, Alfred 64, 83, 156
Mount Lodge, The Mount, St Leonard's, East Sussex 158
Myers and Sons, George 74, 157, 160, 163, 167
Myton Hall, Myton-on-Swale, North Yorkshire 169

Nasmyth, James 33, 36, 153
Nesfield, William Andrews 41
Nesfield, William Eden 29, 81, 85
Netley Castle, Hampshire 176
Neve, the Misses 159, 166
Newman, Thomas Holdsworth 160
Newnham, Philip 159
Niblett and Goddard 176
Nicholson, Peter 47, 153
Nonnington Almshouses, Kent 158
Norris 173
Northampton, Charles Douglas Compton, 3rd Marquess 172
Northbourne, Kent, Church of St Augustine 45, 162
Northbourne, Sir Walter James, 1st Baron 41, 152, 155, 162, 166
Northesk, William Hopetoun Carnegie, 8th Earl 112, 174
Northiam, East Sussex 155
Norton Conyers, North Yorkshire 176
Nunburnholme, Charles Henry Wilson, 1st Baron 125-126, 170, 177
Nunhead Cemetery, Peckham, London 18-19

Index

Oakfield, Smart's Hill, Penshurst, Kent 23, 151
Oldbury Place, Ightham, Kent 74, 77, 173
Ongar, Essex 159
Onslow, William Hillier Onslow, 4th Earl of 172
Orchardleigh Estate, Lullington, Somerset 64, 154
Ormson 178
Orton's Farm, Spencer Estate, Northamptonshire 171
Ossington, Lady Charlotte 172
Owen, Henry 158

Paddington Cemetery 20
Palace House, Newmarket, Suffolk 158
Palace of Westminster, London 63, 176
Park House, Frant, East Sussex 170
Parker, John Henry 38
Parrott, Joseph 160
Pauly, Jean Samuel 14
Paulton, Abraham Walter 164
Pattenson, Mr 177
Pell, Mr 177
Penshurst, Kent 21, 23, 28-29, 32-33, 87, 151
Penshurst Place, Kent 23, 37-41, 151, 152
Perry, Mrs 157
Phillimore, Claud 178
Piccadilly, Westminster, London, No.107 163
Pilgrim, Charles 50, 64, 157
Pink & Son, Thomas 129
Pitchford Hall, Shropshire 130, 176
Plaish Hall, Cardington, Shropshire 177
Pounds Bridge, Kent, Penshurst Cemetery Chapel 152
Poynter, Ambrose 167
Poynton Colliery and estate, Cheshire 115, 171
Proctor Beauchamp, Sir Thomas William Brograve 162
Pugin, Auguste 85
Pugin Augustus Welby Northmore 134

Ralli, Mr 179
Ramsden, Sir John William 169
Ramsgate Harbour, Kent 171
Rangemore, Barton-under-Needwood, Staffordshire 169
Raufenberg, Falkenstein, Frankfurt, Germany 179
Rawcliffe Hall, Goole, Humberside 164
Rebecca, John Biagio 37, 38
Redleaf, Penshurst, Kent 26, 27, 42
Reily, Miss 176
Revelstoke, Edward Charles Baring, 1st Baron 68, 72, 103, 162, 172
Rice, Allen Thorndike 179
Richardson, Dr B.W. 121
Richmond Terrace, Westminster, London, No.1 73, 172

Ripon, George Frederick Samuel Robinson, 1st Marquess 166
Ripple Parsonage, Kent 45, 162
Roberts, Thomas 47, 153
Robertson, Mr 164
Robinson, William 131, 178
Robinson 175
Rochetts, South Weald, Essex 66, 157
Rodda, William John 158
Rogers or Rodriguez, William R. 58
Ronald, Robert Bruce 175
Rose, C.D. 179
Rose, Richard 171
Rosebery, Archibald Philip Primrose, 5th Earl of 172
de Rothschild family 53
de Rothschild, Alfred 58
de Rothschild, Alice 54, 55, 172
de Rothschild, Sir Anthony 54, 155, 156
de Rothschild, Baron Ferdinand James 54, 55, 159, 173
de Rothschild, Hannah 172
de Rothschild, Baron James 157
de Rothschild, Baron Leopold 56, 167
de Rothschild, Baron Lionel 54, 55, 167
de Rothschild, (Hannah) Matilde 157
de Rothschild, Baron Mayer Amschel 53, 54, 155, 156, 158, 163
de Rothschild, Sir Nathaniel Mayer, 1st Baron 58, 174
Rowfant, East Grinstead, West Sussex 163
Royal Institute of British Architects 50, 135
Ruskin, John 18, 24, 27, 80, 81

St Alban's Court, Nonnington, Kent 44, 100-103, 158
St Aubyn, James Piers 106
St John's Wood, London, All Saints Church 19
St Margaret's at Cliffe, Kent 61, 175
Salomons, Sir David 152
Salvin, Anthony 41, 42, 44, 86, 130
Sanderson, Revd Lancelot 164
Sartoris, Charles Urban 64, 157
Sayer, Edward 177
Scot, Revd Robert Francis 159
Scott, A.J. 179
Send Holme, Send, Surrey 74, 77, 163, 170
Shackle, Mr 158
Shafto, Robert Duncombe 158
Shaw, Richard Norman 29, 44, 81, 84, 104, 119
Sheepshanks, John 26
Shelley, Louisa Elizabeth Anne, Dowager Lady 172

Shepherd, Dr 176
Shepherd, William 107, 175, 179
Shepton and Son, Samuel 179
Silesia, Poland 55, 87, 159
Simpson and Son, J. 177
Singleton, Mr 175
Slater and Vernon 166
Smith, Abel 91, 167, 169
Smith, Revd Albert 95, 163
Smith, Eric Carrington 95, 96, 124, 10, 177
Smith's Charity, Henry 122
Smith, Mrs Margaret Louisa Jervoise 96, 179
Smith, Martin Ridley 96, 178
Smith, Lieut.Gen. Philip 95, 171
Smith, Robert 91, 164, 172
Smith & Co., George 160
Smithills Hall, Bolton, Greater Manchester 114, 169
Soane, Sir John 81-82, 118
Society for the Protection of Ancient Buildings 135
Somers Clarke, George 96, 178
South Benfleet Vicarage, Essex 20, 151
South Park, Penshurst, Kent 23, 29, 32, 41, 151
Spencer Estate, Northampton, Northamptonshire 110-122, 171
Spencer, John Poyntz Spencer 5th Earl 119, 168, 171, 175, 176, 177
Staines, Francis William 173
Stanton, William 176
Stapleford, Hertfordshire, Church of St Mary 91, 169
Stapylton, Major Henry Miles 169
Steane Manor House and Manor Farm, Northamptonshire 177
Steinitz 160, 173, 175
Stewart, Maj.Gen. Alexander Charles Hector 124, 177
Stokes, George Henry 54, 55, 90, 156
Stone, Coutts 18, 19, 135
Stone, Percy 44, 50, 87, 135, 137, 139
Stoneley Grange, Kimbolton, Cambridgeshire 163
Stopford Sackville, Mrs Caroline Harriet 177
Stratford de Redcliffe, Stratford Canning, 1st Viscount 170
Strathnairn, Hugh Henry Rose, 1st Baron 173
Strathpeffer Spa, Highland Region 50, 155
Streatfield Collection, J. Fremlyn 30
Street, George Edmund 80, 166
Sturgis, Russell 169
Sudbury Hall, Derbyshire 115, 169
Sudbury, Derbyshire, All Saints Church 115, 167
Surtees, Lady 164
Sutherland, Anne, Countess of Cromartie and 3rd Duchess 50, 155
Sutherland, George Granville Leveson-Gower, 2nd Duke 46, 49, 153, 154, 155
Sutherland, Harriet, 2nd Duchess 46, 153
Swaylands, Penshurst, Kent 33, 107, 162, 174
Sykes, Christopher 66, 160, 166, 169

Tankerville, Charles Augustus Bennet, 6th Earl of 171
Taylor, W.F. 55
Thame, Oxfordshire, No.2 High Street 162
Thynne, Revd Lord Charles 176
Titsey Place, Oxted Surrey 159
Tortworth, Gloucestershire 157
Trentham, Staffordshire 46-47, 153, 154
Trevagethan, Truro, Devon 170
Tring Park, Hertfordshire 54, 55, 167
Trollope & Sons, Messrs 122, 177, 179
Turner, Revd Alfred 156
Twopenny, William 30

United States of America 179

Vernon, Augustus Henry Venables Vernon, 6th Baron 115, 164, 167, 169, 170
Vernon, Robert 26
Vernon, William Warren 160
Victoria, Queen of England 109, 115, 166
Villa Veta, Granville Road, Kingsdown, Kent 61, 164
Vivian, Major Quintus 170
Voysey, Revd Charles 51, 136
Voysey, Charles Francis Annesley 86, 136, 137

Waddesdon, Buckinghamshire 54, 55, 173
Wakefield, William 179
Waldegrave, Frances Elizabeth Anne Waldegrave, Countess 170
Walker, Romaine 178
Walmer Castle, Kent 44, 46, 58-60, 163
Ward, Neville 160
Warren House, Croydon Road, West Wickham, London 96-97, 178
Warren House, Warren Road, Kingston-upon-Thames, London 68, 73, 178
Warren, W. 175
Warter Priory, Humberside 126
Waterford, Hetfordshire, Church of St Michael 95, 172
——————— ——————— Village School 95, 164
Watt, William and Francis 162
Watton-at-Stone Almshouses, Hertfordshire 91, 167
Watts, George Frederick 129
Webb, Philip 138
Weedon Village School, Buckinghamshire 171
Weir, James 160
Welby-Gregory, Sir William Earle 171

Index

Wells, William 26, 27, 33
Wendover Buckinghamshire, Manor 95, 171
———— ———————— Vicarage 95, 163
Wetherell 178
Wentworth Castle, South Yorkshire 172
Wentworth, Frederick William Vernon 174
Westminster, Hugh Lupus Grosvenor, 3rd Marquess and 1st Duke of 47, 157, 166, 174
Wheatland 170
Whitchurch School, Buckinghamshire 64, 156
Whitefriars Glass Co. 67, 70, 71, 159
White-Thomson, Sir Robert Thomas 99, 164
Wickwar Parsonage, Gloucester 156
Wilcote House, Oxfordshire 64, 157
Willesden, London, Church of St Mary, Church End 20
Williams, James 14, 17, 19, 56, 62, 64, 78, 103, 106, 114, 115, 118, 129, 133, 135, 136, 137, 159
Williams 170

Williams, West and Slade 56, 133, 137
Wingerworth, Derbyshire 38, 157
Winkworth, 179
Wolverton, George Grenfell Glyn, 2nd Baron 68, 73, 178
Woodhall Park, Watton-at-Stone, Hertfordshire 91, 167
Wormleighton School, Northampton 176
Worth Park, Crawley, West Sussex 175
Wortley, J. Stuart 160
Wragge, Frederick 176
Wratten, Edmund Livingstone 135
Wyand, Samuel Juler 122, 124, 125, 178

Yates, Miss, cottage for 151
Yewlands 164

Zeals, Wiltshire, Chafyn-Grove Almshouses 84, 156
———— ———————— Zeals House 66, 84, 157